IRON SHARPENS IRON:
Social Interactions at China Shops in Botswana

I0094942

Yanyin Zi

In collaboration

Langaa RPCIG
Mankon Bamenda

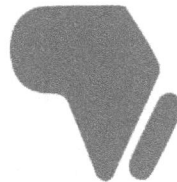

CAAS
Kyoto University

Publisher:
Langaa RPCIG
Langaa Research & Publishing Common Initiative Group
P.O. Box 902 Mankon
Bamenda
North West Region
Cameroon
Langaagrp@gmail.com
www.langaa-rpcig.net

In Collaboration with
The Center for African Area Studies, Kyoto University, Japan

Distributed in and outside N. America by African Books Collective
orders@africanbookscollective.com
www.africanbookscollective.com

ISBN-10: 9956764418

ISBN-13: 9789956764419

First Published by Langaa in March 2017
© Yanyin Zi 2017

Dedication

This book is dedicated to my family, which has been steadfast in sustaining me all these years. I would particularly like to thank my father and mother for their love and support.

Table of Contents

List of Figures and Tables

List of Tables

Preface and Acknowledgement

This book is a revised version of my doctoral dissertation. I am grateful to many people for their contributions to this book, and my greatest debt by far is to my academic supervisor, Professor Akira Takada, who for five years has guided me along with my research; I am truly the fortunate beneficiary of his kindness and genius. I am also deeply grateful to Professor Itaru Ohta and Professor Misa Hirano of the Graduate School of Asian and African Area Studies (ASAFAS) at Kyoto University, Professor Herman Batibo, Professor Frank Youngman, Professor Monageng Mogalakwe and Professor Maitseo Bolaane of the University of Botswana, Professor Yoichi Mine of Doshisha University and Professor Sayaka Ogawa of Ritsumeikan University for their advice and support. Others who provided invaluable comments include Professor Jun Ikeno who tried valiantly to correct my misconceptions and Professor Caroline Hau who contributed her precious time to stimulate me with interesting ideas. I am indebted to ASAFAS for the International Training Program (ITP) and International On-Site Education Program (IOSEP) that supported my field research. I also appreciate the hard work and selfless support of Dr. Yoon Jung Park and other researchers in the Chinese in Africa/Africans in China Research Network (CA/AC Research Network). Specifically for this publication, I thank Professor Francis Nyamnjoh of the University of Cape Town, for encouraging me to revise my dissertation into a book; likewise, I am indebted to Kyoto University for the publishing fund – the Grant for Young Researchers of the FY 2016 Discretionary Budget of the President of Kyoto University.

Special appreciation goes to Samuel Alemu, Sande Ngalande, Fanny Ngalande, Antonie Chigeda and Tadessa Daba for helping me both by reading my paper and their friendship; without their support I could not have completed my work. In particular, I would like to thank my long-time friend Minyuan Li for sacrificing his Christmas vacation in 2015 to comment on a very early draft of this book. My fellow students at the African Area Studies, especially Masaya Hara, Sarama Tsunoda and Georgina Seera, have been very helpful with their encouragement and support. Aino Ikeda at Kyoto University has kindly offered help to design the book cover. I am grateful to the copyeditor at Langga Publishers who took on the highly time-consuming task of copyediting the whole manuscript. I thank my friend Joshua Tan, Jenny Lawy, Joshua Teague, Alexandre Ferreira, and Thibault Moremar who offered extremely generous help and their editing gave new life to the manuscript. For their assistance I am truly grateful.

I owe my deepest gratitude to the Chinese merchants who welcomed me into their homes with open arms and offered unconditional friendship. I must also thank them for allowing me to bother them on a daily basis, and so willingly sharing their personal experiences with me throughout my stays with them. In most cases I have changed their names and other identifying factors to protect their anonymity. I could not have written this book without the friendship, support and generosity of my Setswana teacher, Keitumetse Ositang, as well as Pastor Enock Sitima and Pastor Tshegofatso Sitima of Bible Life Ministries who used the words of Bible to feed my spirit every Sunday and extended their hospitality during my stay in Botswana. Many thanks to the Chinese missionaries, Dejun Yu and Ruiyan Yu, and the many loving brothers and sisters in the Botswana church, who always welcomed me as a family member.

My love and thanks to my friends Rickie and Paul Clark, Dennis Grass, Keith Bouy, Annie Richardson, Manami Kakihara, Kimberly Ayars, Pastor Kang and Pastor Naoko Kang for their care and for always being my antidote to despair. Their strength and courage as well as faith in me were the most important ingredients that kept me going. Big hugs to my roommates, Xiaolan Ying, Yuyan Zhou and Xing Jin for sharing joys and sorrows with me in the past five years, without their company life would have been so much more exhausting.

I would like to thank the Centre for African Language Diversity (CALDi), the University of Cape Town and the Global South Studies Center (GSSC), University of Cologne for hosting me and offering so many opportunities to exchange ideas with scholars abroad. Many thanks to the editors of the *Journal of Chinese Overseas*, *Journal of*

African and East-Asian Affairs and *Psychologia* that allowed me to re-use previously published articles in part of the published data in this book. Finally, I am deeply indebted to my parents in China, without whose understanding and advice as well as affectionate support, I could ever have gone so far. Most importantly I thank the Almighty God for the grace and mercy, without which this work would have been impossible to accomplish.

Such statements of thanks as recorded above might be found in the preface of any book. But perhaps what makes this book special are the intersections of my life story and field experience, which saw this book to fruition. I was born and raised in Suzhou, China, what I believed to be one of the most beautiful cities in the world, and later went to another equally beautiful city – Kyoto, Japan for my undergraduate and graduate education. My life in Japan was blessed, well organised, but organised to a point that it became boring. I started wondering how people lived on the other side of the world and decided to study and explore it. Back in 2011, the population of Chinese merchants was booming in African countries. I was amazed by the bold challenging spirit of Chinese to cope with their daily lives and business in Africa, and developed an interest in Africa–China relations on the ground.

Field research was exciting and frustrating at the same time. Conducting fieldwork in Botswana, I was constantly filled with wonderment at the blue skies, purple flowers, pink haze, cattle on the streets, mango and papaya trees, etc. Those were all novelties to a Chinese city girl like me. Cooking maize meal, eating passion fruit, singing local gospel songs were daily joys for me. However, the biggest lesson I learnt in Botswana was that of patience. To get a document signed from someone in the university could take weeks; I repeatedly heard excuses like the responsible person was on a business trip, sick leave, attending a funeral, and then when he came back the computer did not work, etc. '*Kamoso* (tomorrow)' is the word carved in my mind: 'please come tomorrow' 'I will try tomorrow' 'tomorrow will work'. On some of those frustrating days, I would eat a big frozen *magapu* (watermelon) to cool down my temper. Also, as one of few Asian-looking women in some areas, I endured periodic discrimination and catcalling. Being publicly called 'Chinese sweetie' and 'marry me' on the streets was another thing that annoyed me for a long time. I usually pretended not to hear. Not that I 'feared' the Batswana nationals, but I was advised by friends and colleagues to be vigilant especially in unfamiliar terrain. I was also one of the victims of a deteriorating security situation in Botswana: I had personal items stolen from my bag, and I was once nearly the victim of a street robbery. I later learnt how to hide cash every day before leaving home and wear old, faded clothes every day even when I attended Sunday service at church.

On the other hand, some local people were so kind to me that they wiped away all of these negative experiences and emotions. On the night bus from Namibia to Botswana, I had to get off in the middle of the night to wait for the border post to open the next morning. That night, a group of passengers convinced the driver to leave me at the police checkpoint instead of the gasoline station, considering it was safer for a foreigner. The policemen at the checkpoint kindly opened their office and found a mattress for me to lie on in the office until dawn. In the morning, I met a local gentleman who offered me a free lift to my destination before the approaching storm came. There was a waiter who made a free sandwich for me as my food for the road when he heard that I would spend the next day on the bus. There were countless locals who helped me find my way home, spoke on my behalf when they saw that I was not treated fairly and protected me in dangerous situations. As a scholar these experiences are the pearls in my necklace that was this journey. They compose my perception of a country. I did not try to weigh and balance the positive and negative. Instead I tried to refresh my mind and heart every day, and tried my best to be understanding and forgiving if I had been offended, because emotional burdens and prejudice are counterproductive to anthropological work.

Field research was a truly valuable experience for me, as I stated above, however, I hesitated much when it came to writing a book. It was after reading the famous book, *China's Second Continent*, that I finally felt the necessity to share some of my insights into the living situations of Chinese merchants in Africa. After experiencing 'labour pains' this book was finally born. I hope that this book will serve as a formal introduction to Chinese merchants in Botswana, facilitate Botswana–China relations, and particularly help people on the ground to understand each other better. I have heard many interesting and touching stories from both Batswana and Chinese people, however, in this book I can only touch the tip of the iceberg. I sincerely wish that this book will encourage more Chinese merchants to tell their own stories, and look forward to their autobiographies, as I truly believe that their stories are worth telling. It would be an unexpected pleasure if this book would prompt more grass-roots interactions and cultural exchange programmes in Botswana as well. This book is written for my dear Chinese and Batswana friends, and it is no more than a preface to the ongoing stories among you. For those critics who believe that Chinese merchants in Africa are 'neocolonialists,' I also hope that this book will grant them a better understanding of the situation on the ground. Finally, this book might also be a guide for those potential migrants who have internalised contemporary Chinese stereotypes of Africa as a source of 'easy money'. If you think you can stand the heat, bear the boredom, eat the bittiness and, most importantly, have the guts to initiate a business in a foreign land, then welcome to this *Jumanji* – a game for those who seek to find a way to leave their world behind.

Abstract

China's presence in Africa has been growing since the 21st century. Most African people become aware of this Chinese presence through their daily contact with products made in China, as well as Chinese merchants in China shops. Since the 1990s, China shops in Botswana have expanded from the cities to the rural areas. The boom of China shops created many jobs and provided cheap basic daily goods for the local people. However, local newspapers in Botswana reported that Chinese merchants were confronted by numerous conflicts regarding employment and service issues with the local community.

The aim of my book is to explore how social interactions in China shops help to shape the image of China in Botswana, focusing on the micro-level relations between Chinese merchants and Botswana nationals, including customers, shop assistants, as well as regulatory authorities from the government. The study is motivated by the gap between growing concerns of negative local press coverage regarding China's presence in Botswana and the friendship and cooperation between the two states so far, emphasising the importance of China shops in shaping the image of China and China–Botswana relations at the grass-roots level.

The theory of the 'contact zone' and intergroup relations is applied to consider the interactions between the Chinese merchants and the local community in Botswana. China shops can be regarded as a 'contact zone' where Chinese merchants have face-to-face interactions with local people. The study adopted a mixed methods research design according to the research questions and used data triangulation as a means to validate the study's findings. Informal and in-depth interviews and participant observation were conducted in China shops. Online information and news were gathered from the Embassy of China, local news and Batswana governmental websites.

The study found that the majority of the Chinese merchants in Botswana are Fujianese. They face various challenges in their daily business. Their social position as middleman minority determines their relationships and responses to signs of hostility from the host society. Furthermore, their self-imposed isolation is deeply rooted in their attitudes (combined with their sense of vulnerability as foreigners). On the other hand, the economic situation and geographical location of Botswana offers the Chinese merchants opportunities to avoid competition among them and manage rejection by the local society to some extent by improving business models and moving business to neighbouring countries.

Before the arrival of Chinese retailers in Botswana, shops and stores were mainly concentrated in urban areas, selling items which were priced above what most people could afford. China shops have brought convenience to consumers, particularly those in remote areas, and they play a role in curbing prices. However, Chinese goods sold in the China shops have received widespread criticism in Africa for their poor quality and negative effects on the local marketplace. They are termed 'fong kong' goods and regarded as cheap copies or fakes. In spite of the widespread criticism received and associated illegalities, this research argues that, from a low-end globalisation perspective, fong kong goods have helped the poor and middle class individuals greatly in improving their quality of life, thereby contributing to levelling the socio-economical differences in Botswana society.

Although the jobs offered by China shops have not been very much appreciated by the locals due to their limited skills transformation opportunities and 'low salaries', they have contributed to local unemployment reduction. Concerning the employment relations in China shops, Chinese employers' frugality and exploitative image caused them to receive little respect and trust while triggering many complaints from their assistants, since they usually failed to fulfil the personal needs of the local employees. On the other hand, the local employees' poor work ethics caused loss of trust by their Chinese employers and created a bad reputation for Batswana nationals across the country. These pose a challenge to a good business partnership. The fierce clash in employment relations may be shaped by the frequent face-to-face contact between Chinese employers and Botswana employees in their daily interactions.

Overall, the study found that the image of China in Botswana has been shaped through daily interactions between Chinese merchants and local people on an individual level; at the same time, the abstract group image was shaped by the fame of Chinese mega projects, Chinese organisations as well as local media. The fact that the image of China in Botswana has been negative in recent years is mainly due to the local perception of the abstract image of the Chinese in Botswana through failure of Chinese mega projects and negative local media press, in spite of their undeniable social and economic contribution to local society at a micro level. China's nation branding relies on a top-down model, which continually fails to impact the majority in Botswana. In reality, China's image in Botswana is largely shaped by a bottom-up style through social interactions between Chinese merchants and local people in the contact zone of China shops. So far the important role of the China shops has been recognised by neither the Chinese side nor the Batswana side, despite its potential to serve as a grounded China brand. In this context, the name 'China shop' is like an unauthorised brand name that is not built through nation branding or an image campaign but is coined at the grass-roots level. My main argument is that local customers' negative attitudes toward Chinese goods are mainly influenced by the failure of Chinese mega-projects, local negative media reports and their own economic vulnerability.

The findings pertain to the aspects of Chinese retail business and as such should be interpreted within these aspects of Chinese retail business in Africa. The results, though not representative of all Chinese businesses, serve as an important indicator of potential issues and challenges to the China–Africa relationships.

Chapter 1

Introduction

This book investigates how Chinese merchants and the people of Botswana[1] shape the image of China in Botswana by investigating the social interactions at China shops in Botswana. The study is motivated by the gap between growing concerns over negative local press coverage regarding China's presence in Botswana and the friendship and cooperation between the two countries so far; and the importance of China shops' function in shaping China–Botswana relations at the grass-roots level; as well as the model function of China shop business. Premised on these considerations, the study investigates the migrant motivation of Chinese merchants, reason for conflicts between Chinese merchants and the Batswana in their daily interactions in China shops, particularly against the background of the boom of Chinese presence in Botswana.

This chapter outlines the research problem by focusing on the gap between stereotypical Batswana views on Chinese in Botswana and the reports of the Chinese government. This is followed by a problem statement, a research purpose and questions as well as a justification for the research. The section includes a presentation of the background context and the development of Botswana–China relations. Finally, the research design and organisation of the book will be stated.

1.1. The Research Problem

China's presence in Africa has been a hot topic in the world and is often represented by keywords such as 'poaching', 'land grabbing', 'new neo-colonialism', and 'dumping fake goods' in news headlines that concern China's engagement with Africa. Unfortunately, most people are only familiar with the image of China in Africa through journalists and media analysts. Therefore, the problems hidden behind these representations are: first, the people are only familiar with information to which they have easy access; second, the information is represented by biased sources, even though the role of journalists and media analysts is to bring the comprehensive truth; third, not only is the information biased, the information does not have concrete fieldwork to back it up. Cissé (2014, p. 2) criticises the ironic functions of the media, even some academics in Western countries and China, as below:

> To counter China's growing global expansion and footprint in the world political and economic affairs, some western academics, journalists, and media analysts at times claim to be China experts without conducting any empirical study (on the ground) on any specific research topic regarding China–Africa relations or China's engagement with the rest of the world. The mere repetition of a familiar tune contributes to the so called 'China bashing'. Similarly, with opposing goals, Chinese media experts and academics contribute to official Chinese propaganda by ignoring the situation on the ground and not trying to take a perspective of the affected Africans. Many Chinese scholars working on Africa have never been to the continent – and this is changing only slowly, as there seem to be fears of moving away from the official line and party control.

It is not difficult to see that the top-down perspective of media and academic research is limited to reflect the reality on the ground. Therefore, bottom-up field research is indispensable for us to understand China–Africa relations. With the sharp discrepancies between overwhelmingly negative coverage from the western and African countries, on the one hand, and boastfully positive reports from the Chinese, on the other hand, there is an urgency to discern the reality of China–Africa relations and to understand how different factors come to contribute to shape the image of China in Africa.

1.1.1. Negative Local Media Coverage

In recent years, the majority of the news regarding the Chinese in Botswana issued by Batswana media is negative and resentful. Some notable examples are 'Fake Chinese DVDs, CDs off the shelves' (Gaotlhobogwe 9 April 2009), 'Chinese shops a relief, but they must behave' (Keoreng 30 January 2009), 'Government moves to ban Chinese trade in clothes' (Gaotlhobogwe 27 January 2009), 'Shop assistants in Chinese stores maltreated?' (Bule 13 November 2009), etc. Among all the negative articles, 'We are not a Chinese colony … to hell with the Chinese' (Rasina 20 June 2013) is the one that drew the most Chinese attention. It was written by an individual and published two months later by the local online newspaper Echo. The author's furious words were later translated into Chinese and circulated among Chinese people in Botswana. Although the majority of the Chinese argued that the article was an exaggeration, many did consider it as an ultimatum from Botswana. To give some insight, part of the article is cited below (Rasina 20 June 2013):

> The British came to Botswana in 1895, conquered but finally left when the time was conducive for us to take charge of our own affairs. In the recent years the Chinese came, they conquered and never left. They remain here. They own restaurants, construction companies, our girlfriends, our boyfriends; they steal our wild animals for their skins and tusks. They sell drugs and use our country as money laundering channel. They have imported cheap and unsustainable products to sell to our unsuspecting people. They have more than overstayed their welcome.
>
> The Chinese Community in Botswana constitute amongst the biggest numbers of illegal immigrants. They cost us money through deportations. We are unable to speak to them as they use only their language and thus unable to do business with them. … They fake our national identity cards and passports. They are not the kind of visitors' one wish to have. The Chinese have overstayed their welcome. They continue to bear many children and increase the Chinese population beyond limits. The Chinese refuse to use Botswana local banks. They send all their monies, of every business transaction back to China; they don't have bank accounts in Botswana. …
>
> We are more than a Chinese colony, ours is too bad, they own the land, food, projects, money, labor, and it is an open secret that they own some of our politicians for power and authority. It is

possibly high time that we thank the Chinese for the useless and abusive friendship we have had with them and ask them to leave our country. This is too much, it's out of control. We can't go on like this. We will pay the China Government whatever we owe it and part ways with them. We are surely being milked. We can't pretend to like them. They surely do not like us either; they just love our money, women and land. They must leave. We can't allow ourselves to be Chinese colony anymore. It's enough. To hell with the Chinese and their neo colonialism!

According to local media, the Chinese's offence in Botswana could be listed as this: dumping poor quality goods, violating local business regulations, exploiting local workers, contributing to local officers' corruption, dominating the local market, etc. These offences not only show the key issues concerning Botswana–China relations but also to some extent reveal the stereotypical image of Chinese activity in Africa.

Furthermore, Botswana local media have been influenced by the West for a long time, which is very common among African countries. Mbeki, the then president of South Africa, addressed the launch of SABC News International in 1997:

> For far too long we have relied on others to tell us our own stories. For that long we have seemed content to parrot the words and stories of others about us as if they were the gospel truth … The international broadcast news landscape is not only dominated by a few resource-rich channels, but even when African broadcasters participate in the dissemination of news it is always in the context of stories filed by foreign news agencies, with headquarters in Atlanta, New York, London and other major cities of the powerful nations (Mbeki 2007).

Using random sample and university-based surveys, Sautman and Yan (2009) elaborate on the first empirically based study of what Africans think of their relationships with China. They argue that national attitudinal differences are mainly accounted for by parties making China–Africa links an electoral issue. International media influence is also significant, but secondary (2009, p. 747). They also found that Botswana's newspapers contain a surfeit of headlines and content that invite readers to draw 'anti-China' and 'anti-Chinese' conclusions. Botswana's newspapers draw upon Western sources for their international analysis. Some of the newspapers were founded or are managed by British or South African whites. The primary domestic sources for local journalists on politically charged questions tend to be politicians, as well as academics tied to opposition parties (ibid., p. 754).

1.1.2. Positive Reports from the Chinese Government

Contrary to the negative local media reports, however, the reports of the Chinese government emphasised many positive relationships between the two countries, using the website of the Chinese Embassy. In 2010, on 35th anniversary of establishment of diplomatic relations between the People's Republic of China and the Republic of Botswana, a speech titled 'Memories and blessings of China–Botswana relations' was made by the Chinese envoy, Liu Huangxing (Liu 2010) as quoted below:

> … Much achievement has been made in governmental economic and technical cooperation. Governmental cooperation in economy and technology may serve as the driving force of economic relations between the two countries. To support Botswana's nation building endeavors, China has provided Botswana with certain amount of financial assistance including grant and preferential loans, with which 26 projects have been completed. …
>
> Steady progress has been registered in mutual-beneficial cooperation of enterprises. Chinese companies have all along been actively involved in the activities of economic development of Botswana, with much emphasis on the sectors of contracted projects. … The entry of the Chinese construction companies is helpful in terminating the monopoly of a few foreign companies, reducing the tender price of contracted project to a much more reasonable level. Through their excellent performance, the Chinese companies have won reputation of strict contract execution with high quality. More importantly, they have also created a large number of job

opportunities for local people. According to statistics, the number of local workers employed by the Chinese construction companies has reached 9,000. Some local workers have started their own construction companies after learning technical and management skills from their Chinese counterparts. ...

Chinese wholesale and retail business has benefited local market. Some Chinese nationals are active in running businesses of garment, footwear, baggage, household apparatus, light-industrial product, food, motors and so on. What should be noted is that all the businesses in this regard are private. One may recall that Botswana used to have stores, shops and supermarkets merely based in urban area, and rarely did people in rural areas have access to this kind of services. Such a phenomenon has changed forever since the arrival of the Chinese businesses. They scatter across Botswana and their existence has not only brought convenience to the local people, especially those residing in remote regions, but also helped in lessening the impact of mounting inflation facing the local economy. About 5,000 jobs have been produced in this sector for the local people.

Apart from bringing economic benefit, technology transfers and job opportunities to Botswana as mentioned in the above, the various Chinese businesses here also make their contribution to social and community development of Botswana. ... Generally speaking, most of the Chinese nationals in Botswana are playing their active part in strengthening the friendship and understanding between the two countries. However, some unpleasant behavioural problems have been encountered in certain Chinese individuals living in Botswana. The Embassy does not tolerate such problems and has appealed all the time to every Chinese citizen in Botswana to behave properly and live harmoniously with the local people.

To celebrate the 40 years' anniversary a speech titled '40 Years of Friendship and Cooperation' was given by Ambassador Zheng Zhuqiang in the University of Botswana. He again emphasised the friendship between the two countries and the contributions of China by the government, companies and merchants. He also referred to contributions to the 'China Dream' and reiterated the willingness of China to share development opportunities with Botswana, as cited below (Zheng 2014):

> All these assistance demonstrate that the nature of China–Africa relations is 'sharing of weal and woe', and China's concept on China–Africa cooperation is 'sincerity, real results, affinity, and trustworthiness' through its real action. It also reflects the nature of 'Chinese Dream', which is the pursuit of a common peaceful and prosperous world, not confined to its own territory, but for all human being. 'Chinese Dream' is a dream about peace and development, and China is always ready to share its development opportunities with other countries, especially with African countries.

According to the message of the Chinese Embassy in Botswana, the Chinese government has invested much energy into building a mutually beneficial relationship with Botswana. And both Chinese state-run companies and wholesale/retail business have contributed to the development of Botswana and benefited the local society. Although some unpleasant behavioural problems of Chinese individuals living in Botswana have been mentioned, the conflicts have not been discussed in great detail. However, when we link the reports of the Chinese government to the negative local media coverage, a big gap in their perspectives is distinct. What really happened between the Chinese in Botswana and local people? How was the relationship between them shaped? To understand the reality, a new perspective beyond local media and Chinese government reports is required.

1.1.3 China Shops' Presence in Botswana–China Relations

Mohan et al. (2014, p. 1) argues that much of the discussion of China in Africa has been framed by oppositional discourses, which argue that the presence of Chinese people and firms is either uniformly 'bad' for Africans or resoundingly a 'good' thing. Those are important debates which usually link to change in the global order and the ideological perspectives of the powerful states involved. However, micro-level issues do not take place in the abstract. Those changing relationships are about people on the move and the linkage between places. It is migration that links up the macro-level issue to the micro-level (ibid.).

In this book, the term 'China shop' will describe Chinese-owned shops that sell Chinese made goods to the everyday Botswana consumer. According to the data gathered in the field, almost all of the China shops are operated by Chinese people. In South Africa, Park and Chen (2009) also find the term 'China shops' widely used in the region. In 1995 the first Chinese shop opened in the capital of Cape Verde, Praia. The Cape Verdeans call those shops 'Chinese shops', while the Chinese migrants use the term 'baihuo shops' (general merchandise) (Haugen and Carling 2005). In their research, they use the term 'China shop' to describe textile shops selling a wide assortment of Chinese-made products (usually including clothing, shoes and other 'leather' products, toys and baby items, small electronics and household appliances, and blankets) that are owned and operated by new Chinese immigrants (Park and Chen 2009, p. 31).

Giese (2013, p. 136) emphasises that trading can be seen as central to the understanding of the formation of grass-roots Chinese–African relations, since family-run Chinese trading companies have bloomed in all major urban centres and, for most Africans, the Chinese presence is marked by traders in the markets. Playing a role as a frontline of the Botswana–China encounter, China shops are the bond that ties the closest grass-roots level of Botswana–China relations. Therefore China shops are a good spot for us to gain insights into Botswana–China relations.

Furthermore, the key relationships that can be observed readily between Chinese merchants and the Batswana people in the China shops highlight the face-to-face, ground-level interactions between Chinese merchants and Batswana customers, Chinese employers and Batswana employees, as well as between Chinese entrepreneurs and Botswana authorities. These face-to-face interactions that can be observed in the China shops also represent key interactions operating in any China–Botswana cooperation projects, such as construction and mining projects. However, the interaction in the construction and mining sectors is hidden and not as tangible or visible as that in China shops. Therefore, to some extent, the China shop can be regarded as a miniature model for researching cultural and economic contact and interaction between Chinese and Batswana people.

Here I would like to introduce the 'Building the Image of China' model (see Fig.1) in Botswana. At the top level, China has been increasingly using the soft power of nation branding, such as the Shanghai Expo, Beijing Olympics and Confucius Institute (Barr 2012, p. 83) to improve her international image, due to the fact that she does not have a strong national brand like Toyota, Sony or Chanel. In a developing country like Botswana, the impact of the image campaign that China adopted manages to impact local people to some extent. However, it is somehow limited to a short period of time (Shanghai Expo, Beijing Olympics) and some can only impact an educated group (Confucius Institute). At the middle level, Chinese companies, particularly construction companies do impact locals' development in a significant way, however, it also comes at a high risk. As I will explain in more detail in Chapter 8, the Chinese who work for Chinese companies are usually 'hidden' from the public scene (Lam 2015). Even Chinese companies are seldom known to the public until things go wrong; then related negative news will be seen in local newspapers. Compared to national brands like Toyota and Benz that are familiar to a wide range of consumers, China's image campaign is less effective in capturing the majority's hearts and minds. To the majority in Botswana, the most familiar presence of China is the China shop, not the Confucius Institute or pandas. Therefore, the bottom level, the private-sector exchange (China shop), becomes a medium of nation-branding at the grass-roots level spontaneously without any involvement of the central government. The interactions conducted between Chinese merchants and local people infleunces the foundation that builds the image of China in Botswana. In daily interactions between Chinese merchants and local people, *suzhi* (素质) – the quality of Chinese merchants as well as the quality of Chinese merchandise are the determining factors. *Suzhi* of Chinese merchants, as revealed through the manner of individual Chinese merchants and their daily interaction with local people, also influences the image of China. Here I quote the definition of *suzhi* from Yan Hairong's work. It usually refers to the somewhat ephemeral qualities of civility, self-discipline and modernity (Yan 2003). Furthermore, Chinese racialisation also rests on the concept of 'quality' conceived in terms of discipline, honesty, industriousness and skill (Sautman and Yan 2016). During interactions with African local people, *suzhi* can also be translated into manner, shared common sense in African local culture and even, to some extent, ablility to speak English (since many Botswana locals judge people's education level by the measure of their command of English).

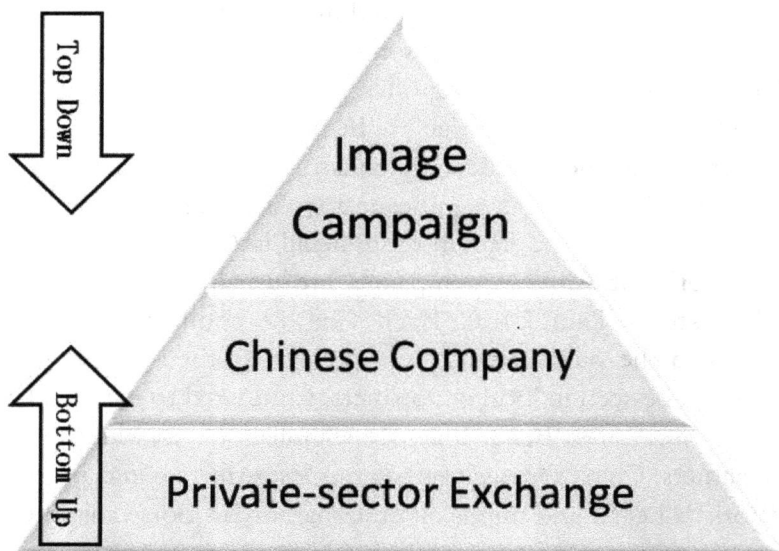

Figure 1. Building the Image of China

The few academic studies on the topic of Chinese trading in Botswana are limited to the work of Kalusopa (2009), which is based on a few cases regarding China shops and relies primarily on local news. As Youngman (2013, p. 14) states, at this point in time there is a lack of empirical information that can provide a reliable guide to those who wish to enhance the relationship between Botswana and China; to bridge this knowledge gap, a wide range of studies are required to identify the challenges and opportunities in the relationship. So far, past work conducted has dealt little with fieldwork, and in comparison my research is novel as it is based on close ethnographic field research.

1.2. Research Purpose and Research Questions

The aim of the research is to explore how social interactions in China shops help in shaping the image of China in Botswana and how the interactions influence Chinese merchants on an individual level, focusing on the micro-level relations between Chinese merchants and Batswana locals, including customers, shop assistants, as well as regulatory authorities from the government.

The research questions examined are:

1. What are the experiences of Chinese merchants as they move to and live in Botswana?
2. What challenges are encountered by Chinese merchants in Botswana? What strategies do they put in place to combat the challenges?
3. How do Chinese merchants interact with the local customers, local employees and local authorities? How does the social interaction with local people shape the *suzhi* (quality) of Chinese merchants as well as the quality of Chinese merchandise?

1.3. Justification for the Study

It is common to find a gap between local media reports and Chinese governmental reports (Cissé 2014). The large imbalance between the local media reports and Chinese governmental reports on the China–Botswana relationship is concerning and necessitates field research, as in this study, to clarify the issues and the discourse behind it in greater depth. In addition, understanding the relationship between the Chinese and Batswana people in China shops can elucidate the cultural similarities and differences behind their conflicts. In turn, mutual understanding on these differences can offer concrete cross-cultural solutions to resolve conflicts. This research hopes to provide first-hand insight into the widely discussed industrial labour conflicts caused by Chinese enterprises in Africa (Giese 2013), by highlighting the cultural similarities and differences between the two involved parties. Furthermore, this study will also help to raise awareness of other potential cultural-economical conflicts similar in nature and provide a basis for future research studies on intercultural relations.

Botswana is well known as a stable and peaceful country in Africa. Although it has been 20 years since the first bunch of Chinese merchants went to Botswana and a lot of changes have occurred due to China–Botswana interactions on different levels, not much attention has been paid by scholars concerning China–Botswana relations, particularly the relationship on the ground.

1.4. Contextual Background

1.4.1. General Economic Summary of Botswana

Botswana is one of the most dynamic economies in Africa. However, according to the Botswana Economic Outlook, current unemployment stands at 17.8 per cent, and 18.4 per cent of the population live below the poverty line. Mineral extraction and diamond mining are the principal economic activities, although tourism is a growing sector because of the country's conservation practices and extensive nature reserves. The Mbendi information service (2014) states that the manufacturing sector in Botswana is relatively small, accounting for only an estimated 5 per cent of its GDP; this is due to the small domestic market, and the fact that South Africa supplies most of the country's needs. Aside from meat processing, Botswana has had no notable manufacturing activity since its independence in 1966.

According to Best (1970), for a considerable period, people originating from Europe and India occupied crucial roles within Botswana's economy, while the Batswana were relative newcomers to the trading community. Because of Botswana's inexperience and undercapitalisation, the country was highly dependent upon European and Indian wholesalers and transporters (ibid., p. 610). Even now, Botswana remains influenced by many South African investments, including large supermarket chain stores such as Shoprite, Pick n Pay, and Spar, and clothing and apparel chain stores, examples of which are PEP, Ackermans, Mr Price and Bata. These chain stores can be found distributed throughout the cities' shopping malls and, in some cases, even in medium-sized towns. Therefore, despite Botswana having attained independence some time ago, the economic influence from South Africa remains or has even increased.

With Botswana's economic boom in the 1980s due to the livestock industry and diamond mining, plus the high mortality rate caused by HIV, it faced a manpower shortage. There were not enough local talents to satisfy the needs of a growing economy, which attracted an influx of expatriates from all over the world. Better pay and working conditions attracted professionals from various African countries to South Africa's homelands (and later to black-ruled South Africa), Botswana, and Zimbabwe, until many Zimbabweans began leaving because of the failing economy and repressive government. This kind of brain drain helped the prosperous and politically stable Botswana to attract professionals, particularly to the private sector and university, from South Africa, Ghana, Zambia, Zimbabwe, Nigeria and Kenya (Shinn 2008). Later, most of the leading positions and rewarding careers were occupied by foreigners because of their superior education and skills. According to Kalusopa (2009, p. 126), the items listed below are believed to be the advantages that attracted foreign investment and trade in various fields:

- political and social stability
- least corrupt government in Africa (rule of law and transparency)
- stable economic and financial situation and prudent economic management
- government's commitment to adoption of serials of preferential policies that target foreign investors, e.g. provision of a 25 per cent tax refund on exports
- existence of relatively harmonious relations between Botswana and its neighbouring nations (these mutual relations include SACU and SADC establishment)

However, on the other hand, the Batswana's xenophobia is widely recognised by people from other African countries (Lesetedi and Moroka 2007). As the following citation shows (Sayila 2002):

> The locals (Batswana) accept the fact that they cannot do without the immigrants who are here simply to make money and improve their lives, yet they are cold towards them. However, the cold attitude is not extended to Westerners, which may be due to the colonial history. But Chinese businessmen have become the latest on the list of abhorred aliens from neighboring countries like Zimbabwe, South Africa and Zambia.

1.4.2. Overview of Botswana–China Relationship

One of the most important events in the history of relations between China and the entire third world, and Africa in particular, is their establishment of the government in Peking to China's seat on the United Nations Security Council in 1971 (Achberger 2010, p. 369). The displacement of Taipei and the Republic of China and the seating of Peking and the People's Republic of China was because of the diplomatic recognition and United Nations votes of African nations (ibid.). During the period of anti-colonial nationalism and the struggle for independence in Africa, China made its contribution to the political liberation of African countries by providing both moral and material support (Bolaane 2007, p. 144). Given a history of the struggle against colonialism and imperialism, their support to one another is based on the common cause of safeguarding national sovereignty and developing the national economy. Since independence many African countries have established diplomatic relations with China that provided the political foundation for later economic and trade contacts between China and Africa (ibid.). During the period of Cold War geopolitical alignment, Chinese government officials repeatedly stated that their only aim in Africa was to provide the economic investment that the new nations so desperately needed. This manifested itself in a number of different projects throughout the continent (Achberger 2010, p. 371).

Botswana and the People's Republic of China established diplomatic relations in January 1975. Based on the principles of sincere friendship, mutual respect and trust, equality and mutual benefit, the friendly relations and cooperation between the two countries have been developing at a very fast speed (Embassy of the People's Republic of China in the Republic of Botswana 2008). Both countries have related on a stable basis and have established strong political ties. The closeness and friendliness of this relationship have been expressed in frequent exchanges of high-level visits, steady progress in all fields and good coordination in international relations. Both sides have been supportive of each other's stance on major international issues. China is especially indebted to Botswana for its firm adherence to the One China principle (ibid.).

Significant efforts have been committed by both countries towards the development of socio-cultural exchanges and cooperation. In 1991, according to local news, China and Botswana signed the Agreement on Cultural Cooperation and since then various events have been exchanged (Liu 2010). China also has been supportive of cooperation in education and human resources development in Botswana. Since 1984, China has provided Chinese Government scholarships annually to Botswana students to pursue masters and doctorate degrees in China. To support human resources development in Botswana, short-term training opportunities are offered to Botswana by China, covering areas of informatics, agriculture, business and commerce, industry, sport, military and more. Short-term training now plays a very important role in the human resources cooperation between the two countries. As a new form of technical cooperation, China would like to send young volunteers to work in Botswana in areas needed by Botswana (Embassy of the People's Republic of China in the Republic of Botswana 2008).

Furthermore, the University of Botswana (UB) signed an agreement at the headquarters of the Confucius Institute to establish the Confucius Institute at UB in October, 2007. The opening ceremony of the Confucius Institute was held in November 2008, and by 2010 there were more than 200 Batswana students studying in the institute, specialising in Chinese language and culture. Besides, Chinese medical teams have been servicing in Botswana for many years. Since 1980, China has consecutively dispatched to Botswana more than 300 medical personnel, under a bilateral agreement. The government of China paid all the salaries starting from 12th contingent of the Medical Team (Liu 2010).

It is also worth mentioning that cooperative projects between China and Botswana have reached remarkable achievements in recent years. It is believed that governmental cooperation in economy and technology has served as the driving force of economic relations between the two countries. To support Botswana's nation-building endeavours, China has provided Botswana with a certain amount of financial assistance including grants and preferential loans to support the projects such as the renovation of the Botswana railway, low-cost housing, land survey and planning, road construction, health facilities, agricultural technology, human resources development and so on.

Since Botswana established diplomatic relations with China, inter-governmental co-operation in the fields of economy and technology has been a driving force in their relationship. In parallel, over the past decade, Chinese merchants have migrated on a global scale, distributing made-in-China goods (Ma Mung 2008, p. 648). Currently, it is estimated that there are approximately 1,000 China shops distributed across the cities and rural towns. The spread of these shops to villages throughout the country has brought a great deal of convenience to consumers, particularly those living in remote areas; Chinese products have also curbed price rises, especially in response to pressure caused by mounting inflation of the local currency (Bolaane 2007, p. 164).

1.4.3. Botswana–China Trade Relations and their Social and Economic Impact

The first Chinese who come to Botswana were in the construction industry. They arrived after the signing of an agreement in 1977 on technical cooperation by President Seretse Khama and the Chinese, and the agreement focused on railway rehabilitation (Youngman 2013; Mathangwane 2015). Trade between Botswana and China started in the early 1980s. In June 1980 the Vice-President of Botswana, Quett Masire, visited Beijing to exchange experiences in economic construction, which was later followed by the visit of a Botswana delegation in December of that year. In 1984, the first Chinese construction company, China Civil, started business in Botswana and was later followed by other companies. Those companies worked on small projects such as building houses, junior secondary schools and some private buildings (Youngman 2013; Mathangwane 2015, p. 51). The bilateral trade operations are boosted by the Trade Agreement signed in 1986 (Liu 6 January 2010). China was eager to strengthen commercial links with Botswana and sent a trade mission to participate in the Gaborone International Trade Fair in 1998, which resulted in a large increase in imports from Botswana. On the other hand, to attract Chinese commerce, in 1991 the Botswana President appealed to Chinese industrialists to help with the industrial development of Botswana (Taylor 2006). Chinese investment in the wholesale and retail enterprises has benefited from the good relations between the two countries as well. As the economy grew rapidly during the 1990s, the country became more and more attractive to Chinese investors and traders (Mathangwane 2015, p. 51). In 2004 the Gaborone Oriental Plaza, a large wholesale shopping complex selling Chinese goods, opened (Bolaane 2007; Mathangwane 2015, p. 51).

Concerning the recent situation regarding retail and wholesale trade, in an interview with Business Week, the Chinese ambassador to Botswana, Ding Xiaowen, said that more than 1,000 Batswana went to China in 2008 and imported containers of clothing and electronic gadgets. He suggested that Chinese traders may have virtually taken over the clothing shop business at the expense of the Batswana because of globalisation and the immaturity of the Botswana market. He said:

> I hope Batswana will learn from the Chinese and do as China does. If the local entrepreneurs want to push the Chinese out of business, I think they should just simply do better than the Chinese. They should bring in more of the low cost goods, with a wide variety

for the convenience of the consumers and then the Chinese will leave gradually. At the end of the day, with this globalisation, business is still business. For the consumers, no one wants to buy less and spend more. ... But I believe the current situation is temporary and the solution lies with Batswana as they should try to be more competitive and go to China and import the gadgets and the clothes. ... So I believe that in an immature market like Botswana, it is better for the locals to learn from the Chinese than to try and install protectionism at the expense of the consumers. However, I still believe there should be some preferential treatment for the locals as the economy is still very young (Embassy of the People's Republic of China in the Republic of Botswana 2009).

It is said that Botswana–China trade relations have brought positive socio-economic results (Kalusopa 2009). The cooperative projects and investment ventures have contributed to Botswana's development, and the creation of job opportunities for Botswana citizens. On the 33rd anniversary of the establishment of diplomatic relations between China and Botswana, the Chinese Embassy declared that approximately 9,000 locals had been employed by the Chinese construction companies, whereas 5,000 jobs had been created by wholesale and retail business. This constitutes six per cent of the jobs in this sector. Beside the benefit gained from job opportunities, technical and management skills are transferred from Chinese experts to Botswana as well. Apart from this, Chinese investors and traders have also ventured into textile and clothing factories. Those factories are not only dedicated to employment creation but also to foreign exchange because the products from these factories are exported to USA, South Africa and European countries (Embassy of the People's Republic of China in the Republic of Botswana 2008).

The Chinese top leaders' visit to Africa marked the programme of aid and economic cooperation (Bräutigam 2009). According to Bräutigam's research, in 1995 three Chinese vice-premiers visited a total of 18 African countries. Compared to neighbouring counties in Southern Africa, Botswana had not been well visited by Chinese top leaders from 1995 to 2009. However, in Novermber 2010 the then Chinese Vice President and now President, Xi Jinping, met with Botswana's Vice President Mompati Merafhe in Gaborone, capital of Botswana, and signed a cooperation deal bringing around six million US dollars to the Southern African country (News of the Communist Party of China 22 November 2010). In 2011, the then State Councillor and now Vice Premier of China, Madam Liu Yandong visited Botswana (Zheng 2014). When it comes to trading relations, China is now the third largest trade partner of Botswana and the third largest consumer of Botswana diamonds (Batlotleng 18 July 2013). Chinese companies are active players in Botswana's construction, service and manufacturing industries and have made contributions to Botswana's economic diversification (ibid.).

On the other side, the perceptions of local people seem contrary to the governmental report, which unveiled the other side of the China–Botswana relationship. According to Sautman and Yan (2009), a university-based survey showed that the small businesses in Botswana and Zambia 'help with the local economic development but also a source of problem for local people', the percentage of which is extremely higher than any other items (Figure 2). Furthermore, as shown in Figure 3, the impression of Chinese presence in Botswana has gained the highest percentage for being unfriendly when compared to other African countries.

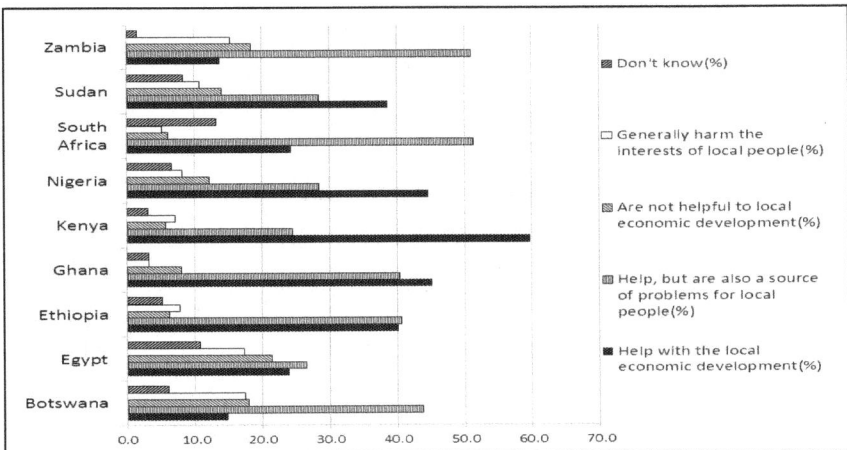

Figure 2. View of Chinese Small Businesses in My Country[2]

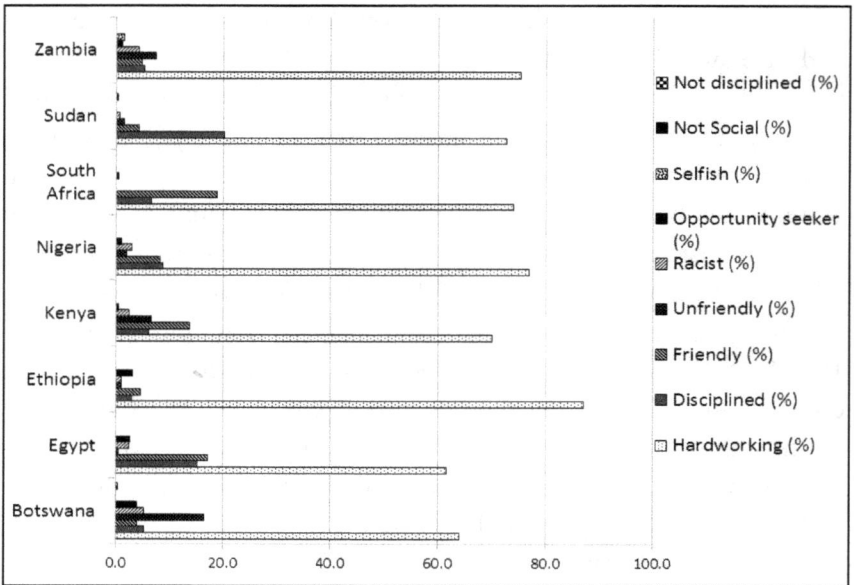

Figure 3. Impression of the Chinese Presence in My Country[3]

In 2008, the Ministry of Trade and Industry updated a new list of business reserved for citizens of Botswana or for companies wholly owned by the citizens of Botswana in accordance with the new trade law of 2003, which came into operation in May 2008. The list of 13 includes licences for general clothing, general dealer, car wash, auctioneer, fresh produce, funeral parlour, hairdresser, laundromat, petrol filling station, fast food, cleaning services and curio shop businesses (Embassy of the People's Republic of China in the Republic of Botswana 2009; Trade Act 2003).

According to local news Mmegi (Gaotlhobogwe 27 January 2009), the government of Botswana moved to ban Chinese trade in clothes. The Botswana licensing department issued special licences to protect local traders from the non-citizen investors engaged in specialised trades.[4] However, Chinese traders exploited a loophole in the system, applying for special licences to sell almost anything in the same shop. The government decided to ban non-citizens, especially the Chinese traders, from dealing in clothing at a time when Chinese traders were found in every corner of the country, selling all types of clothes, mainly fake overseas clothing brands. With 654 China shops holding special licences, the licensing department was forced to abolish the licence system in May 2008. Chinese traders were given two years to rearrange their businesses or face the loss of their licences (ibid.). After the news of the local government's decision to close foreign-owned clothing shops was spread, many local people, especially needy people, stood up for China shops, saying that they appreciated the cheap goods sold in China shops, without which they could not make ends meet (Keoreng 30 January 2009).

Permanent Secretary B.K. Molosiwa of the Ministry of Trade and Industry put on record in an article titled 'Government Moves to Ban Chinese Trade in Clothes,' that appeared in the Mmegi issue of 27 January 2009. Later, Mr. Molosiwa clarified his declaration, saying that the government does not have a policy that discriminates against any nationality or any businesses entities including the Chinese business community residing in Botswana:

> The truth of the matter is that the ministry of Trade and Industry has, in respect of existing business, directed that operators that sell goods that were unrelated, that is, those that were essentially General Dealers, which are reserved for citizens only under the new Trade Act, should be licensed on condition that they rearrange their operations, within a period of 24 months. This decision was made in recognition of the fact that certain non-citizens previously circumvented the reservation policy and used the Specialized Dealer's license to operate essentially as General Dealers. Under the new Trade Act, the miscellaneous license specifies that goods or services should be of a similar range of products.

The Embassy of the People's Republic of China in the Republic of Botswana (2009) responded to the action of Ministry of Trade and Industry as below to justify the mandate of the Botswana government, so as to help adjust the disturbed trading order:

> The mandate of the Ministry of Trade and Industry is to facilitate trade and at the same time ensure that the business environment is not fraught with unfair business practices. This is done by amongst other things, monitoring that businesses adhere to the requisite

statutes and taking action as may be required to remedy any unlawful practices.

In addition, the regulation of Chinese businesses has tightened in recent years as a result of local policy changes. Botswana had so far relied on imports, but in recent years the local government has established new policies to initiate business and manufacturing instead (Ministry of Trade and Industry 2011). The local government, through the Economic Diversification Drive (EDD) and Citizen Entrepreneurial Development Agency (CEDA), provides a holistic approach to the development and promotion of viable sustainable citizen-owned enterprises in order to promote the growth of a vibrant and globally competitive private sector. In this political environment, many Chinese merchants are experiencing difficulties with government officials due to increased inspections targeting sales of counterfeits, tax evasion and other illegal/informal business activities. In 2015 the government of Botswana even planned to drastically reduce the number of retail licences issued to Chinese people, with the aim of preserving the retail business for Batswana locals (Motsamai 1 July 2015).

1.5. Organisation of the Book

Chapter 1 describes the study, outlines the context of the research and provides a statement of the problem as well as an overview of the structure of the book.

Chapter 2 presents a review of the related literature. It reviews studies on China–African relations, the Chinese in African countries, Africans in China as well as their impact on local societies. The chapter also summarises the research on the China shop phenomenon in Asian and African countries to further situate the research problem. It discusses the theoretical framework adopted in this study and its justification. The chapter concludes by the typology of ethical problems in retail sales.

Chapter 3 presents research methodology, design and methods used in the study. It discusses the advantages of mixed methods research adopted in this study through reviewing related anthropological references. The weaknesses inherent in these approaches as well as the specific research questions of the study are presented as a justification for choosing methodological eclecticism. The chapter further discusses research design and methods employed in data collection and analysis as well as the scope and delimitations of the study.

Chapter 4 focuses on the first question of the research: What are the experiences of Chinese merchants coming and living in Botswana? The first part of this chapter introduces the logistical chain of Chinese merchandise and the Chinese markets in Botswana. Then it focuses on the chain of migration of Chinese merchants, their family background and daily lives in Botswana. The quantitative findings presented in this chapter suggest the composition of Chinese merchants and migration wave of their coming to Botswana. However, the qualitative findings reveal a variety of migrant experiences, life situations and migration plans among the Chinese merchants. Both quantitative and qualitative data help to grasp the changes in the local market situation over the years.

Chapter 5 discusses the second research question: What are the Chinese merchants' businesses challenges in general in Botswana? The theory of a middleman minority is used as a theoretical perspective to assess both the challenges and the strategies employed to meet them. It argues that Chinese merchants' self-imposed isolation (combined with their sense of vulnerability as foreigners) is deeply rooted in their attitudes. Their social position determines their circumstances and their responses to signs of hostility from the host society. On the other hand, the particular geographical location and economic situation of Botswana offers Chinese merchants opportunities to avoid competing among themselves and to manage their rejection by local society. Based on the background of Chinese merchants and their business in Botswana, this section gives a panoramic picture of the key issues between Chinese merchants and local society. From a middleman minority perspective, this section locates the social position of Chinese merchants in order to explain the nature of business challenges the Chinese face as well as the business strategies they employ. However, the details concerning social influence brought by Chinese merchants and their interaction with local assistants will be discussed in the later chapters.

Chapter 6 addresses the first part of the third research question: How do Chinese merchants relate to and affect local customers and local authorities? How does the social interaction between Chinese merchants and local people shape the quality of Chinese merchandise? 'Made-in-China' goods have received widespread criticism in Africa for their poor quality and negative effects on the local marketplace. They are termed fong kong (Barrett 2007), and in Southern Africa including Botswana, are regarded as cheap copies or fakes (Park 2013a). In Botswana, fong kong is linked to Chinese merchants, bringing a negative image to Chinese businesses and triggering governmental restrictions on Chinese businesses. However, surprisingly, fong kong continues to be sold on the local market. This chapter aims to address two sub-questions. First, why fong kong are prevalent despite of the quality and legal issues, as well as the governmental regulations in Botswana society? Second, what is the social and economic influence of fong kong? In the first part of the chapter I will give a brief introduction to the arrival of fong kong, the push and pull factors on them as well as local government's attitudes towards them. In the second part, this chapter mainly introduces fong kong's influence on local industry and retailers, the local demand for various types of fong kong and the related policies of governmental regulation of China shops.

Chapter 7 answers the latter part of the third research question: How do Chinese merchants relate to and affect local employees and local authorities? How does the social interaction between Chinese merchants and local people shape the quality (*suzhi*) of Chinese merchants? This chapter analyses the employment relationships between Chinese merchants and Batswana employees, focusing on organisational commitment and interpersonal trust at work. After investigating recruitment processes, daily employer–employee conflicts, treatment and work attitudes were analysed with consideration of the social status of the Chinese merchants and Batswana employees. From the perspectives of occupational psychology, I found that there was little respect or interpersonal trust between Chinese merchants and local employees, mainly due to local employees' poor work ethics. On the other hand, Chinese merchants' frugality and exploitive image failed to fulfil the personal needs of local employees, which invited complaints and a bad reputation. Although employment relations – the closest interaction between Chinese merchants and local people – seem the fieriest, it requires a more patient and long-term view to see the improvement achieved in social and culture exchange.

Chapter 8 presents how factors outside of China shops influence the image of China and the relationship between grass-roots interactions in China shops and the failure of Chinese companies charged with mega-projects. This chapter also answers the remaining question posed in Chapter 6 as to why local customers in Botswana have negative attitudes towards Chinese goods despite the fact that their quality has improved. My main argument is that Batswana customers' negative attitudes towards Chinese goods are mainly influenced by the failure of Chinese mega-projects, local negative media reports and their own economic vulnerability. Furthermore, I argue that China shops play a lens role by indicating the macro-level China–Botswana relationship by catching micro-level interactions and perceptions in society.

Chapter 9 discusses the geographical mobility of Chinese merchants, analyses their short-term vision as well as the influence of government regulations on China shop business. This chapter aims to find the link between the business climates of Botswana and the movement of Chinese merchants, as well as their businesses. Furthermore, this chapter reveals the fact that grass-roots level China–Africa relations are greatly affected by the relationships at higher governmental levels, as the China shop business in Botswana has suffered as scapegoat when the relationships at higher levels deteriorated. The geographical mobility of Chinese merchants, caused by market saturation and government regulation, explains the presence of a China shop in every village and promotes them as a national brand of China in Botswana.

Chapter 10 presents a summary, conclusions and implications of the findings. It highlights the key questions of the study, the findings of the study and the study's conclusions. The chapter then presents the possible implications of the findings on both theory and practice in improving Botswana–China relations.

Notes

[1] 'Botswana' is a noun that represents the Republic of Botswana. The people of Botswana are called 'Batswana'.

[2] Adapted from Table 5 in Sautman and Yan (2009).

[3] Adapted from Table 10 in Sautman and Yan (2009).

[4] A special licence permits merchants to sell the applicable merchandise that is usually beyond the allowed range. For instance, with only general clothing licence, the shop cannot sell furniture; however, if the owner holds a special licence for furniture, he can sell both clothes and furniture in the same shop.

Chapter 2

Literature Review and the Theoretical Framework

This chapter presents a review of literature related to the study topic. It begins with a background of China–Africa relations and is followed by introduction of the Chinese diaspora in Africa and African diaspora in China. The chapter then discusses the concept of 'China shops', their presence in African and Asian countries, as well as Chinese merchants' business experience and their interaction with local people. This is followed by a discussion on the theoretical framework of the study based on the theory of contact zone and intergroup relations. The chapter concludes with the typology of ethical problems in retail sales and a framework of analysis for this research.

2.1. China–Africa Relations

China's presence in Africa today is undeniable. New economic ventures abound in oil, minerals, timber and factories, not to mention Chinese consumer goods flooding African markets, create tensions and global unease, particularly in the West. Too often however, Africa's history of interactions with China is ignored in current coverage. African nations have more than half a century of interaction with the People's Republic of China (Achberger 2010, pp. 368–369). One of the most important events in the history of relations between China and the entire third world, and Africa in particular, was Peking government's assumption of China's seat in the United Nations Security Council in 1971. Then, the displacement of the Republic of China by the People's Republic of China was the result of diplomatic recognition and United Nations votes by African nations (Achberger 2010, pp. 369–370).

China is essentially a determined and value-maximising state, operating in an environment perceived as disadvantageous to itself. Southern Africa in particular has been a constant focus for China, and the PRC's policy pursuance in Southern Africa has exhibited a constancy that has survived the radical developments in the post-Mao era (Taylor 2006, pp. 3–4). On the African continent Southern Africa has traditionally been the focus of attention for Beijing. It was here that China first engaged with the anti-colonial movements and certainly expended the most energy, and it was in Southern Africa where China expanded its economic ambit. Southern Africa also hosts the continental economic – and arguably political – hegemony and thus any discussion of China's policy on Africa cannot avoid a discussion of China's links with South Africa. But equally, Southern Africa is seen as emblematic of various historical and current tendencies that have staked out Beijing's engagement with the wider continent (Taylor 2006, pp. 4–5).

According to Thrall's (2015, p. xii) analysis, China's government and commercial actors have three primary economic interests in Africa: a source for natural resource imports, a growing and relatively underutilised market for exports and investment, and an opportunity for Chinese firms to increase employment and gain global experience. China's investment in Africa occurs in the broader context of Beijing's 'Go Global' (*zou chu qu*, 走出去) commercial strategy, intended to increase outgoing Chinese investment and commercial presence. Contrary to the model of Chinese firms' operations being driven by Beijing's geopolitical strategy, the vast majority of Chinese economic interactions in Africa are profit-driven, and Beijing has struggled to maintain oversight of its firms' overseas activities (ibid.).

Chinese commercial actors can be loosely grouped into three categories: large, state-owned enterprises (SOEs) pursuing infrastructure and resource projects; large-to-medium private interests pursuing a range of markets; and small, private merchants farming or selling within African marketplaces (Haroz 2011, p. 23). China's citizens in Africa can be envisioned in three major communities, facing different security threats. The first group consists of officials associated with embassies and state-owned companies; these people often stay in an African state for a few years before moving to other foreign states, similar to their Western counterparts. Second are Chinese labourers brought in for major infrastructure projects; they tend to live in Chinese enclaves, interact little with the local population and return to China upon project completion. Finally, there are private Chinese citizens and small-business owners who have expatriated to Africa, have little contact with the Chinese government and are building their businesses in local markets, farms or small-scale production (Haroz 2011, p. 59). Concerning the last group, Bräutigam (2009, p. 86) argues as below:

> The pattern we see today of a Chinese presence in African markets is partly due to the success of government programs to push Chinese export businesses to expand into Africa, but there is no evidence that the Chinese government sends workers to Africa under a plan to have them remain behind as traders. These are individual decisions.

Of course, the movement of Chinese retail traders is not unrelated to the domestic changes in China. Tania Li (2010) uses 'surplus populations' to describe a group of people that have been expelled from rural agricultural production systems but not incorporated into urban industrial working classes, mainly due to land seizures in China since the passing of a new land regulation in 1987 (ibid., p. 7). Ferguson (2015, p. 90) based on his research in Southern Africa holds that the surplus populations excluded from any significant role in the system of production, are either distributing goods produced elsewhere or making claims on the resources of others. This 'surplus populations' phenomenon occurs both in China and in Africa, to some extent, is the engine that drives Chinese merchants and African rural people to meet together in the informal section of retail trade.

In the next section, a review of recent research concerning Chinese small-business owners who expatriate to Africa on their own decisions will be taken.

2.1.1. Chinese in Africa

In the last two decades, new entrepreneurial migrants went to countries in Africa which have no previous history of Chinese immigration, but where there was high demand for low-cost consumer goods produced by China and a lax regulatory environment. Nyíri (2011, p. 145) states that what enabled this migration was the 1986 Law on Exit and Entry Management, which facilitated the issuance of passports, especially so-called service passports, which could be issued to any state employee travelling on business. What propelled it was the situation of the Chinese economy in the late 1980s, when inflation combined with an overproduction glut, and state 'work units' attempted to trim their workforce by encouraging employees to go into business ('plunge into the sea') while retaining some of their workplace benefits (such as housing, health care and pensions). Between 1989 and 1992, a recession and fears of a rollback of economic reforms were additional reasons for fledgling business people to want to leave the country (ibid. 145).

The People's Republic of China's (PRC) change in policy regarding the emigration of Chinese nationals has a big influence on the phenomenon. Xiang (2003) argues that diaspora policy and labour export could be counted as the most significant factors that have influenced the increase of Chinese migrants to African countries in the last several decades. First, over recent years, China's overseas policy has gradually brought 'Chinese overseas' including Chinese descendants and 'new migrants' under its new migrants.[1] Furthermore, the rapid increase in number of the new migrants, and the emphasis on 'new migrant,' is inherently related to China's overall development strategy such as China's progressive integration into the world's economy, international exchanges in the high-technology sectors and the expansion of Chinese firms' international markets. Besides, labour export from China has increased rapidly since the 1980s and has made significant contributions to developing a migration system. According to Xiang (2003), labour export is the practice where companies organise and send workers overseas to meet a destination country's demand for labour. Organised labour export can take two forms. First, companies send workers overseas as 'project workers' to carry out certain projects that are subcontracted to the companies. Second, specialist labour-supply firms send workers overseas and the labour-supply companies are not involved in other aspects of the project.

Ma Mung (2008) gives a succinct description of three kinds of migrations and explores their possible relation with the new foreign policy of the People's Republic of China. The three kinds of migrations are: labour migration within the framework of public works realised by big Chinese enterprises, an entrepreneurial migration composed mainly of traders and a proletarian migration in transit in Africa waiting for opportunities to go on to European countries. According to the paper, recently many of the migrants whose principal activity is distributing Chinese-made goods[2] are settled in the large cities of France, Italy and Spain, in central Europe and in African countries. Entrepreneurial immigration to Africa is part of a widespread movement. In the last decade, soaring numbers of Chinese merchants have migrated on a global scale in conjunction with China's rising production of consumer goods. Guangdong, Fujian and Zhejiang provinces are the main departure zones, which shows the significance of the migratory networks. The paper concludes that the migrations directly connected with China's policy of cooperation with Africa[3] suppose good relations between the government of China and the African countries. Merchant migration, on the other hand, is an active part of PRC policy to expand their export market, since it consists mainly in distributing Chinese industrial goods in the receiving countries. Additionally, migration not only helps reinforce the diaspora and strengthens its autonomy, but also consolidates the physical and symbolic ties between the diaspora and China.

Chinese merchants initiate 'Chinese markets' such as China town, Chinese wholesale markets and retail shops where they conduct business.

> From the shuttle trade of the early years – which involved selling goods brought from China in a market or on a street and then returning to China for the next consignment – the migrants rapidly progressed to a structure that is defined by a network of larger and smaller 'Chinese markets'. These markets function as regional, national, or local clearinghouses for consumer goods (Nyíri 2011, p. 146).

However, the image of the Chinese in Africa and South America is generally negative. Nyíri (2011, p. 149) states that the Chinese dispose of unsold stock, taking advantage of the complementarity of the seasons between the two hemispheres and making use of kinship and native-place connections, particularly among migrants from Fujian. The appearance of these networks has elicited both praise and hostility: praise for supplying a large number of Africans with consumer goods while hostility for unfair competition, smuggling, inferior quality, illegal immigration, ruining local industries, taking local jobs and simply 'invading' foreign countries by virtue of sheer numbers, if not already then surely in the immediate future (ibid.).

2.1.2. Africans in China

While Chinese traders are rushing to the African continent for business opportunities, Africans are also going to China for prosperity. Based on five years' research involving qualitative methods and quantitative methods, Bodomo and Pajancic (2015) came to the conclusion that there would be around 400,000 to 500,000 Africans in China who are present in China in any twelve calendar months' period, including at least 300,000 to 400,000 traders, 30,000 to 40,000 students, 4,000 to 5,000 professionals, 10,000 to 100,000 tourists and 10,000 to 20,000 temporary business travellers.

With China's entry into the WTO in December 2001, there was a dramatic increase in the number of Africans going to China to buy goods for sale back in Africa. This has created a visible presence of Africans in Guangzhou, which has been receiving, in many cases, a lot of negative coverage in newspapers and magazines on issues of immigration irregularities (Bodomo 2015, p. 2). The main parts and cities in China where there is African presence includes six main places: Guangzhou, Yiwu, Shanghai, Beijing, Hong Kong and Macau. Beyond these six cities, African communities are beginning to be noticed in other major cities in China such as most provincial capitals, especially those in the southern parts of the country (ibid., pp. 2–5).

Cissé (2015) gives us an example of Yiwu, a city in eastern China, which has become a new destination for African traders due to comprehensive policy reforms by the local officials to transform the city into an international trading hub. With production bases around the city, district markets established to enable trade activities within and outside of China and a host of facilities implemented, Yiwu has attracted traders from all over the world, not least of all African traders. The presence of African traders in the 'world's largest commodities city' has connected African trade networks around the world. Even though they have trade connections with their home countries while in China, some of the African traders in Yiwu also have trade ties with other African trade networks in Africa, Europe, the United States and Asia (ibid., p. 45).

African traders have secured niche markets in Africa for 'made-in-China' goods. Products shipped to Africa are often sold to wholesalers in different African markets. Those wholesalers supply retail traders who are in the informal trade sector. With the flows of Chinese imports to African countries, many young people, particularly vendors or peddlers, have found business opportunities to support themselves and families (Cissé 2013).

A recent research on Africans in Guangzhou examines how the Chinese perceive Africans vis-à-vis other foreigners and how contexts and conditions of Chinese–African encounters affect attitudes and racial formation (Zhou et al. 2016). The analysis of data from surveys, interviews and participant observations reveals that the attitudes held by local Chinese residents in Guangzhou towards African migrants are ambivalent. The Chinese tend to perceive Africans negatively in general, but they also look upon African students' presence in a positive way and express openness to interacting with them. The research indicates that the mechanisms of social exclusion and inclusion are shaped by the intersection between the types and levels of contacts and the social contexts in which intergroup encounters occur. Furthermore, it also indicates that the Chinese have not yet formed a collective xenophobic consciousness, nor have their attitudes been racialised in ways that are explained by theories of threat or ethnic economy developed from the Global North (ibid., pp. 157–158). The researchers argue that the consequences of Chinese–African encounters are paradoxical. At the institutional level, lack of official endorsement and visa restrictions put Africans in a vicious cycle of exclusion; however, at the micro level, greater contact reduces social distance, which in turn facilitates greater cooperation and nurtures closer relations, leading to a virtuous cycle of inclusion (ibid., p. 158).

2.2. Previous Literature on China Shops

This section of the literature review mainly covers perspectives concerning Chinese merchants' moving to different countries in the world to open China shops, including the influence they bring to local societies and the relations between the migrants and the policy of the Chinese government as well as that of receiving countries.

2.2.1. China Shops in Africa

China shops in Africa have attracted considerable local and international attention among researchers (Bräutigam 2003; Carling and Haugen 2004; Mohan and Kale 2007; Park 2009; Sautman and Yan 2009). Both the local population and the Chinese merchants operating in Botswana employ the term 'China shop' to describe their businesses. Approximately 99 per cent of China shops in Botswana are Chinese-owned and generally sell goods made in China to African customers, which is similar to the situation in Namibia (Dobler 2009). The Chinese have been welcomed by ordinary Africans (particularly those on low income) because they provide affordable Chinese products and create job opportunities (Carling and Haugen 2004; Cissé 2013; Codrin 2014; Giese 2013; Giese and Thiel 2012; Tanga 2009). However, a number of negative sentiments associated with economic and political concerns also exist (Mohan 2008, p. 8), and these are expressed mainly by the local government and the media. China shops are often considered a threat as competition to local retail businesses (particularly in countries with a small population), and as such they are restricted, to varying degrees, by the local government (Carling and Haugen 2004; Dobler 2009; Kalusopa 2009; Tremann 2013).

34

In the majority of cases, local regulations and trade policies control the development of Chinese investment (particularly industrial). In Namibia, Chinese businesses face strict regulation in an increasingly hostile political environment, leading to slow and extremely volatile conditions for investment (Dobler 2009). Bräutigam (2003) states that Nigeria's policy is not conducive to exports and that there are no resident Chinese. Links between Asia and Africa are therefore limited to information and to consulting services and technical assistance, which are considered portable if faced with policy constraints. Mauritius, on the other hand, has a policy of encouraging Chinese merchants, and hosts a sizeable Chinese population involved in textile industry (ibid.). Botswana encourages industrial and technical investment, while its policy on trade has been gradually tightened since 2008 (Kalusopa 2009).

Transnational Asian entrepreneurs[4] also strive to forge strong connections with local entrepreneurs and invest in joint ventures to form successful export-oriented industries (Bräutigam 2003). However, fierce competition between Chinese and local traders caused by market saturation has been considered as the reason for conflict between Chinese merchants and the local population (Carling and Haugen 2004). In recent years, a large number of African traders have travelled to China as 'suitcase traders,' although these involve relatively small amounts of capital (Mathews 2011) and still bring more competition into the Chinese market. However, Laribee (2008) argues that as long as the Chinese traders control supply chains more effectively[5] than the non-Chinese, China shops will maintain an edge over the competition. This factor partly explains why China shops continue to survive in a competitive business environment in many African countries.

Working as the goods' distributers, Chinese merchants have many opportunities to interact face-to-face with local communities, and therefore trading can be perceived to be central to the understanding of the formation of grass-roots Chinese–African relations (Giese 2013). Research recently released by Khan Mohammad (2014, p. 96) emphasises the influence of individuals in international trends, establishing that in Africa, state-to-state Sino–African cooperation and collaboration arises from the bottom up, implying that grass-roots level Sino–African relations influence state-to-state relationships. So it is important to understand the extent of Chinese migrants' integration by demonstrating the 'everyday interaction' between Chinese and Africans (Mohan and Tan-Mullins 2009). After researching employer–employee relations between Chinese merchants and Ghanaian employees, Giese (2013) concluded that dissatisfaction at the micro level on both sides is caused by a mutual lack of awareness of culturally grounded reciprocity expectations. The majority of Chinese traders prefer employing family members (or other Chinese) to local workers, despite the fact that Ghanaian labour costs far less. The Chinese deny racism as a motivator, asserting that the reason is the lower transaction costs for routine operations when language[6] and social and cultural backgrounds are shared. On the other hand, Chinese merchants in Ghana forge close relationships with one another, in order to face a potentially hostile environment characterised by high levels of competitiveness and frequent extortion by officials (Giese and Thiel 2012, p. 1115). Additionally, Akhidenor (2013) and Deumert and Mabandla (2013) stress that language and cultural barriers deter both labour and business relationships between Chinese merchants and the local population, although many Chinese employ code-switching[7] to improve relations with local customers or adopt English as a lingua franca.[8]

From a panoramic perspective, migration research concerning Chinese merchants' migration history, localising and relationships in the community are mainly conducted in South Africa (Lin 2014; Park 2008, 2009; Wilhelm 2006). However, several research studies focus on the logistical chain of Chinese goods and business networks of African traders who conduct business in western Africa (Cissé 2013, 2015; Haugen and Carling 2005). Besides that, the situation of Chinese business in Namibia (Dobler 2009), Lesotho (Tanga 2009), Congo (Makungu 2012), Nigeria (Xiao 2015) and Lybia (Wang and Stenberg 2014), etc. have been researched. Chinese business in Botswana was only mentioned in a small section of Kalusopa's report regarding Chinese investments in Botswana.

The research regarding Chinese merchants in Africa has so far covered almost every country in Africa. However, concerning the relationship between Chinese merchants and the local society, little research has so far taken the function of interaction between the Chinese and the local society into consideration. In most of the research, analysis was limited to fresh interview or survey data, while neglecting the changes undergone in the relationship within rapidly developing African societies. In particular, the change of local needs follows the development of African society, which may bring about a direct change in the China–Africa relationship. Furthermore, when analysing the relationship between Chinese merchants and local people, the existing research is limited to their interaction in the business context while ignoring the social background or financial stress that both sides are encountering. Usually, people's background and financial situation can provide some clues for their performance in business and jobs. So far, research has, respectively, covered areas like the history of Chinese migration, the economic impact of Chinese business on local society, local government's policies and regulation of Chinese business, as well as interpersonal relationships between Chinese merchants and local people, etc. However, a comprehensive overview is lacking, as we understand that through journal papers it is difficult to describe the links between the different parts. In the end, despite the fact that the interactions between Chinese and African people were analysed in some research, language and culture have been over emphasised as the factors that cause conflict between the two parties in their interpersonal relations.

2.2.2. China Shops in Asia

Chinese presence in Africa is a more recent phenomenon that occurred during the rise of China (Tjon Sie Fat 2009). When we study the Chinese merchant community in Africa, it is crucial for us to review some literature on Chinese merchants and their business in Asia. Historically, the oldest Chinese merchant communities outside China were established in Southeast Asia over centuries (Skinner 1996). It is important to note that, in the 20th century, even though the ethnic Chinese minority was often historically perceived as a threat and a potential 'fifth column' through which Communist China could extend their political power (Tong 2010), the ethnic Chinese nonetheless joined in the nation-building in Southeast Asia (Suryadinata 2007; Wang 2004). On the other hand, Chinese ethnicity can be used as a form of social capital as Chinese communities provide a network of linkages and contacts for economic success (Lin et al. 2001). In this section, I would like to introduce Yao's work on Chinese merchant families in Malaysia, focusing on the family business system and the trusting relationship in the China shop. On the other hand, Hau's work on the Chinese in the Philippines will also be introduced within the perspective of the local society. How Chinese merchants are perceived will be the key issue in the discussion.

According to Yao (2002, pp. 2–3), in Malaysia, China shops are called *za huo dian* (literally 'variety goods store') or *pei huo dian* (hundred goods store) in Chinese, and kedai runcit in Malay. All these names go to the heart of the 'economic principle' of the store: the offering of a wide range of goods in order to serve a large catchment of customers. In economic terms, being open at all hours and never turning away customers makes sense because of the need to improve the poor economies of scale of an enterprise typified by low capital, high labour input and non-standardised goods and service delivery.

As much as Confucian capitalism would like to perceive culture as a unifying force in the Chinese family business, both management authority and work demands are in fact unevenly distributed among workers of different positions: between kinsmen and outsiders, men and women, young and old, with some crucial consequences (Yao 2002, p. 84) The shop is thus a social world in which family life and business are closely intertwined. In the flux of daily life, it is difficult to see where one begins and the other ends. The business depends on low-cost family labour and requires long working hours as a way of cutting down on overhead costs. Like the immigrant enterprise, the Chinese family business emphasises consensus and cooperation by tying its financial success to the collective prosperity of the family. This as we quickly recognise, is the familiar feature of 'collectivism' described by the literature on

Confucian capitalism. But 'collectivism' is often another word for 'forced industrial peace' in a situation where family members are unable to voice their discontent and negotiate their own interests in the hierarchy of relationships (Yao 2002, p. 86).

The deployment of family in the shop harnesses instrumental values and culture significance, driving at times a tortuous negotiation between management and workers, which is illustrated through 'huo ji'[9] or the apprenticeship system (Yao 2002, p. 88–89). The *huo ji* system achieves its aim by recruiting outsiders into the family, and in doing so enlarges the catchment of labour beyond that which the immediate kin can provide. At the same time, workers are bound within the same ethics of obligation and loyalty that are prescribed for family members (Yao 2002, p. 91).

'Kan dian' (mind the shop) is usually considered as something 'useless old men' do to pass the time. Really it is just about keeping an eye on things. One of the family members always has to be in the shop, to watch over things, sometimes the *huo ji* may not be trusted, or still lack experience at work. So someone who can greet the customers and suppliers is necessary. It is like telling people there is someone in charge, and the shop is not in the hands of outsiders (Yao 2002, p. 93). Yet the casualness of the practice and the easy way it is being talked about, belie the social effectivity of the practice. In truth, *kan dian* is about signifying the fact of economic ownership and management control through the physical presence and visual power of the proprietor. The idea is that some member of the family will be there among the 'outsiders' working in the shop. *Kan dian* operates, in short, by signifying power and structural relationship as unmistakably originating from the towkay his family (ibid.). Therefore, what *kan dian* aims to achieve is no less than the making of a hierarchy between family members and outsiders, employer and employees, business interests and workers' aspirations. It installs a set of power relations in the workplace by the forceful visual presence of 'family ownership.' Yao emphasises that *kan dian* is really a sign of the general lack of trust in employees, in their work and honesty while living in the shop. If the practice is about ensuring work efficiency among the employees, it is even more primarily about casting doubt on outsiders who are, in different degrees, not to be trusted because they are not 'one of the family' (Yao 2002, p. 94).

Through Yao's work on *kan dian*, it is not difficult for us to sense that Chinese merchants are very sensitive and suspicious. Even the *huo ji* living and working with family members together can barely obtain the full trust of the boss. The control coming from the boss is prudent, although what seems like killing time in the shop, his/her presence is enough to control the behaviour of *huo ji*. From this case, we question if the outsider and family member is determined by a blood relationship. If one was born as outsider, is it almost impossible for him to obtain the trust that the boss gives to family members? So, what if the *huo ji* has no kinship with the boss? Or put differently, how would the *kan dian* system be practiced differently, if the *huo ji* is a foreigner?

Hau (2014) however, emphasised the local perception of Chinese merchants. She states that in the Philippines, it was not the Chinese labourer, but the Chinese merchant, who became the specific target of postcolonial official nationalism. The economic importance of the Chinese in the Spanish and American colonial eras became a 'problem' that had to be addressed through commonwealth and postwar legislation aimed at breaking Chinese 'dominance' over certain economic activities, such as the retail trade, and barring Chinese entry into the professions by limiting the right to exercise professions, such as law and medicine, to Filipino citizens. This strain of decolonising nationalism viewed economic and political rights competition from 'foreigners'. The historical conflation of Chinese ethnicity with commerce and capital found expression in the stereotypical image of the rich, avaricious, and (often sexually) predatory Chinese merchant and capitalist – almost always men – whose economic activities, bordering on the illicit because they involved collusion with, if not corrupting of, officials of the state, had to be curbed in order for wealth to accrue to its rightful owners, the Filipino people (Hau 2014, p. 6).

Hau further explains why Chinese merchants are often targeted by nationalist criticism and action. American application of the Chinese Exclusion Act to the Philippines drove the Chinese even more deeply into the mercantile niche (in 1930, Chinese controlled

90 per cent of the retail trade) while creating the legal fiction that 'all' Chinese immigrants were merchants. Operating mainly in the domestic market at a time when the Philippine economy was becoming increasingly tied to the US market on a preferential basis, Chinese merchants with their limited capital outlay, intensive labour input, small employment number, and high liquidity faced rising competition from foreign and Filipino entrepreneurs and became visible targets of nationalist legislation. Far more crucially, their visibility as merchants and 'alienness' made these merchants the targets of popular nationalist criticism and action, as Hau explains below:

> The visibility of the merchant and his exclusive confinement to the equally visible public sphere of circulation means that even though the merchant performs only one among many functions in the capitalist system, capital itself appears prima facie in 'his' sphere and comes to be associated with and is taken at face value as the exclusive function of the merchant as a specific agent of circulation distinct from the producer. This may explain why the merchant and his shop are often the first and favorite targets of mass action during moments of crisis. The 'alienness' of the Chinese cements, and is cemented by, this association of the 'alien' merchant with alienating capital, so that the merchant appears in the public imagination as the personification of capital with a consciousness and will (ibid., pp. 149–150).

Therefore, in Philippine, Chinese merchants on the one hand are attacked due to their small scale business investment and limited visible contribution to local society, while on the other hand, criticised for their 'alienness'. Although useful at times, they are easily seen as a threat to local business. However, can this formula also be adopted to societies with different races? Do Chinese merchants in Africa experience the similar treatment for the same reason? And to what extent will the image of China in Africa reveal the factor of 'alienness'? This book seeks to answer these questions.

2.3. Analytical Framing

2.3.1. Intergroup Relations

Intergroup relations involving natives (insiders) and immigrant or racial/ethnic minorities (outsiders) are often conflict-prone (Zhou et al. 2016, p. 142). Allport in his book The Nature of Prejudice (1954) argued that positive effects of intergroup contact occur only in situations marked by four key conditions: equal group status within the situation; common goals; intergroup cooperation; and the support of authorities, law or custom. More recently, Zhou et al. researched social relations between Africans in China and the local Chinese. In their research, threat, ethnic economy and contact were introduced as three central sociological perspectives for analytical framing of the study. Before this kind of conflict started taking place in China between African merchants and Chinese local people, it had existed decades before in African countries between Chinese merchants and African locals. Here I would like to briefly introduce the three perspectives mentioned in their paper.

1. The Threat Perspective

The threat perspective conceives economic competition and cultural differences as main sources of intergroup conflict. From the individual threat approach, hostility towards immigrants emerges when natives in the host society feel threatened by the possibility, or reality, of being out-competed in local job and housing markets and access to public resources (Bonacich 1973; Zhou et al. 2016, p. 142). Blumer (1958, p. 4) lists four basic types of feeling that seem to be always present in race prejudice in the dominant group. They are (1) a feeling of superiority, (2) a feeling that the subordinate race is intrinsically different and alien, (3) a feeling of proprietary claim to certain areas of privilege and advantage, and (4) a fear and suspicion that the subordinate race harbours designs on the prerogatives of the dominant race.

2. The Ethnic Economy Perspective

Ethnic economies consist of businesses owned and run by members of ethnic or immigrant minority groups. From this perspective, intergroup relations are conditioned by the types and locations of ethnic businesses (Zhou et al. 2016, p. 142). The middleman minority economy is most relevant to the understanding of in-group–out-group dynamics. Middleman minority entrepreneurs usually operate between the dominant and subordinate groups with customers generally being members of marginalised racial or ethnic groups (Bonacich 1973). Details of the middleman minority will be introduced in chapter 5.

3. The Contact Perspective

Robert Park's race relations theory (Park 1950) sees intergroup relations as moving in a natural cycle of competition, conflict and accommodation. When different racial or ethnic groups first come into contact with each other (e.g. through immigration or colonisation), their interactions tend to be conflicting because of competition for scarce resources and pre-existing prejudices about an out-group's supposed perception of competition and socioeconomic inferiority. Competition for economic and territorial dominance causes intergroup conflict; racial prejudice and social distance intensify this conflict. Park cautions that conflict should not be confused with racial prejudice or social distance, since conflict sets the precondition for change, leading to accommodation as in-group and out-group members make adjustments towards reducing conflict and achieving coexistence (Park 1950; Zhou et al. 2016, p. 144).

These are the mainstream theories of intergroup relations. However, these existing theories leave some obvious gaps. First, most established theories assume that the host country is a migrant resettlement society that promotes the eventual integration of immigrants (Zhou et al. 2016). In host societies where immigrant integration is highly selective and restrictive, such as those in the Global South, the sources of intergroup threat may be different (ibid.). Furthermore, so far the research is limited to the two opposite groups, usually conflict-prone two groups. However, more subcategories are needed for further analysis since not every local person (insider) holds the same opinion about outsiders. The opinion will vary according to local person's economic class, educational background, etc.

2.3.2. Contact Zone

Pratt (1992), in her book Imperial Eyes: Travel Writing and Transculturation, attempts to use 'contact zone' to invoke the spatial and temporal co-presence of subjects who were previously separated by geographic and historical disjuncture and whose trajectories now intersect. The 'contact' perspective emphasises how subjects are constituted in and by their relations with each other. It treats the relations among colonisers and colonised, or travellers and hosts, not in terms of separateness or apartheid, but in terms of co-presence, interaction, interlocking understandings and practices, often within radically asymmetrical relations of power (Pratt 1992, p. 7).

I adopt 'contact zone' as a theoretical orientation for this study. As we mentioned in previous chapter (1.1.3) the China shop can be regarded as a 'contact zone' where Chinese merchants meet local people face-to-face to interact. The term 'contact zone' was initially used to refer to a social space where cultures meet, clash and grapple with each other, often in contexts of highly asymmetrical relations of power, such as colonialism, slavery, etc. (Pratt 1992, p. 4). I use the term to consider the interactions between the Chinese merchants and the local community in Botswana. The original concept is normally used for colonial relationships, and 'West and Rest' relations, whereas my research highlights contact between non-Westerners, in the context of rising China and its growing economic and geopolitical clout inside the economic sector (not mega-corporation, but petty trade) rather than a post-colonial realm.

2.3.3. Shaping Process

The theory 'contact zone' is not limited to the actions of 'cultures meet, clash, and grapple with each other,' but is also linked to a process of shaping in society both on a micro (individual) level and macro (group, nation) level. As we discussed in 1.1.3 about building the image of China, there are top-down and bottom-up approaches. In this section, we explain the linkage between 'building the image of China' in relation to the bottom-up daily interaction in China shops.

Herbert Blumer (1958, p. 5) offers a position theory that contributes a further understanding of the shaping process in individual level and group level. He argues that the sense of group position is not a mere summation of the feelings of position such as might be developed independently by separate individuals as they come to compare themselves with given individuals of the subordinate race. The sense of group position is clearly formed by a running process in which the dominant racial group is led to define and redefine the subordinate racial group and the relations between them. He offers two important aspects of this process of definition.

First, the process of definition occurs obviously through complex interaction and communication between the members of the dominant group:

> Leaders, prestige bearers, officials, group agents, dominant individuals and ordinary laymen present to one another characterizations of the subordinate group and express their feelings and ideas on the relations. Through talk, tales, stories, gossip, anecdotes, messages, pronouncements, news accounts, orations, sermons, preachments and the like definitions are presented and feelings are expressed. In this usually vast and complex interaction separate views run against one another, influence one another, modify each other, incite one another and fuse together in new forms. Correspondingly, feelings which are expressed meet, stimulate each other, feed on each other, intensify each other and emerge in new patterns.... If the interaction becomes increasingly circular and reinforcing, devoid of serious inner opposition, such currents grow, fuse and become strengthened. It is through such a process that a collective image of the subordinate group is formed and a sense of group position is set (Blumer 1958, pp. 5–6).

Secondly, the process of group definition is necessarily to be concerned with an abstract image of the subordinate racial group. The subordinate racial group is defined as if it were an entity or whole. While actual encounters are with individuals, the picture formed of the racial group is necessarily of a vast entity which spreads out far beyond such individuals and transcends experience with such individuals. He also offered four implications of the fact that the collective image is of an abstract group:

1. Public Arena. The collective image of the abstract group grows up not by generalising from experiences gained in close, first-hand contacts but through the transcending characterisations that are made of the group as an entity. This occurs in the 'public arena' where the spokesmen appear as representatives and agents of the dominant group. The extended public arena is constituted by such things as legislatives assemblies, public meetings, conventions, the press and the printed word (ibid., pp. 5–6).

2. Big Event. The 'big event' that is felt to be of major importance in developing a conception of the subordinate racial group. The happening that seems momentous, that touches deep sentiments, that seems to raise fundamental questions about relations, and that awakens strong feelings of identification with one's racial group is the kind of event that is central in the formation of the racial image. The definition of this event is chiefly responsible for the development of a racial image and of the sense of group position (ibid., p. 6).

3. Leader. The major influence in public discussion is exercised by individuals and groups who have the public ear and who are felt to have standing, prestige, authority and power. Intellectual and social elites, public figures of prominence and leaders of powerful organisations are likely to be the key figures in the formation of the sense of group position and in the characterisation of the subordinate group (ibid., p. 6).

4. Strong Interest Groups. We also need to perceive the appreciable opportunity that is given to strong interest groups in directing the lines of discussion and setting the interpretations that arise in such discussion. Their self-interests may dictate the kind of position they wish the dominant racial group to enjoy. It may be a position which enables them to retain certain advantages, or even more to gain still greater advantages. Hence, they may be vigorous in

seeking to manufacture events to attract public attention and to set lines of issue in such a way as to predetermine interpretations favourable to their interests. The role of strongly organised groups seeking to further a special interest is usually central in the formation of collective images of abstract groups (ibid., p. 6).

In this research, I adopt the framework of Herbert Blumer's (1958) position theory. In his work more thoughts were given to the abstract image of the group, while only a few paragraphs were given to complex interaction and communication at individual level. To extend the framework, I aim to focus on the individual-level dynamics of perceived threat and theorise about the attitudes of both dominant and minority racial group members (Chapters 5, 6 and 7) and also shed some light on the abstract image of China in Chapter 8.

Both individual *suzhi* and nation image can be adapted in Herbert Blumer's (1958, p. 5) position theory. At a microlevel, *suzhi* usually refers to the qualities of civility, self-discipline and modernity (Yan 2003), therefore it is adjustable according to the social enviroment and interactions. At a macrolevel, according to Fan (2006, p. 11), in the context of the nation brand, the image of a nation (customers' existing perception of the nation) may be based on the following factors:

1. personal experience, e.g. visiting the country;
2. education or knowledge;
3. prior use or ownership of a product made in that country;
4. the depiction of the country through media channels;
5. stereotypes, etc.

Therefore, the image of China (local perception of China) in Botswana is also assessed by individual local people through these factors. Of course, the image of a nation also depends on the background of the audiences, as audiences of a different intellectual and social class see nations in various ways:

The image of a nation is so complex and fluid as to deny the clarity implicit in a term such as brand image. Different parts of a nation's identity come into focus on the international stage at different times, affected by current political events and even by the latest movie or news bulletin. Moreover, national images exist at different intellectual and cultural levels, and for different audiences, they have different meanings according to class, demography, and so forth (O'Shaughnessy and O'Shaughnessy 2000, p. 58).

In the 'contact zone' China shops, through social interactions between Chinese merchants and local middle/low class members not only the image of China (the collective image of the Chinese) in Botswana but also individual quality of Chinese merchants is shaped. In this research I aim to focus on the interactions between middle and low economic class Botswana and Chinese merchants who have the most chance to meet in China shops. To the majority, interacting with Chinese merchants and using Chinese merchandise are the most common means to assess China besides stereotype and media channels. In this context, the image of China (local perception) in Botswana is made clear mainly through exchanges of social interactions between Chinese merchants and the Batswana who meet in the China shops, as we explained in 1.1.3. In other words, the image of China/Chinese people is not self-built but shaped through the interactions with the Batswana in the contact zone of China shops and at the same time influenced by the abstract image of the group. In the same process, individual Chinese person's *suzhi* as well as the quality of Chinese merchandise are under the process of being shaped through daily interaction, self-examination and reformation of self-image.

The theory of 'contact zone' is, therefore, very relevant to this study because it addresses interactions in the contexts of highly asymmetrical relations of power and further blends the ideas of social interaction into shaping self-images and nation-image while attending to possible challenges of an adoption in petty trade and non-Western setting.

2.4. Typology of Ethical Problems in China Shop Business

I adopt ethical issues as a typology for China shop research, due to the fact that retail sales people are most likely to encounter situations that could be ethically troublesome (Dubinsky and Levy 1985). Dubinsky and Levy (1985, pp. 2–3) point out four main reasons for this. First, retail salespersons are in a boundary-spanning role where they interact with individual customers from outside the store as well as with members from within their own organisation. The individuals with whom salespersons interact are likely to have disparate needs and problems that salespersons might find incompatible. As a result, retail sales personnel may often face ethical dilemmas when torn between short-term pressures from management (to achieve a sales quota or some other objectives) and long-term goals of achieving customer confidence and goodwill. The second reason for studying ethical issues of retail salespersons is that their environment is conducive to the development of ethical problems because of the variety of tasks they perform, from 'ringing up' a sale to handling returns or exchanges. Third, the nature of the job itself could foster ethically troubling situations for retail salespersons. That is, the pressures of the job and the need to be a consistent producer may place salespersons in uncomfortable situations that might be expediently addressed using questionable behaviour. Last, previous research has found that retail salespersons tend to receive little formalised sales training. As a result, they may not know how their company would like them to act in a potentially ethically troubling situation because they have not been adequately instructed regarding company policies (ibid.).

Chinese retailers confront numerous situations that may pose potential ethical problems. The potential ethical problems they face are most likely to be generated from the diverse individuals with whom the Chinese interact in their daily business. For the Chinese retailers, the key individuals who may engender ethical problems generally will be the customers, local assistants and local authorities of China shops. Consequently, when using these three groups as a frame of reference, ethical conflicts between the Chinese and

Batswana people can be classified into three broad areas: customer-, employee-(peer-), and local authority-related situations.

Customer-related situations encompass those situations that entail involvement with customers and have a direct impact upon customers. Examples of such situations may include failing to assist customers or failing to give them a replacement when there is an issue over the quality of merchandise that has been paid for. Employee-related situations involve interaction with Chinese retailers' non-work peers (business rivals and relatives) and employees (Batswana assistants). Examples of such situations may include competition, or employee theft, or dismissal of employees without following local legislation. Local authority-related situations entail circumstances that may be precipitated by bribing issues, or seeking loopholes in regulations. Examples of such situations may include failing to obtain a check authorisation or selling products without proper licence. The preceding typology (Figure 4) will be used in Chapter 5, Chapter 6 and Chapter 7 (issues between the double-circled oval and rectangular characters) to classify the situations examined in the present study. On the other hand, the relations between the double-circled and single-circled oval characters will be discussed in Chapter 4 following a background of the Chinese merchants who operate China shop businesses in Botswana. The single-circled and double-circled oval characters represent Chinese merchants, while the rectangular characters represent local people. The lines and arrows show the relations between the characters.

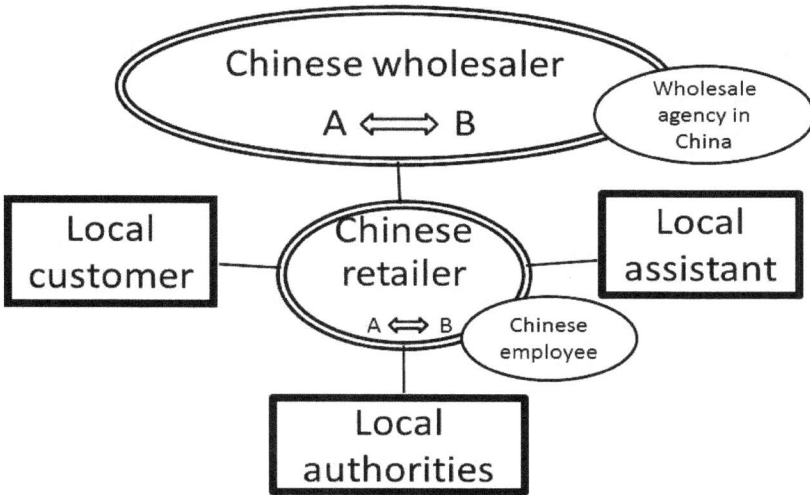

Figure 4. Stakeholder Analysis of Trade Relationships

2.5. Summary

This chapter has reviewed literature on China–Africa relations in general, Chinese merchants in Africa and African traders in China. It has discussed the challenges inherent in existing research to situate the present study. This is followed by a discussion on the theoretical framework of the study based on the theory of intergroup relations, contact zone and shaping. Finally, the chapter concludes with the typology of ethical problems in retail sales and an analysis framework of this research providing a background on which the rest of the study is premised. The next chapter discusses the methodology adopted in conducting this research.

Notes

[1] 'New migrants' are the Chinese who left China after the 1980s.

[2] Textiles, clothes, shoes, electronics, trinkets and so on.

[3] Such as medical, technical, agricultural aid, etc.

[4] Mainly entrepreneurs from China, India and Pakistan.

5 Chinese wholesalers are usually offered cheaper prices by manufactures in China than are non- Chinese traders, due to the fact that Chinese orders are far larger.

6 Most Chinese merchants (particularly newcomers) are fluent in neither English nor the local language.

7 The practice of moving back and forth between two languages, or between two dialects or registers of the same language.

8 Commonly used for commerce between peoples of diverse speech.

9 *Huo ji* is recruited from among the poor relatives or other towns, who send their young sons to earn a 'rice bowl' and to learn the business ways by serving as an apprentice or a shop assistant.

Chapter 3

Methodology and Research Design

This chapter discusses the methodology and research design used in this study. A discussion of the challenges associated with qualitative and quantitative research approaches is presented to justify the choice of mixed methods in this study. The methodology section is followed by a discussion on research design and methods as well as their justifications in the study.

3.1. Methodology

3.1.1. Review on Methods Paradigm

Bodomo and Pajancic (2015) have criticised existing research of Africans in China as many of these works – mainly sociological, anthropological and journalistic in nature – have mostly pursued a so-called qualitative approach to the neglect and even disdain for quantitative approaches:

> Many scholarly studies thus adopt more qualitative interview methods than quantitative methods of questionnaire surveys. This is especially so with the journalistic type, where someone just flies into Guangzhou[1] and spends a few days, with a microphone in hand, asking people quick questions that require short answers and flies out to their station and the next day we read a sensational news headline: 'Africans in China Face Racism!' Even the more sober academic, sociological and anthropological, participant-observation methods that should permit the author to stay longer and mingle with the research subjects shy away from interviewing large numbers of people. There are papers that have been written on Africans in China with the authors hardly ever interviewing more than 10 Africans, and some authors do not even go into Guangzhou at all (Bodomo and Pajancic 2015, p. 129).

Bodomo and Pajancic argue that it is more plausible in the 21st century as migration and 'diasporisation' get more complex, these complex humanities and social science issues require a mixed methods approach. The use of both qualitative and quantitative approaches is often referred to as a triangulation of methods (ibid., pp. 137–138).

According to Carling and Haugen (2004), increasing competition among the Chinese has contributed to apprehensive and sceptical attitudes. Laribee (2008) points out that visiting many shops helps one obtain more information and thus find out the tendency and variety in different cases. However, visiting certain shops frequently is also important, especially when one needs some information that can only be gained after a trustworthy relationship has been established between the interviewee and interviewer.

3.1.2. Justification for Methodological Approach

This study examines the relationship between Chinese merchants and local people. It focuses on the micro level relations between Chinese merchants, their relations with local customers and local assistants, as well as local authorities who represent local government to regulate the legitimacy and management of shops. Consequently, Chinese merchants' experiences in Botswana and their relationships with the Chinese community as well as their experiences in business need to be researched. As discussed before, a comprehensive understanding of these aspects cannot be achieved by using only qualitative or only quantitative methods.

Qualitative approaches are necessary to explore Chinese merchants' business experiences as well as general experiences in Botswana society, because experiences represent a humanly constructed reality. The experiences and views of Chinese merchants and local people do not constitute an objective reality that can be fully captured in purely quantitative approaches. Thus, a qualitative paradigm is better suited to learn from Chinese merchants regarding their experiences in business how they deal with issues with local customers, their local employees as well as authorities.

On the other hand, quantitative approaches can better establish trends and patterns of relationships between Chinese merchants and local people. The migration experiences of Chinese merchants, the challenges they face in business as well as their relationship with local customers, employees and authorities can be 'parameterised' by concrete events and characteristics. These aspects of the research require quantitative approaches, especially collecting and analysing aggregated datasets.

Thus, the complex nature of questions examined in this study provides a primary justification for using mixed methods in this study. In addition to the inherent limitation of qualitative and quantitative approaches, combining methods (or methodological eclecticism) will also allow for possible corroboration of the study's findings, ensuring the accuracy of research findings and conclusions.

3.2. Method

3.2.1. Research Design

I randomly chose China shops to visit in Gaborone and rural towns and visited the shops twice every month, so as to take a balanced view in the qualitative research. To create an atmosphere that is easy for Chinese merchants and local people to talk frankly, I used anthropological methods such as participant observation, informal interview and conversation with Chinese merchants and their workers. The primary sources of data are mainly based on informal and in-depth interviews with Chinese merchants, concerning their life experiences and opinions of local people. Participant observations were conducted in China shops, while observing the interaction between Chinese merchants and local people and assisting in China shops during their busy times.

Bodomo and Pajancic (2015, p. 138) also discuss the facilitation of the interdisciplinary aspects of various academic fields involved in the study of Africans in China. Research on the diaspora links several different academic areas such as African and Asian studies, linguistics, sociology, political sciences and history. This combination has been proven to lead to an in-depth study of the phenomenon. Thus it is obvious that, with this interaction between different academic areas, an interaction of different methods is also inevitable to make sure that as many relevant issues as possible can be examined and analysed accordingly. In this research, methods of anthropology, sociology and history are adopted to show the depth of Chinese merchants' interaction with Botswana society.

3.2.2. Site Selection

I chose as my research site the shopping malls in Gaborone where China shops are found. The site was selected to take advantage of an overview of the management of China shops and the Chinese merchandise transportation system and to understand the complexity of the relationship between Chinese merchants, the Chinese and the local people.

Chinese wholesale markets in both Gaborone and Francistown[2] were visited in order to gather information concerning the supply chain of Chinese merchandise and the history of pioneer Chinese merchants, due to the fact that Chinese wholesalers were usually the first to come to Botswana. Besides that, China shops in other cities and small towns were also visited to assess the general situation of the China shop business and the movement of Chinese merchants.

3.2.3. Data Collection Process

Data used in this thesis were obtained from both primary and secondary sources and collected between November 2011 and September 2015 (Nov. 2011–Jan. 2012; Sep. 2013–Nov. 2013; Sep. 2014–Nov. 2014; Aug. 2015–Sep. 2015) during my total 11-months of fieldwork in Gaborone, Francistown and rural towns. I used Mandarin Chinese with Chinese merchants and English with local people. Setswana usage was limited to greetings and ice-breaking. The primary sources are mainly based on the following:

Most of the time, Chinese shopkeepers would ask me what I was doing in Botswana in my first visit to their shops. When I told them that I was a student, coming to collect data for my thesis regarding China shops most of them responded with questions and comments such as 'Why do you choose this topic? Looking after shops here is a terribly boring job!' Therefore, our conversation usually started from how boring the job was. I did not take notes during conversations, but wrote down key points of the conversation after visiting, and filled in as much detail as I could.

Table 1. Survey data (sample size)

Number of visited shops	No.	Number of visited Chinese merchants (CM)	No.	Number of visited local assistants (LA)	No.
China shop in Gaborone	47	CM in Gaborone (who has shop)	90 (75)	LA in China shops	20
China shop in other towns	17	CM in other towns	18	LA in local and ethnic shops	4
China wholesale store in Gaborone and Francistown	13				
Local and ethnic shop in Gaborone	24				
Total	101		108		24

(1) Both informal and in-depth interviews with Chinese merchants, concerning their life stories and interactions with local people were held. In order to relate their background to the development of their businesses, information like gender, age, marriage status, years in Botswana, home town, business type, education status, job experience and English level was gathered by interviewing and will be analysed in the coming chapters. Besides, the stories of interactions with local people will be used as case studies. Voices from both Chinese merchants and local employees who work for Chinese, other ethnic shops and other local people are heard. Furthermore, interviews conducted at large South African retail chain shops (e.g. PEP, Ackermans, and Mr. Price), the Chinese Embassy and the Chinese Chamber of Commerce will be used to check the validity of the data gathered at China shops.

(2) Participant observation was mainly conducted at China shops through observing the interactions between Chinese merchants and local people and helping the Chinese arrange goods in their busy times. Besides, I managed to observe the interactions among Chinese merchants after they closed shop to rest at home, by living in the same yard with them. Information gathered in this section will mainly be used to help understand what Chinese merchants said in the interviews and to express their feelings.

(3) Online News published by the Embassy of China in Botswana (both in Chinese and English) were gathered for recent updates on Botswana–China relations and the shift on both sides. Furthermore, at times some information was found on the Chinese pages of the Embassy website.

(4) The Botswana Online news, named 'Mmegionline', which is in English and was issued daily. This news was collected to learn about the current public opinion on various issues.

Secondary data on the relationship between Botswana and China, as well as policy and market situations on both sides were collected from published written resources, namely books, journals and governmental documents. Through these resources, the outline of the China–Botswana relationship was sketched and the current situation of Botswana society was readily understood.

To check the validity of the data, I conducted crosschecks of my personal observations, communication with Chinese shop owners, the Embassy of China, the Chinese chamber of commerce, Chinese merchants who are doing business other than in China shops and local people. This way, the differences in perspective will be clarified, and therefore the solution to the existing friction can be expected.

3.2.4. Ethical Issues[3]

According to the research guidelines of University of Botswana and regulations set by the Government of Botswana, all research involving human subjects should be conducted in accordance with the basic ethical principles, namely respect for persons, beneficence and confidentiality. Therefore, the applicant will obey the following items:

(1) Respect for persons:
- The applicant will explain regarding the purpose, risks, and benefits of this research study to participant.
- Participant has the right to refuse to take part, or agree to take part now and change his/her mind later.

- Participant can ask any questions before he/her makes a decision.
- Participant's participation is voluntary.

(2) Beneficence: The participants will be paid a token payment in appreciation of their time and effort involved in the various data collection exercises of the study.

(3) Confidentiality: Data collected in this study will be used for academic purposes only and participants will be duly informed of such use and their voluntary acceptance obtained. No personally identifiable information including names of the participants will be used in the research reports and publications. Where names are required codes will be used to protect the privacy of the participants. The codes are chosen to provide the following general information regarding the informants:

C: Chinese business
B: Botswana business
F: Foreign business
T: Trade
E: External service provider
M: Middle size company

G: Government informant
S: Scholar informant
P: Pilot interview informant
0,1,2 etc. differentiates: between respondents of the same affiliation

c: Chinese individual
b: Botswana individual
i: foreign individual besides Chinese; e.g. Indian; Zimbabwean
o: owner
m: manager
e: employee
f: family member

3.3. Scope and Limitations

This study looks at the China–Africa relationship at a grass-roots level. This scope is chosen because of the increased attention paid to ethical issues in cross-cultural business practices and the booming interest in the gaps in ethics between China and Africa as the interaction increases (Giese 2013, 2014; Lee 2009). Giese (2015, p. 3) emphasises the importance of clarifying the scope of research on China–Africa as below:

When we talk regarding 'China in Africa', we should always remember to differentiate between the various actors and scales that are too often conflated and hidden behind such large and all-encompassing labels like 'China' or 'Africa'. Common containers and the homogenizing of diversity seldom help to broaden our knowledge or deepen our understanding of the various phenomena which can be observed at the various scales of the multiple relationships that have evolved between this East Asian country and the African continent.

Therefore, this research focuses on the interpersonal/intergroup relationships between Chinese merchants and the Batswana people who meet each other in China shops. Ethical issues between the Chinese and Batswana will be used as a framework to organise this book and separate discussion topics into different layers. This research attempts to bring a new perspective on China–Africa relations, which is different from the one widespread in media and the one predicted in diplomatic relations. Along with the investigation on the interactions in China shops, the conflicts and the contributing factors will also be analysed in different layers.

This study includes almost half of the China shops in Gaborone. The limited sample size discourages generalisation of the conclusion beyond the area where the study was conducted. However, the findings of the study are still expected to be illustrative of the interaction between Chinese merchants and local society in Botswana in general. The study further recognises the multiplicity of avenues through which the relationship between Chinese merchants and local people may be shaped beyond China shops and local culture. In this respect, the study should be understood within the role of China shop as a 'contact zone' that provides the opportunity for Chinese and Africans to interact with each other. The study also recognises that Botswana is a country comparatively rich among African countries with a good social welfare system. In addition, most of the Chinese merchants from Fujian province have strong family ties, have a worldwide family network and invest mainly in business interests when going to Botswana. All the above define the social context within which the findings should be understood.

Despite a careful preparation of this research, there are limitations and shortcomings, especially when some of the opinions collected from the local population can be affected by the fact that I am a Chinese national. Furthermore, since the interviews were mostly conducted in China shops, the voices of local people were limited to the group that purchased products from China shops and the opinions of people who do not visit China shops are absent. Furthermore, my perspective of the opinion of the local people on Chinese merchants is limited. I tried to hear more voices of local people, particularly local assistants who work in China Shops. However, some local people were afraid to express their honest views towards their Chinese bosses in the presence of their bosses and others only uttered several words such as 'my job here is fine' and 'my boss is good to me' when being asked about their relationship with Chinese merchants. I wish I could spend more time building a relationship of trust with the local assistants. Nevertheless, I highly appreciate those local assistants who frankly explained their feelings and struggles with their Chinese bosses.

3.4. Summary

This chapter discussed the methodology and methods employed in the conduct of this study. It highlighted the necessity to adopt mixed methods as a research paradigm that capitalises on the strengths of both quantitative and qualitative research paradigms. Research design and methods have also been discussed to demonstrate how the research was conducted and data analysed. The next chapter presents results obtained from the field research.

Notes

[1] A city in China where there are many Africans.

[2] The second largest city in Botswana.

[3] According to (1) Government of Botswana: An Act to Regulate Anthropological Research, Chapter 59: 02, Printed by the Government Printer, Gaborone, Botswana. (2) Guidelines on the ethical conduct of research involving humans as participants at the University of Botswana.

Chapter 4

China Shops and Chinese Merchants in Botswana

China is very rich, why do you come to Africa? – Batswana national
I studied geography very well in the middle school, but I have never heard
there is a country named Botswana until I came here. – China shop employee

This chapter has four subsections. The first part of this chapter will introduce the supply chain logistics of Chinese merchandise and the Chinese market in Botswana. The second part focuses on the development of Chinese business in Botswana, with an emphasis on wholesale and retail China shops (Figure 4). The third part introduces the background of Chinese merchants, their system of chain migration, family background and daily lives in Botswana. Last but not least, I would like to highlight some key challenges that Chinese merchants are coping with in their daily life in Botswana.

4.1. An Overview of the Chinese in Botswana

According to the Chinese Embassy, there have been approximately 20,000 Chinese living in Botswana since 2011. Besides, merchants who run wholesale or retail businesses, there are construction companies and textile companies, and a few people work in Chinese medical teams, Chinese restaurants and the Confucius Institute. According to the information provided by the Chinese embassy in 2014, there were 17 Chinese construction companies in Botswana besides small Chinese private construction companies. According to the Chinese Embassy, Chinese Associations in Botswana are loose and not functional since the majority of the Chinese in Botswana are new migrants arriving after 1990.

4.2. Distribution of Chinese Merchandise

4.2.1. Wholesale Markets in China

In China, Yiwu (义乌, Zhejiang Province) and Jinjiang (晋江, Fujian Province) are the places famous for wholesale markets. The majority of the Chinese wholesalers source Chinese merchandise from these two places. In August of 2005, Yiwu was certificated to be 'the world's largest commodities wholesaling market' in a China Development Report jointly issued by the UN, World Bank and Morgan Stanley. Yiwu Market covers a business area of 2,600,000 m², with 50,000 booths. The market boasts a daily visit of over 2,000 persons, sells 320,000 kinds of products in 34 industries, ranking first among all big markets in China for 14 successive years.[1] On the other hand, Jingjiang has a big wholesale market of shoes.[2]

Besides the big markets mentioned above, Chinese wholesalers in Botswana also import merchandise from Guangzhou, send orders directly to factories or even book through the internet, but it seems that majority of the Chinese merchandise is still imported from Yiwu and Jingjiang.

4.2.2. Merchandise to Botswana

Chinese wholesalers in Botswana go to China to order merchandise and entrust some export agencies in China to send the merchandise for them in containers on ships. It usually takes 70 to 90 days for containers to be delivered to Botswana. In Botswana, containers are delivered to Gaborone and Francistown, where Oriental Plazas or Chinese wholesale markets are. From these two wholesale markets, merchandise is further distributed inland to other cities and towns through retail trading activities. This retail trading is conducted by both Chinese merchants and local merchants. The majority of local merchants and street hawkers prefer to buy clothes and shoes from Chinese wholesalers, since their merchandise is comparatively cheap and easy to access. However, a handful of local merchants travel to South Africa, China, even Southeast Asia (e.g. Thailand, Malaysia) and the Middle East to purchase unique goods in order to avoid direct competition with the Chinese merchants. These local merchants have usually accumulated some capital from previous business and now open retail shops in big shopping malls, targeting local rich customers.

4.2.3. Merchandise to South Africa

According to the Chinese merchants in Botswana who are doing wholesale trading between Botswana and South Africa, the Chinese wholesale market in South Africa is approximately 20 times bigger than the one in Botswana, and it has been the wholesale resource for retailers from neighbouring countries. There are wholesalers in Botswana who specialise in importing merchandise called 'South African goods' from the Chinese wholesale market in South Africa (mainly Johannesburg). Most of these goods, especially clothes, are originally made in China as well, but designed according to the requirements of fashion and the body style of African people.

4.2.4. Quality Issues

Made-in-China goods have received widespread criticism in Africa for their poor quality and negative effects on the local marketplace. They are termed 'fong kong' (Barrett 2007) goods, and in Southern Africa, including Botswana, are regarded as cheap copies or fakes (Park 2013a; 2013b). In Botswana, *fong kong* is linked to the infamy of Chinese merchants, bringing a negative image to Chinese businesses and triggering governmental restrictions on Chinese businesses. However, surprisingly, *fong kong* goods continue to be sold on the local market. Generally speaking, the quality of goods exported to Africa is inferior to those exported to America and Europe due to the differences of consumption levels. Local people make jokes regarding China shops, saying 'once you buy a pair of sandals in a China shop, you need to go back to the shop again and again, because those sandals only last couple of weeks and you need to keep on buying new ones'. To give an explanation of this phenomenon Mathews and Vega (2012, p. 12) state:

> Poor quality China-made goods are imported to Africa largely because the Chinese merchants in Africa focus on price as the primary determinant when purchasing. People tend to judge overall

65

quality of China-made goods as a whole, while in fact China produces goods in different qualities.

Generally, among the imported Chinese clothes in Botswana, 'South African goods' have the best quality, and then the goods ordered from Chinese wholesale markets rank second. The worst are the so-called 'leftovers' that are usually sale remains gathered from closed down factories in China.

The quality of Chinese merchandise exported to Botswana has improved over the years following the development of China shops in Botswana. However, there are still some issues between Chinese merchants and the local society concerning made-in-China goods. It takes years for local people to understand that 'China creates room for every customer according to their buying power'. Details of the issue will be discussed in Chapter 6.

4.3. China Shops in Botswana

4.3.1. Wholesale Stores

In Botswana, there are two Chinese wholesale markets. One is at the Oriental Plaza in Block 8 in Gaborone, and the other is settled near the bus rank in Francistown. The wholesale of Chinese clothes is totally under the control of Chinese merchants. These Oriental Plazas have a different appearance from China Town and look more like stores.

Oriental Plaza, the wholesale market in Gaborone, was founded in 2006. There are approximately 80 to 100 stores, all of which are doing wholesale business only, although several years ago retail business was also allowed. Most of the stores open between 9:00 am and 5:00 pm. The majority of the owners of the stores are Chinese and every store hires one to two local assistants to arrange the merchandise. Many wholesalers have their own retailer Chinese customers, so once they have new stocks they will circulate information among their customers.

In the stores, only samples of the different merchandise are displayed on the shelves and the rest remains unpacked in boxes, which could explain why people call them storehouses. Different stores sell different types of merchandise imported from China, which range from furniture, appliances, tools, clothes and shoes to small accessories. Not only Chinese and Botswana retailers but merchants from neighbouring countries (e.g. Zimbabwe and Zambia) also come to buy goods from the wholesale markets. Compared with the wholesale market in Gaborone, the one in Francistown has more shops selling electronics, in order to feed the demands of retailers from neighbouring countries like Zambia and Zimbabwe. On the other hand, the wholesale market in Gaborone mainly deals in clothes and daily necessities.

The wholesale market in Francistown is located near the bus rank on the sides of the streets. There are approximately 100 stores set over several blocks. The stores in Francistown are usually bigger than the ones in Gaborone. Furthermore, wholesalers there are also allowed to do retail business, which makes wholesale stores look more active than the ones in Gaborone. Additionally, the wholesale market in Francistown has more stores selling appliances such as TV sets, stereo speakers, DVD players, etc. There are also Indian stores in the wholesale market that sell appliances with various levels of quality, some of which are imported from South Africa, others from China.

Many local people see the type of segregation presented by the Oriental Plazas in Botswana as voluntary segregation. Comparing them to the case of a China Town in some of the big Western cities, we tend to assume that the Chinese community intentionally chose to operate their businesses in an exclusive location. However, according to Mathangwane (2015) who researched Oriental Plazas in Botswana, economic and cultural factors play major roles in the type of voluntary segregation in Botswana. Mathangwane (2015, p. 56) argues:

> First, and from an economic perspective, Chinese businesses stand to benefit from using a location that virtually closes out competition from locals. Additionally, Oriental Plazas, just like Chinatowns, are a tourist attraction to many people who visit the city, because they constitute a one stop shopping experience for visitors.

Secondly, the Chinese feel safer as a homogenous cultural group trading on the same premises in large numbers.

In 2011 some wholesalers in Gaborone considered moving to Francistown, expecting the move would provide them with a more active wholesale market because the market in Francistown was not saturated. However, field research in 2014 showed that business there was also getting worse due to market saturation and devaluation of the Pula. In Francistown an Oriental Plaza was developed by a Chinese businessman after the success of the Oriental Plaza in Gaborone. However, the project suffered a setback later on (Mathangwane 2015).

4.3.2. Retail Shops

It is said that there is at least one China shop in every town of Botswana. There are more Chinese merchants operating retail businesses than operating wholesale businesses. Retail shops can be regarded as one of the crucial factors that promote the image of China, because a China retail shop is the place where local people can readily contact Chinese people face to face.

Among the retail shops, there are also Indian shops, shops managed by local people and large South African retail chains (e.g. PEP, Ackermans, I wana, Mr. price, Bata, etc.). However, Indian shops usually sell traditional Indian clothes, hair extensions, shampoos and detergents. Therefore, they do not provide much competition in the trading relationship with China shops. Retail shops run by local people are usually smaller and sell more expensive goods than China shops, targeting a class of customers different from most of the China shops. Some large South African retail chains, however, have become competitors of China shops in recent years.

1. Retail Shops in Gaborone Shopping Malls

In Gaborone, China retail shops are mainly scattered in different shopping malls and on the sides of streets. There are more than 12 shopping malls that have China shops in Gaborone. In some shopping malls, China shops occupy the majority of the shops. The merchandise sold in the China shops is usually stocked from the wholesale stores in the Oriental Plaza. However, in order to avoid competition with other Chinese, some Chinese retailers import small quantities of unique goods by themselves from China. The practice has been ongoing for several years.

In every shop, there are one to three local people hired as assistants and one to two Chinese people who look after the shop.[3] These shops normally open between 8:00 am and 7:00 pm, with the only resting day on 1 January. Generally, every shop has at least one fitting room, a store and a bathroom in the back. The rent varies from 7,000 Pula to 20,000 Pula (900 to 2,600 US dollars)[4] depending on location.

In Gaborone, China retail shops were not allowed to open in several 'fancy' shopping malls where attracted brand shops and shops owned by South Africans. For instance, there is no China shop in River Walk, Game City or Airport Junction. According to Chinese merchants, those shopping malls are for rich people and the other shop owners in the shopping mall do not want Chinese businessman to be there for Chinese merchants tend to compete with rivals by selling their merchandise at a cheaper price.

2. Retail Shops in Rural Areas

In Botswana, retail China shops have spread from shopping malls in cities to rural towns in recent years.[5] The China shops in rural areas sell similar goods to the ones in cities. Those shop owners usually have relatives managing wholesale businesses in Gaborone or Francistown,[6] or have other shops in cities. Details of the shops in rural areas will be introduced in Chapter 8.

3. A Story of the Beginning of Retail Shops

I met CTcof 93, a Fujianese young lady in 2014. She has been in Botswana for more than 10 years. Her father was one of the pioneers among Chinese merchants who came to Botswana in 1990s. CTcof 93 came to join her family business after getting graduated from high school. When being asked about the life in earlier days and China shop history in Botswana, she told me:

We (my parents and I) lived in a rural town for two to three years before coming to open a shop in Gaborone. Those days in the rural town were boring and scary …

One day my father came to Gaborone to restock goods, leaving my mother and me at home. In those days the house did not have a wall, only a fence, anyone could climb over. We had five dogs, but strangely enough none of them barked that day. They slept until the next morning. I did not dare to sleep until 3:00 am. When I was just about to fall asleep, I heard the glass of our living room window breaking. Then I woke up my mother immediately. My father had taught me how to use a gun, because we sold hunting guns in the rural shop. I handed a gun to my mother. Turning off all the lights, we started to shoot, regardless if people outside had guns or not. While I was shooting, I called other Chinese in the town to help. When they arrived they told me to stop shooting. An uncle told me to go to sleep, saying they would watch out for our safety. I was so scared. I wanted to cry, but I thought if I cried what would my mother do, so I held my tears. After that incident, we decided to move to the city.

In 2002 or 2003 when my father came to Botswana, he found that there were only two China shops at Gaborone station in the centre of the town. There was only one shopping mall near the railway station. The police station was there, but was no other shopping mall. The land was muddy and business was very good. The China shop owner only allowed 20 local customers into the shop at a time. Once they had paid and left the shop, the owner would let another 20 people come in. There was a long queue outside of the shop. In those days, the Chinese could close the door and go somewhere else for half a day without worrying local customers would go to other shops.

At that time, my father had a shop in a rural town and thought that business in the rural area was good enough. My father was very shocked, because business in the in the city was better. In those days, the quality of merchandise was worse, and profits were higher. No matter how bad your attitude was, the local customers supported us. Chinese merchants would say: 'Do you need? If not, you shall go, other people need it.' In those days, Chinese merchants did not even display clothes on shelves; they put them on the floor, and local assistants only needed to watch out for thieves. The Chinese merchants shipped containers by themselves from China (the supply chain had not been built yet). Back in 2007 business was good here, but since 2011 business became worse, because too many Chinese had come.

Looking at the China shops one after another in the railway station area, it is difficult to imagine that such rapid change has occurred in the past 10 years. If life in the city centre of the capital city Gaborone was like this, then what kind of life did local people live in the rural area? And what kind of life did Chinese merchants live in rural areas?

4.3.3. Local Trading Regulation

In the course of my field research, I noticed one puzzling aspect of the system which these Chinese merchants operated within: the local trading regulation concerning retail business. Local regulation seems to have reserved 'selling clothing' for Batswana citizens only; however, Chinese merchants have been doing it year after year. Regulation 28 of the Trade Regulations, which came into effect on 31 March 2008, clearly stipulates the licences that are reserved for citizens only. The regulation states that:

> The following licences shall be reserved for citizens of Botswana or for companies wholly owned by citizens of Botswana: (a) auctioneer's licence; (b) car wash licence; (c) cleaning services licence; (d) curio shop licence; (e) fresh produce licence; (f) funeral parlour licence; (g) general clothing licence; (h) general dealer's licence; (i) hairdresser's licence; (j) hire services licence; (k) laundromat licence; (l) petrol filling station licence; and (m) takeaway licence (Regulation 28(1), Laws of Botswana CAP. 43:02).

Restriction of the above licences to citizens only is not unique to Botswana (Mathangwane 2015, p. 55). In other African countries such as Zambia, Malawi and Ethiopia, foreign nationals are totally barred from operating in the small and medium scale wholesale and retail sector, as these are reserved for locals (Hanisch 2013, p. 91). In all these countries, including Botswana, these restrictions are meant to promote local entrepreneurship by minimising competition from foreign traders (Mathangwane 2015, p. 55). According to the Chinese Embassy in my interview in 2014, no new working permits have been issued to Chinese merchants since 2010. Furthermore, it has been difficult to extend the working term unless the Chinese shifted their retail business to business requiring bigger investment. According to the local government, determination of a successful application is objectively performed through a point-based system.

This regulation issue has been a potential threat to China shop business, as I will explain in more detail in later chapters. Some pioneering Chinese call this 'neck cutter for Chinese merchants'. No doubt, a reasonable explanation is that local government simply seeks to reserve these businesses for local people. However, some Chinese merchants assume that before this sector has grown to maturity in Botswana, local people still need the Chinese to fill their needs. Although the regulation is already set, the execution is intentionally delayed so that local government can control the development of Chinese business according to the situation on the local market.

4.3.4. The Uniqueness of China Shops

1. 'Lay-bye' System

China shops in Botswana have adopted the local 'lay-bye' system[7] to facilitate business. Customers can pay in instalments, usually more than one third of the price at the beginning in order to have the goods reserved for one month. Before the deadline, the customer can take the goods back home at any time as long as s/he pays the rest of the instalments. If the customer does not come to take the goods before the deadline, the shop owner can keep both the goods and the money. Owners of China shops write receipts as proof to the customer who has as paid for a lay-bye purchase and usually keep the goods longer than one month, waiting for the customers to finish the payments.

2. Security Problem

Theft is a very serious problem in Botswana, particularly in China shops. Most of the China shops have adopted security video cameras and beeping boards to reduce the incidence of theft (Figure 5). However, the average loss caused by theft in every China shop is still around 2,000 Pula per month. To both Chinese people and local assistants who work in China shops guarding against thieves is one of the most important tasks. Sometimes, not only customers but local assistants who know the security system better than customers also steal from the shops. This problem causes a lot of issues between Chinese and local people, and even disturbs the building of a trusting relationship. Related issues will be discussed further in Chapter 5 and Chapter 8.

Figure 5. Theft Prevention in China Shops

4.4. The Background of Chinese Merchants

4.4.1. Statistics

Figures 6 to 10 show the statistics of 81 Chinese merchants who established their shops in Gaborone; Figure 11 shows the data gathered from Chinese merchants in Botswana, although not limited to Gaborone.

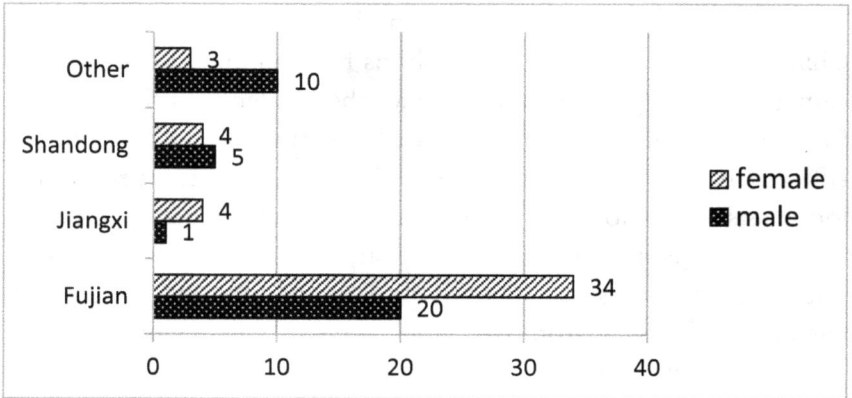

Figure 6. Distribution by Region

According to the statistics, the population of Chinese merchants from Fujian province is far more than that of any other place (Figures 6, 10 and 11), particularly during the newcomers' rush between 2002 and 2011 (Figures 10 and 11). Gender difference exists but does not seem drastic according to Figure 7. No matter which age group, more than 64% of the Chinese merchants could not speak English before coming to Botswana (Figure 8). A wide range of educational levels can be observed among Chinese merchants; most of the Fujianese received no more than a middle level of education (Figure 9).

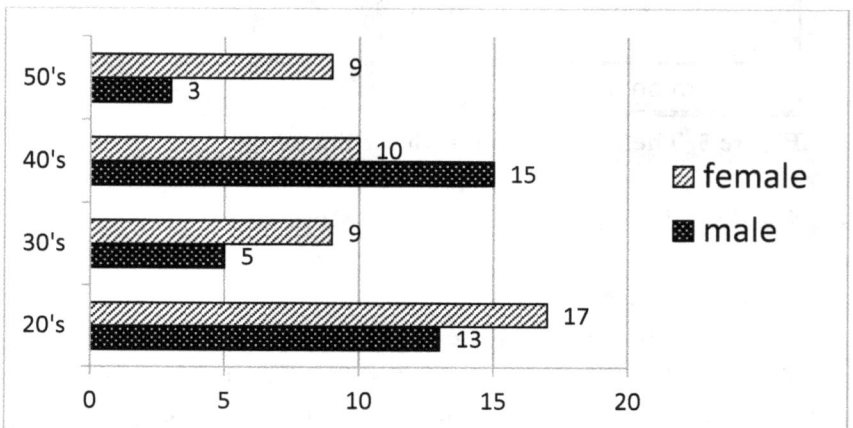

Figure 7. Gender Rate by Age

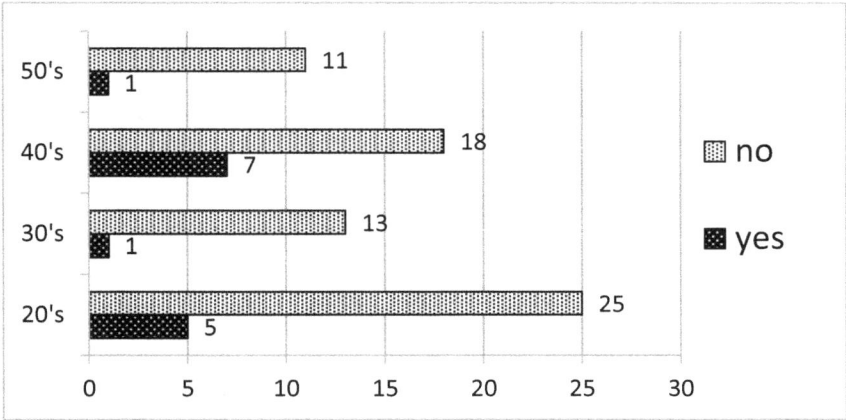

Figure 8. English Ability by Age

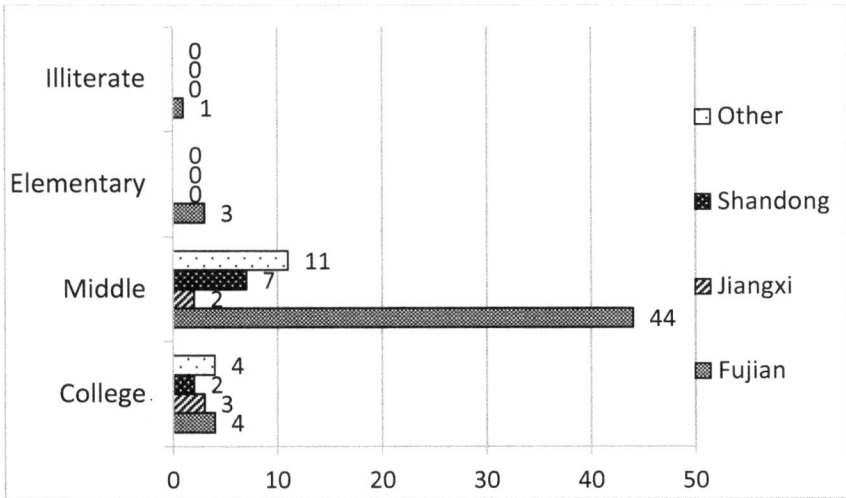

Figure 9. Education Level by Region

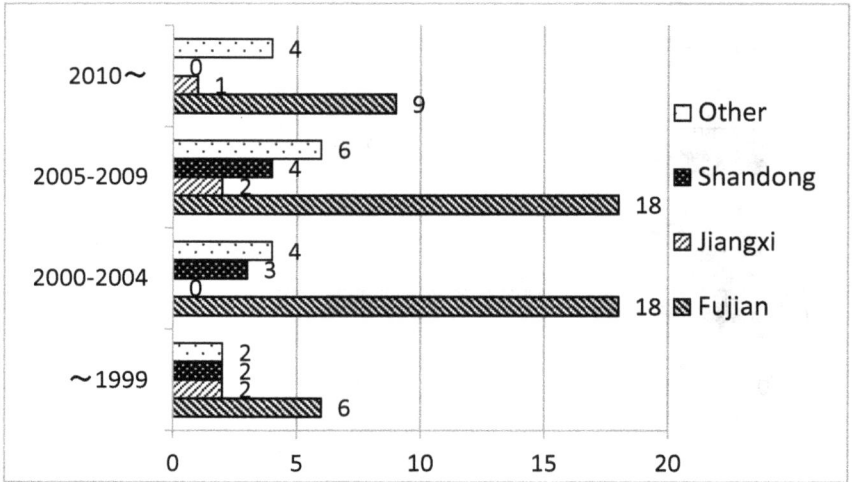

Figure 10. Arrival Year by Region – A

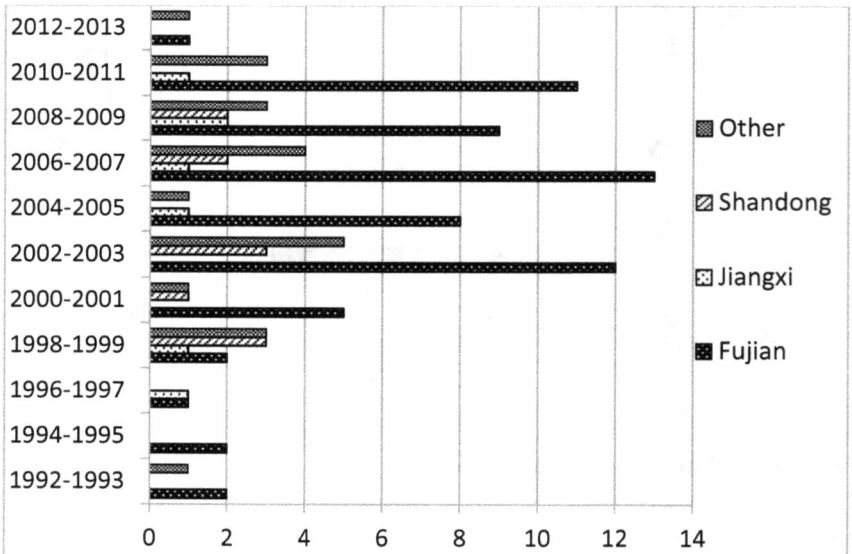

Figure 11. Arrival Year by Region – B

4.4.2. Historical View of Fujian

As mentioned above, the majority of the Chinese merchants in Botswana came from Fujian province. It is necessary to review the historical background of Fujian, in order to explain that phenomenon. Fujian lies on the east coast of China and between 1949 and the 1970s was on the frontline of a potential war between mainland China and Taiwan, so it received considerably less investment from the government of the People's Republic of China than other province. As a result, the area lacked financial support from central government and was economically impoverished but, on the other hand, the Fujianese faced less administrative interference from the government in their day-to-day life compared to the inhabitants of other provinces (Liu 1992; Thunø and Pieke 2005). Partly because of this, Fujian developed private economies much earlier than other parts of China, which is an important reason for the large-scale emigration (Xiang 2003). Furthermore, since 1978, when China opened up to the world, Fujian became the first economic experimental zone targeted for modernisation. Substantial autonomy to open up for foreign investment was given to local authorities (Thunø and Pieke 2005), which is believed to promote the trading activities between Fujianese and foreign investors. Fujian migrants and emigrants have been around the world, and relevant research has been done since the 1990s (Xiang 2003). In the Fujianese family, once the adventurer of the family who is usually the eldest brother, manages to make a life in a foreign land, then he would help his wife and siblings to immigrate, because the economic situation and living environment are too severe to bear. Especially after foreign investment came into Fujian, living costs and house rents escalated, which meant that ordinary salaries were no longer adequate to fulfil daily needs. Thus, to the majority of the Fujianese, doing business and living abroad is the most effective option for a better life for themselves and their relatives. This background explains, to some extent, why people from Fujian province make up the majority of the Chinese population in Botswana.

Besides Fujian, the other coastal provinces of China, particularly Guangdong and Zhejiang have been, for many centuries, regions that have sent migrants out into the world. Park (2009) gives a general introduction to Chinese migration to Africa from their hometown as below:

Most of the world's overseas Chinese are from particular areas within these few provinces. In some villages, over 80% of the people have migrated over that past three to four centuries; these areas are 'characterised by a long-standing tradition of emigration that has gained self-sustaining momentum'. It has become a rite of passage for the men (and more and more women) of these villages to spend at least some time overseas. Young people from these areas are under social pressure to go out into the world and return successful. Migration, then, becomes a measure of one's courage, worth, and success; it has become culturally valued (Park 2009, p. 5).

In Chinese there is a term 'qiaoxiang' that popularly refers to an area where a considerable number of inhabitants have emigrated abroad (Li 2005). From tracing the history of the emergence of Mingxi *qiaoxiang* in Fujian, Li (2005, p. 16) concludes that the migration wave has resulted from the following 5-I's. They are information; interaction (functioned along the kinship, township and friendship); ingress (the possibility of ingress into the destination state); income (the expected profits of migration); and the potential to identify the legal status. These 5-I's have interacted each other and shaped the size and orientation of the migration wave.

4.4.3. Migration Chain

Chinese merchants, who came to Botswana in the beginning of the 1990s, came as adventurers; however, latecomers came through chain migration. According to the information gathered during field research, the pioneer Chinese merchants can be divided into several groups. The first group is Chinese merchants who started their businesses in South Africa and later shifted the businesses to Botswana due to deteriorating security and the competitive market in South Africa. The second group includes some Chinese who were once employees of Chinese state-owned enterprises (SOEs) and turned to be merchants after they discovered the potential business opportunities in Botswana. This corresponds with what was reported by Mathangwane (2015) and Youngman (2013):

In 1984, the first Chinese construction company, China Civil, started business in Botswana and was later followed by other companies. These companies worked on small projects such as building houses, junior secondary schools and some private buildings (Youngman 2013). As the economy grew rapidly during the 1990s, the country became more and more attractive to Chinese investors and traders (Mathangwane 2015, p. 51).

The third group, despite of its small number, are migrants arriving in Africa from other overseas Chinese communities in Europe. As mentioned by Park (2009, p. 5), there are linguistic connections between groups of migrants.

The chain migration system among Chinese merchants observed in Botswana is very similar to the descriptions in other African countries, such as South Africa (Laribee 2008), Namibia (Dobler 2009) and Cape Verde (Haugen and Carling 2005). When it comes to retail business, once the pioneers, usually men, settle and have stable businesses, they invite their wives and children to Botswana. When they open their second shops, they invite their trustworthy relatives and friends to help. In the majority of the cases, their relatives and friends also desire to have shops of their own in the future. Therefore several years later, when sufficient resources and experience are gained, they start to open shops of their own. As shown in the Figure 12, chain migration is the system not only to multiply Chinese migrants but also increase China shops.

However, due to restricted working permits and the fiercely competitive market in recent years, fewer and fewer people want to open retail shops in Botswana; even those who have already been working as employees in China shops are contemplating going back to China. Because of the reduced profit margins, shop owners, despite the lack of Chinese employees, hesitate to invite their relatives or friends into what they perceive as an increasingly unfavourable market.

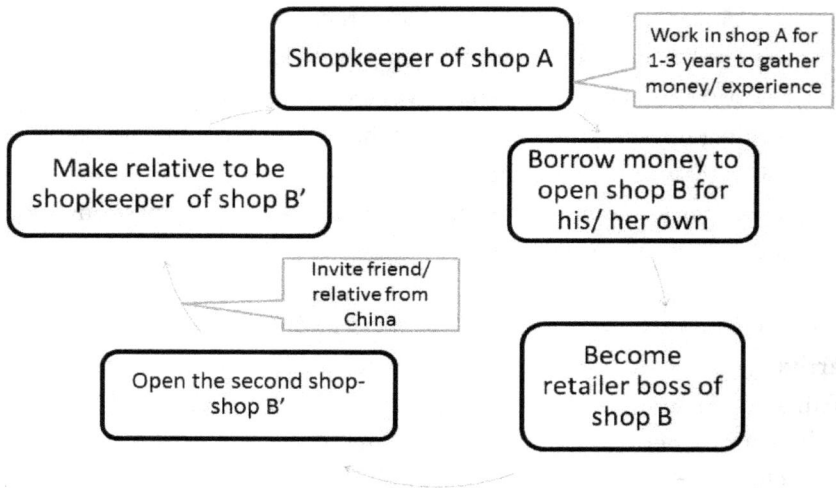

Figure 12. Employee to Owner Process

Figure 12 shows no more than a normative sequence of events; in reality there are many varieties, especially, in recent years. Due to the instability of the trading policy, the final goal of being a shop owner has been diluted to some extent. The purpose of employees' going to Botswana also varies from receiving an eye-opening experience to seeking job opportunities.

Rapid economic growth in China and the restricted trading policy in Botswana influence the purposes of coming and future plans of Chinese newcomers. Their family backgrounds and education levels determine their decisions. Since 2008 the trading policy has become very unstable making it difficult for newcomers to decide whether to open their own shops or not. Actually fewer new shops have opened since then because of the high risk of failure. Facing this kind of challenge, the existence of a senior family member, especially a successful one, is a kind of insurance, encouraging and assuring the newcomers not to give up. This tendency is shown clearly in the following case:

> YZ: When did you open this shop?
> CTcof21: My husband worked for his aunt for three years, and finally decided to open a shop of his own. We just opened this shop this year.

YZ: How do you feel about having a shop of your own?

CTcof21: In October, we had few customers and also suffered a loss as a result of goods being stolen by the man who came to decorate the room. When we went back home we reflected on whether it was our own fault. During that period of time our relationship was totally influenced by the business circumstance.

YZ: I heard that the trading policy was becoming strict these days. Weren't you afraid of that when you opened a shop of your own?

CTcof21: Of course, we were. As soon as we borrowed money to open this shop, we got the information that we could not extend our licence from the next year. Both of us were deeply shocked and felt frustrated.

YZ: How did you overcome it?

CTcof21: Because our aunt is a very clever lady and she comforted us, our parents told us to rely on her when we are here (15 December 2011).

It is not rare to find people who ask for help from relatives such as to save some money for future investment. Many Chinese are convinced that African countries can make them rich more quickly. Thus opening a China shop is regarded as the most efficient and effective way to materialise the dream. Although working in a China shop is boring and not the job most Chinese desire, they consider this period of time as purgatory while looking forward to the easy and happy life afterwards as CTco74 stated.

I want to go back home after we fulfil the five year contract with my relative. I think China is better than here. I do not enjoy a job that makes you do the same thing every day. Neither do I enjoy a busy life, only to earn a little more money. I would like to go shopping and spend time with my family. I do not want my husband to be very busy with work. I wish that he can spend some time with me. So I would like to invest in real estate and then rent houses to others; by doing that I do not need to work all day long (30 October 2011).

81

This kind of thought is very common among Chinese merchants, especially among those who failed to receive a good education. To these people, the working experience in Botswana does not necessarily relate to their future careers, nor are they interested in Africa. They go to Botswana as sojourning merchants rather than anything else. Those Chinese merchants in Western African countries may look for opportunities to immigrate to Europe (Haugen and Carling 2005), however, most Chinese who go to Botswana are not looking for immigration, but a market to achieve their quick rich dream. Bräutigam (2003) argues that when Asian business networks extend their global reach to sub-Saharan Africa, they can provide an important catalyst for local industrialisation. However, according to Chinese merchants, due to water scarcity, the distrustful relationship with locals and their short-term vision, few people want to invest in industries in Botswana.

On the contrary, to some university graduates, the purpose of working in China shops in Botswana is not limited to finding a job or earning some money. Fulfilling the dream of travelling in African countries and gaining some exciting experiences are more important.

CTce59: Being attracted to Africa because of a novel

YZ: How did you come?

CTce59: Our employer came to our school to recruit students. In our university there are many students who come to different African countries, such as Ghana, Zimbabwe, Uganda and Zambia. We are the first two people to come to Botswana from our school. Our university tries to increase the employment rate of its graduating class this way.

YZ: What attracted you to come?

CTce59: My motivation of coming to Africa was stirred by San Mao[8] I was so attracted by her book Stories of the Sahara, and have been yearning to travel to Africa by myself for a long time.

YZ: What did your parents think about your plan?

CTce59: I did not tell my parents that I wanted to come to Botswana until I signed the three year contract with my employer.

Because my university was not far from my home, I went back home three times every month during my college years. I had been sick and tired of living life under the shield of my parents.

YZ: You are very bold!

CTce59: One of our seniors in South Africa also told us that it was a good experience to come to work in Africa. Our seniors in African countries are doing different types of work, such as arranging goods, selling, etc. (17 December 2011).

It shows that the educated Chinese especially young people adopt certain values that are different from the majority of Chinese merchants. They value experience and fulfilment of their dreams higher than good job positions. Of course an understanding family, self-confidence and an adventurous heart also play crucial roles.

4.4.4. Why Botswana

For Chinese, particularly those from Fujian Province, there are many countries to choose from for a migration destination. Why do they choose Botswana? Even if many of them came through the family chain, then what convinced them to come to Botswana? I would like to introduce a few conversations I had with Chinese merchants.

Some Chinese merchants who ran businesses somewhere else saw Botswana as a better market:

> It's too competitive to do business in China (CTco34 2011).
>
> Security is bad in South Africa, and there are too many Chinese there (CTco134 2011).

Some young people who worked in Chinese factories come to get better pay when they work for their Chinese relatives and others come for adventure:

> The factory I worked at pays a low salary. My relatives here pay me better, plus I was curious about Africa (CTce79 2011).
>
> I was told that I could go to watch wild animals any time in Botswana (CTce84 2013).

There are also a very few cases of Chinese who were cheated by a 'snakehead'[9] and ended up in Botswana:

> I was cheated when I was sent here. I thought I would be sent to South America. After coming I regretted it but it was too late. I looked after the shop for a Chinese for several years and even sold goods at a market ... later I managed to open this small shop for myself (CTco55 2012).

Although Chinese merchants have their own stories of coming to Botswana, I found one thing common among them: they knew very little almost nothing about Botswana before arriving. As many Chinese merchants state: 'I have never heard there is a country in the world named Botswana until I came.' This to some extent foretells that they will encounter many challenges during their adventure in Botswana.

4.4.5. Daily Life in Botswana

The majority of the Fujianese merchants were not born into rich families. Some of them were from fishing villages and have old parents and young children to feed back home. Some of them take out loans to start their businesses, and therefore they experience a very stressful and frugal life in the early state of business.

1.   Daily Life Schedule

The Chinese merchants' daily life is very busy, especially those retailers who have to mind their shops. Owners of the shops are in charge of handling merchandise, and Chinese employees do house chores. Chinese employees, who are usually relatives or friends of the owners, work all day long in the shops. In most of the cases, for security during transportation of goods, male owners are on duty to receive goods from wholesale markets. CTco34 is a Fujianese retailer who came to Botswana in 2007 with her husband and other two Chinese employees. Based on my observation and CTco34's narration, the daily schedule of CTco34's family is summarised in Table 2.

Table 2. Retailer's Daily Schedule

Time	7:00 -8:00 am	8:00 am	8:00 -1:00 pm	1:00 -2:00 Pm	2:00 -6:00 pm	6:00 -7:00 pm	8:00 pm	9:00 -11:00 pm
Owner A (wife)	---	Open shop A	Work at shop A	Lunch	Work at shop A	Close A	Dinner/ Bath	TV Prepare
Owner A' (husband)	---	Open shop B	Restock at wholesale market	Lunch	Work at shop B	Close B	Dinner/ Bath	TV Prepare
Employee A (female)	Cook	Open shop A	Work at shop A	Lunch	Work at shop A	Close A	Dinner/ Bath	TV Chore Report
Employee B (male)	Cook	Open shop B	Work at shop B	Lunch	Work at shop B	Close B	Dinner/ Bath	TV Chore Report

In the morning, Chinese employees wake up early to prepare breakfast and lunch, because most of the Chinese retailers bring lunch to their shops instead of buying from outside. In the evening, Chinese television channels and the internet are the only source of entertainment for most of them. After listening to the reports about chain stores, the owners prepare business for the next day. After that, bathing and doing laundry usually occupies most of the remaining time.

2. Living Environment

The majority of Chinese merchants feel more secure living together in Chinese communities rather than staying among the local society. If they have to live among local people, they usually choose to share a yard with other Chinese merchants and raise some aggressive guard dogs in the yard for security purposes. Even when they live in the Chinese community, they are still very cautious. Some of them lock every door from the gate to bedroom and put alarm systems on four sides of the yard.

For those Chinese merchants who have not been in Botswana for a long time or those who have just started their own businesses, a cheap and safe yard is the best choice for their dwelling. Most of those merchants who arrived in Botswana five or ten years ago when the local market was not under fierce competition have already earned much money. A considerable number of people in this group have shifted their business from retail to wholesale or have opened many chain shops, thus they hired Chinese employees from China.[10] This group of people was much more concerned about security and would never live in a yard among local people. Because they have experienced theft and robbery to a greater extent, they know how devastating it can be.

3. Food

Generally speaking, Chinese merchants still very much rely on Chinese food. Some Chinese pioneers report that when they came in the 1990s, there were only beef and carrots. Thanks to the Chinese grocery stores that provide rice, fish, tofu and snacks, which are imported from South Africa, Chinese people can still have Chinese dishes every day. Particularly for the Fujianese who are used to eating seafood, Chinese grocery stores helped them to allow them to maintain their dietary preferences. Chinese people do buy food from local supermarkets but those purchases are limited to beef, dairy and fruit. Since most of the Chinese people have big spaces in their yards, planting vegetables for their own use is essential, in order to avoid the limited variety of local vegetables that can be found at local markets.

Furthermore, when compared with buying processed food from the supermarket or eating at Chinese restaurants, the merchants prefer cooking by themselves. For them, eating dinner around the table with family members while watching Chinese channels is a way of relaxation after a tiring day. Eating at home can also save much money, since most of them have to live frugally due to the devaluation of Botswana Pula.

After years of living in Botswana, the Chinese avoid the local cuisine due to health concerns but not sanitary reasons. Many of them think Tswana food is too oily. They would feel uncomfortable if they do not eat some fresh vegetables every day. Many Chinese enjoy beef and fruit in Botswana very much. The most unacceptable food is local salad which is mixed with too much dressing.

4.5. Struggles in Daily Life

4.5.1. Security Issues

Although Botswana has been ranked as one of the safest countries in Africa, security has been getting worse in recent years. Consulting my field notes, there is no Chinese merchant who did not complain of security issues in the interviews. Almost every Chinese merchant I spoke to has either experienced robbery, or heard of their relatives or close friends being robbed. Some have experienced robbery on the way back home from their shops, some in their shops and a handful of them have encountered robbers at home.

Having experienced living in the Chinese community, I observed how nervous and stressful their and my daily life was. Because retail businesses usually have to deal with large quantities of cash every day, the process of knocking off business, walking from shops to the parking lot and driving back home are full of tension. Even on some bad business days, where shop owners leave with only some coins in the hand, tensions and nerves remain the same.

Since 2014, there have been several local groups targeting Chinese people on the road. Some of these local thugs might smash car windows at night when drivers (particularly female drivers and Asian drivers) stop at the traffic light. After the news circulated, my host family and I were always nervous when we found a car following us for a while on the way home. We would speed up or change our route in order to get rid of the following car. Before getting into the car, the first thing we did was to double check the back mirror and rear-view mirrors; we always adjusted them to the best angle in order to secure our safety.

Some Chinese even suffered trauma after a robbery, as they say they could not sleep well for weeks. Some of their young children who experienced a robbery would cry when they saw local people. Some Chinese do not dare to sweep the leaves in their backyard, saying that in case robbers or thieves climbed in during the night, the sound of the leaves would alert them to the presence of intruders.

The majority of the Chinese call policeman after any incident, however, very few cases have been successful resolved. Few Chinese expect the robbers or thieves to be caught. 'Even if the policeman caught the robbers or thieves, after writing a statement, the police will release them very soon', echoes a common complaint by countless Chinese. In an interview, a representative of the local police gave the explanation as follows:

> After catching a suspected thief, we can detain the suspect for no more than 40 hours, and if the court finds the thief guilty, the thief will be arrested. That is why there is a perception that the suspected thief is released soon. We do spend time on searching for the suspect but it also takes time to get the stolen goods back … Theft does not only affect the Chinese… there are many others victims too (Mainmall police station 2014).

'Look at us, what kind of life we are living? We live in a prison!' a Chinese mumbled when he was opening two iron fences before reaching his door. He lived with his Chinese friends and their house was broken into by robbers the week before and all their computers, phones and cash were taken. The Chinese's complaint of 'no life quality' in Botswana is not a sarcastic comment but a voice screaming for help and protection.

4.5.2. Isolation and Self-isolation

The language barrier is still the main reason that isolates Chinese merchants from local society. Concerning the Chinese merchant's communication with local people, English is the most used language. The majority could only speak a few English words when they came but usually after several months of working in the shops they gradually manage to understand the English dialogue used daily. The merchants who have been in Botswana for a long time can speak some local languages as well, but the majority is usually limited to greetings and short sentences, like 'no problem' or 'how much.' Since English was already a big challenge for Chinese merchants, few of them are enthusiastic about learning the local languages. During my field research I met at least two Chinese merchants who can speak Setswana fluently after staying in Botswana for more than 10 years. Their language ability to communicate with locals earns admiration and praise from both their Chinese and Batswana friends. Some Chinese are curious about local society, but usually lose heart when encountered with many barriers. As one Chinese merchant stated:

> We cannot interact well with locals; first because of language barriers; second there are few places to visit here. When we go into a bar, the local people start to shout 'China'... I cannot remember local people's faces, even if they visited my shop just the day before. Old local people do not speak English, and I have to rely on the local assistants in my shop to communicate with them (CTco116 2014).

The hectic daily schedule and security concerns also limit social activities of Chinese merchants. Chinese merchants have little connection with Indians or other Chinese who work for Chinese companies, mainly because watching the shop is a time-consuming job as explained in 4.4.5. Some Chinese have business connections with Indians and some have local friends but it seems that communication beyond business is limited. The Chinese merchants express extra caution when they associate with people of a different culture.

Class differentiation also, to some extent, contributes to the isolation of Chinese merchants. There are different cliques among the Chinese. Chinese who work for Chinese state-owned companies, Chinese private companies or even established merchants have their own circles. According to my several communications with Chinese who work as employees in Chinese companies and pioneer merchants, there is a tendency to see newcomer merchants as 'low quality' and 'poorly behaved'. Such social differentiation is also apparent in other overseas Chinese communities, as illustrated by Lam (2015) in her research in Ghana. She argues that the class question will continue to play a significant role in investigating the intra- and inter-ethnic dynamics of Chinese migration in the future (ibid., p. 37). Xiao (2015) who researched the Chinese community in Nigeria also revealed a similar situtation:

Small-scale Chinese entrepreneurs in Nigeria do not have much in the way of social connections with institutions like the Chinese embassy and consulate, state-owned enterprises (SOEs) and big private corporations. They may earn more money compared to levels of income at home in China, but actually they tend to make less than the Chinese staff in the institutions mentioned above; moreover, they generally have a lower social status and live with the uncertainties that accompany transnational business (Xiao 2015, p. 76).

Due to the growing of competition among Chinese merchants, many Chinese do not associate much with 'outsiders' including other Chinese who may be their business rivals. More details on this point will be discussed in 5.2.1. Besides, Lam also found that the self-imposed isolation (self-alienation) among the Chinese comes not only from the fierce competition between Chinese businesses, but also from the circulation of 'Chinese-cheating-other-Chinese' stories (Lam 2015, p. 30). In Botswana, this kind of negative story also circulates but it seems that those Chinese with bad reputations had already returned to China for they could not survive in the small Chinese community in Botswana.

The Chinese newspaper Oriental Post (*hua qiao zhou bao* 华侨周报)[11] has been the main resource helping Chinese merchants to catch up with local news and news concerning the Chinese living in Botswana. Mr. Nan, an entrepreneur who came to Botswana in 1990s, founded the Oriental Post in 2000. In the interview in 2014 he told me that:

> Investing in Media is my hobby (side job). In the beginning, I initiated the Chinese newspaper to help Chinese merchants in Botswana to get to know local culture and society. It causes misunderstanding and conflicts if Chinese do not know local society very well. Now we print approximately 3,000–5,000 copies of the newspaper in Botswana and 10,000 in Zambia. The newspaper is founded by commercials and not supported by government. The newspaper has been distributed free and it brought deficit to my business. However, I am hesitant to close the press, since it has been

serving the Chinese community in an important way. Now we also try to use our website and social media to share the news.

With the internet and social networks, the social life of Chinese merchants has greatly improved. They can communicate with family back in China as long as they are connected to the internet. Watching movies or playing games on cell phones helps them to kill time when they watch shops. Recalling life back 10 years before, CTcof 93 said:

> Nowadays we can access the internet with our cell phones. In the old days, we could only sit like a block of wood. After dinner my parents watched TV, but I felt the TV programmes were so boring that I would rather watch the ceiling in my room. Later my father bought me a computer, but we had no internet connectivity and very few movies were accessible. In those days, we connected the computer to the telephone to access the internet and it cost 10 Pula per hour, which was very expensive. Even Mascom the telecom company had no internet, and when we made calls back to China we called directly. The fee was very high. One day when I could no longer bear the boredom, I got angry at my mother and said: 'it was you who brought me here!'(CTcof 93 2014).

In recent years, cyberspace serves the function of cohesion that the Chinese Embassy and Consulate cannot achieve (Xiao 2015). Xiao who conducted research on the Chinese community in Nigeria, argues that QQ – the social informality of the transnational online community has helped Chinese petty entrepreneurship to overcome some vulnerability. For instance, when Nigerian immigration officials began to arrest the Chinese in Nigerian markets in May 2012, the QQ group members used a chat room to inform each other about where the immigration officers were going, and even suggested that their members stay indoors (Xiao 2015, pp. 96–97).

4.5.3. Homesick

As mentioned previously, many Chinese merchants, particularly young couples left their children with their parents or relatives back in China, and came to Botswana to start up their businesses. With social networking, communication with family members back home is not a problem anymore. However, for mothers leaving children back home, the emotional burden is not easy to bear. Many Chinese merchants could spend hours talking about how they miss their children back home. With WeChat some of them manage to video chat with their children every day, listening to their school reports and their issues with grandparents. CTco34 left two young children back in China. Her feelings and struggle are universal among the female Chinese merchants who left their children back in China:

> I miss them a lot when I watch the videos taken by my husband and sometimes I cry at night. When I call my children they say: 'Why do you always lie to us, saying you are coming back?' I am afraid of calling back home sometimes, because I do not know how to face my children ...
>
> I will buy anything for my elder son even if people around me accuse me of spoiling him. I feel guilty about my absence and would like to make up for it by supporting him financially. Several days ago, my son sent me a message saying his new cell phone had been stolen. (She had paid 3,000 RMB for it and he liked it very much.) I told him not to feel too bad about it and that I would buy him a new one when I went back home again.
>
> I know that my son is suffering during my absence. I know my son has questions and doubts if his mother really loves him. If I do not provide for my son's needs I would feel bad (CTco34 2011).

4.5.4. Lack of Rest

Wholesalers may take one week off after the Christmas season for a family trip to a remote area. But to most of the Chinese retailers, especially the Chinese employees, 1 January is their only day-off. On that day, shop owners arrange some activities or short trips. Due to the limited number of parks and entertainment places in Gaborone, many Chinese complain that their only holiday in the year is spent in crowded places:

> After Christmas Gaborone is almost empty because the majority of the local people have returned to their home towns. In spite of that, I open my shop in the hope that some customers will come. If I stayed at home, I would be watching TV and playing cell phone games which I could do in the shop ... The only rest I get is on New Year's Day. Our family always visits 'Lion Park'. You will find many Chinese visitors in the Park on that day.
>
> The Indians all close their shops on Friday afternoons and go to Indian Temple but the Chinese cannot be united in this way. Even if someone suggests that all Chinese merchants should close shop for one day in a week, I am sure you will still find some Chinese open their shops secretly. We think even selling a roll of tissue brings in some profit and selling a battery, another several Pula; however, if we stay at home, we still pay rent for the shop for the day ...Why do we leave family back home and travel so far to this country? Of course, for running businesses!
>
> We are really greedy sometimes. We don't think one Pula is too little, neither do we think one million Pula is too much ...The principle of opening this kind of retail shop is 'As long as you open it, there are customers, they will come to buy, whether more or less' (CTce79 2012).

For retailers, staying in the shop is the only way for them to do business. Even during the days when only a few customers visit their shops, they still choose to open the shop to earn as much as possible. For most of them, daily life is therefore unbearably 'boring.' Some of them admire those wholesalers who can have longer days off work, and admire those people who open shops in European countries, saying they can even have time to go fishing and enjoy beautiful views. Wholesalers in Botswana do not improve profits by extending business hours; they usually only open their store for a limited time and some only open when they know some retailers want to resource stocks. In that sense, the lives of wholesalers are much more relaxed compared to the retailers.

Because of the dull routine, some male merchants gamble to entertain themselves. It is said that many male Chinese merchants spend their weekends in the hotels where casinos can be found, leaving the shops to their wives. Although some of them do not have time to meet each other on weekdays, gambling brings them together and even provides the place for them to conduct further communication.

4.6. Summary

This chapter has focused on the first question of the research: What are the experiences of Chinese merchants coming to live in Botswana? How do Chinese merchants in Botswana start business as 'suitcase travellers', and later build up China shops and China towns in the world? In the first section of the chapter, the logistical chain of Chinese merchandise and the situation surrounding retail and wholesale shops have been introduced. The quantitative findings presented in this chapter suggest the composition of Chinese merchants and significant changes in the coming of Chinese merchants to Botswana. However, the qualitative findings reveal that Chinese merchants usually have a low English language ability, the majority come from Fujian and have a poor family background, and their status as foreigner merchants makes them easily isolated from the local society and even established Chinese. The chapter acknowledges that the experiences of Chinese merchants' coming to live in Botswana essentially arise from the business challenges they face daily. This issue is taken up in the next chapter.

Notes

[1] http://www.amandaiec.com/category/yiwu_market/.

[2] http://jjxy.hhczy.com/.

[3] This situation was common in 2011, but fewer Chinese employees could be found in 2013 due to the restricted regulation of Chinese retail business.

[4] Information gathered in 2011 according to the Pula–USD currency rate in 2011.

[5] Several cases showed a development in the opposite direction.

[6] The early comers who started business as retailers run wholesale stores once they have earned enough money. They will allow their relatives to continue running their retail shops and also open retail shops in some rural areas.

[7] Shopping on credit.

[8] A famous Chinese author who went to the Sahara Desert in 1974 and published her novel Stories of the Sahara in 1976.

[9] Snakeheads are Chinese gangs that smuggle people to other countries.

[10] Based on the situation in 2011; few Chinese employees could be found since 2013.

[11] The first and only newspaper published in Chinese in Botswana. http://observers.france24 .com/content/20090710-oriental-post-africa-first-chinese-paper-botswana."

Chapter 5

The Business Challenges and Strategies in China Shops[1]

Security is getting worse and worse. Most of us have experienced being robbed. We get little profit in the business as if we are selling cabbage but are so worried on a daily basis, it's as if we are selling heroin[2]. — Chinese pioneer

This chapter discusses the challenges faced by Chinese merchants when engaging in retail activities in Botswana. The theory of a middleman minority will be used as a theoretical perspective to assess both the challenges and the strategies employed to overcome them. It argues that Chinese merchants' self-imposed isolation (combined with their sense of vulnerability as foreigners) as mentioned in the last chapter is deeply rooted in their attitudes. Their social position as middleman minority determines their circumstances and their responses to signs of hostility from their host society. On the other hand, the particular geographical location and economic situation of Botswana offers Chinese merchants opportunities to avoid competing among themselves and to manage their rejection by local society. Based on the background of Chinese merchants and their business in Botswana, this chapter gives a panoramic picture of the key issues between Chinese merchants and local society. From a middleman minority perspective, this chapter locates the social position of Chinese merchants in order to give an explanation of the nature of business challenges the Chinese face as well as the business strategies they employ. However, the details concerning the social influence brought by Chinese merchants and their interaction with local assistants will be discussed in later chapters.

5.1. The Middleman Minority Perspective

The middleman minority theory has been widely employed to explain the concentration of immigrant groups within the small business sector (Bonacich 1973; Min 1990). The theory refers to entrepreneurs operating between the dominant and subordinate groups with customers generally being members of marginalised racial or ethnic groups. According to Zhou et al. (2016, p. 142), the entrepreneurs have several marked characteristics that reinforce their double outsider status. First, they intend to return to their community or country of origin after accumulating some capital and are, thus, socially isolated from the host society's dominant group. Second, they aim to profit quickly from their portable and fluid businesses and then reinvest their earnings elsewhere. Therefore, they are not socially rooted in, nor do they belong to, the communities where they conduct business. Third, they most commonly establish their business niches in poor racial minority neighbourhoods, and thus are a socially in-between group (Bonacich 1973). However, the theory can be fully applied to immigrant groups, observing the continually changing nature of immigration and racial/ethnic relations (Douglas and Saenz 2007). The concept of the middleman minority is therefore flexible.

Nyíri (2011) conducted a study in Eastern Europe, which argued that Chinese merchants in various colonial and imperial economies occupy the position of 'middleman minorities', i.e., functioning as economic and political intermediaries between the rulers and the populace while being regarded as outsiders. The emergence of networks of Chinese importers and shopkeepers in Africa (and other developing countries) since the mid-2000s replicates this Eastern European pattern. Nyíri (2007) stated that Chinese merchants are referred to as a 'transnational middleman minority' able to import goods and labour flexibly from China without reliance on locally accumulated capital. Due to globalisation, the Chinese merchants' position as a middleman minority appears to be increasing on different continents, while mediating between dominant and subordinate groups.

As discussed in the previous chapter, Chinese retailers in Botswana distribute to local low-income customers merchandise imported from Chinese wholesalers, both locally and directly from China. While Chinese wholesalers mainly distribute Chinese merchandise to Chinese and Indian retailers, they also deal with traders from neighbouring countries, as well as some that are local. Both Chinese retailers and wholesalers encounter hostility from the host society as a consequence of their dependence on subordinate and ethnic groups. Chinese merchants (particularly retailers) are criticised as occupying jobs suitable for local people and for exploiting local employees. Parallel to the logic of the 'transnational middleman minority' as discussed in Nyíri (2007), Chinese merchants in Botswana are situated between the dominant (local rich and middle class customers) and subordinate groups (local low-income customers, Indian retailers and traders from neighbouring countries), making the middleman minority theory a useful perspective from which to analyse the challenges they face.

5.2. Nature of Challenges

This section presents the nature of the challenges faced by Chinese merchants in their daily business interactions. According to my observations and informal interviews, Chinese merchants face internal challenges related to their shops and external challenges posed by local authorities. Internal challenges include: price wars, overwork, internal competition between Chinese retailers, theft by local assistants and problems of service involving merchants and local customers. External challenges mainly consist of regulation and extortion by local authorities. Furthermore, the majority of the external challenges are actually triggered by internal challenges, which will be discussed in greater detail below.

5.2.1. Internal Competition between Chinese Merchants

Most Chinese retailers stock goods from the wholesale market in the Oriental Plaza, so that similar goods tend to be sold in all China shops. Large South African retail chains and local shops operated by Indians and Africans sell merchandise at a higher price, while China shops mainly sell cheap goods. In recent years, profit margins have fallen as the result of lowering prices to attract local customers. This has led to competition between China shops. I was warned by many Chinese retailers: 'If you are not close friends or relatives of other China shop owners, you had better not visit other shops. They would suspect that you are trying to check their goods and prices.' According to my observations, many shops do not even put price tags on their goods. Chinese merchants and local assistants give prices only when customers ask.

A price war is gradually destroying the relationship of trust among Chinese retail merchants, since the absence of price tags could be regarded as a way to compete with other Chinese merchants while maintaining harmony on the surface. Most of the merchants in Botswana admit that, as merchants in the same foreign country, they try to be friendly with each other, and considering themselves as compatriots. However, when facing a stiff competitive situation, they have to employ some strategies to survive. They manage to keep the competition underground in most cases, but conflicts do surface sometimes. For instance, when there was a goods shortage in the wholesale market before the Christmas season, Chinese retailers were fighting each other for new stocks (CTco38 2011).

Price wars are gradually destroying relationships among Chinese retailers. However, the Chinese community maintains its unity in the face of adversity. Chinese businessman have a cultural urge to make peace with each other, in line with the saying harmony brings wealth (*heqi shengcai*, 和气生财). This is thought to be particularly so abroad, as many believe that in unity there is strength, particularly when the Botswana government restricts Chinese business. Hence, price wars lead to competition with other Chinese, but there is a general desire for harmony. The majority are linked through groups on social networks in order to exchange information, so if an inspection occurs in one shop, the information will be shared with group members – to the annoyance of the local government. Thus, despite the price war and hectic daily life, Chinese merchants understand the necessity to remain united.

Due to the rapid rise in the number of Chinese merchants and China shops recently, the local market (particularly in Gaborone) is becoming saturated. Market saturation has severely influenced local businesses and brought fierce competition among Chinese merchants, forcing them to engage in a price war in order to survive (Carling and Haugen 2004). In Botswana, the strong ethnic cohesion among Chinese is not as obvious as it once was, although it still exists, despite saturation and competition. However, competition drives Chinese merchants into a vicious circle that leads to an extension of opening times as explained previously in section 4.5.4., the overworking of local assistants and the search for loopholes to cover the profits lost. This then triggers labour and legal conflicts as well as external challenges.

5.2.2. Labour Issues

Local assistants arrange the goods in the China shops and help Chinese merchants and local customers understand each other. The roles they play in the shops are invaluable. Before their arrival in Africa, most Chinese merchants neither speak English nor know anything regarding Botswana's culture. They begin by learning the names of the goods in the shops and use code-switching (Akhidenor 2013) to express simple meanings. After working for several months, local assistants can understand commands from their employers by grabbing at key words. However, language and cultural barriers cause misunderstandings when it comes to values, principles, structure, decision-making and leadership preferences (Yang and Doh 2013, p. 51), so that Chinese merchants experience rejection by local assistants and their own vulnerability as foreigners (Giese 2013).

Two features apply in most China shops: firstly, Chinese merchants stand by the cash machine; secondly, there is a large monitor for the security cameras. Chinese merchants seldom let local assistants handle cash, and security cameras are used not only to scare away thieves but also to monitor the activities of local assistants. The latter know how the shop is managed and spend a considerable amount of time there, giving them ample opportunity for theft. It is difficult for Chinese merchants to dismiss employees without solid evidence, hence the reliance on security cameras. A Chinese commented: 'It is difficult to fire a local assistant without cause and solid evidence, but once you record her stealing, you have the proof to fire her (CTce44 2011).'

Chinese merchants value trusting relations with employees and recognise that they cannot run their businesses smoothly without the cooperation of local assistants. However, many have become disillusioned. Some Chinese merchants repeatedly seek to build a trusting relationship with their local assistants, but others draw conclusions from poor reports by senior management, as the following comments indicate:

> I tried to trust him, but he is heartless, biting the hand that feed him. I gave him what I eat and took him wherever I went ..., but one day I saw him stealing money from my daughter's wallet (CTco134 2012).

> I was told that they are untrustworthy. When we go to the bathroom we close the shop and let the local assistants wait outside. Even when we are in the shop they steal; it would be terrible if we left them with cash (CTco74 2011).

Theft by local assistants is considered by Chinese merchants to be a moral defect (Giese and Thiel 2012, p. 1114) and a betrayal. Once local assistants are found stealing, they lose the trust of their Chinese employers. However, Giese and Thiel (2012, p. 1114) argue that theft is deviant behaviour by which local assistants express their dissatisfaction with the relations they exchange with their Chinese employers. Some local assistants in Botswana are required to work six days a week and ten hours a day for a minimal salary. Although most Chinese employers claim that they pay for overtime, the salary offered fails to satisfy the assistants. As a result, they come to expect free goods from the shops as a 'bonus' or 'incentive' in return for their hard work. Or it may be 'a weapon of the weak' (Scott 1987) to express silently their resistance to Chinese merchants or to the job in the China shop itself (more details will be discussed in Chapter 7). Few Chinese relate the thefts to their own failure to fulfil the needs of local assistants; or perhaps they deliberately ignore the connection. The Chinese are fearful of being overgenerous to local people, lest the latter expect still more or come to believe that their Chinese employers are rich. Many Chinese merchants ignore their assistants' thefts as long as they remain minimal, or possibly record them as a means of countering their assistants' wage demands. Some Chinese consider themselves lucky to get a really loyal local assistant who has never been found stealing things from the shop.

A further issue is truancy. Most Chinese merchants regard local assistants as lazy. I observed that they usually move slowly and with reluctance when requested to act, and tend to chat with each other during the working day if they have the opportunity. According to Chinese merchants, local assistants seek various excuses for taking time off during the busy season, thus disrupting the business. One Chinese noted: 'They nag for leave to attend funerals in home village no matter who passed away in the family. We have to let them go even if we are aware of their lies sometimes. ... Some of their mothers have died twice.' (CTco22 2012) Of course, cultural differences cannot be ignored, since many Chinese merchants do not understand the local attitude to funerals.

There is an imperative to attend funerals in order to 'show love' (*go bontsha lerato*) by participating in the work of death (Klaits 2010, p. 38). Funerals often direct attention to the question of who is helping or refusing to pay for whose burial, and to the long-term consequences of such exchanges for a variety of relationships. For many reasons, then, death is a site of identity creation, a site of differentiation – and also a site where mutuality is recognised and created (Durham and Klaits 2002, p. 781). Therefore, funerals play a crucial social role in Botswana, particularly with the impact of AIDS on the overall mortality rate.

Among the Tswana, funerals are typically carried out on weekends so that people can attend. Nightly radio programs such as Ditatolo or Dikitsiso tsa Dinstho come on around 8: 00 p.m. and announce the names of people who have recently died so that people who are living in rural areas or traveling or working far from their homes can listen and learn if any of their friends or loved ones have passed away. With the impact of AIDS on the overall mortality rate and especially that of young people, even those in their twenties and thirties now listen to such programs every evening in hushed silence. They may then decide to attend a funeral if it is not too distant and there is enough time to get there.

In traditional funeral rites, the corpse is brought to the deceased family's home the evening before the burial, where people come to pay their last respects, say prayers, and partake of tea and snacks. Funerals are expensive because the deceased's family is expected to provide food for everyone who attends; it is standard practice for those who can afford it to kill a number of cows (Denbow and Thebe 2006, pp. 185–186).

To local assistants, a funeral is a social obligation that consumes time and money. They expect understanding from their Chinese employers and even some extra money for their long trip. Nevertheless, the Chinese employers usually see it as an unnecessary activity or an excuse for being absent from work, which only deserves a bonus reduction. This kind of discrepancy causes both sides to harbour grudges against each other. However, the motivation of local assistants and the value they place on their jobs in the China shops, should also be taken into consideration. Many local assistants consider their jobs in the China shops to be part-time and leave if offered the opportunity to go back to school or to a job with a better salary. One local assistant noted:

> If I could find a better job I would not be working in this shop. I work six days every week. … When do I have time to do my laundry? My boss comes to count the goods every day. If we make a mistake, or goods are stolen, we have to pay. Even if we do well we only receive about 200 pula (23 US dollars) as a bonus in December (CTbe10 2013).

Since there are many job opportunities in the China shops in Gaborone, local assistants are not afraid of being fired. Few plan to work long term in China shops, due to the low wages and long hours. Meanwhile, many Chinese merchants fail to understand the point of view of their local assistants and consider the assistants' disrespectful attitude to be racially motivated or due to their own low social status as shop owners. Even when they do see their employees' point of view, they cannot satisfy the demand for higher wages, because of the fierce competition with other Chinese. Concerning the employment relations between Chinese merchants and local employees, a further detailed analysis will be given in Chapter 7.

5.2.3. Business Loss

As mentioned above, Chinese merchants invest heavily in theft-proofing, as evidenced by the security cameras in every China shop. However, a certain amount of loss is unavoidable. Firstly, China shops sell diverse merchandise, which provides thieves with many opportunities. Secondly, almost half of Botswana's population lives on less than 2 US dollars a day (Benza 2012). People receive financial support from the government but their income still falls short of their needs. Surprisingly, although many are angry regarding theft, many Chinese merchants have sympathy for the thieves:

> They need to steal to survive. Some goods are stolen at my shop every month. … It annoyed me before, but now I regard it as charity. I have already put in a security video camera and should accept what I cannot change (CTco22 2012).

Theft destroys the trust between Chinese merchants and locals, since merchants now view every local as a potential shoplifter (Carling and Haugen 2004). If theft is a chronic disease facing Chinese merchants, robbery is fatal and even more necessary to avoid. 'You should not carry a bag when you are walking around in this season,' Chinese merchants are frequently warned around Christmas time. A Chinese merchant (who had been robbed a few weeks previously) commented: 'Our habit of carrying cash is well known to local people. Indians and white people all use plastic cards to pay.' (CTco1 2011) The Chinese newspaper the Oriental Post prints reminders from the Chinese embassy, particularly around Christmas and New Year. This also explains why Chinese merchants typically buy second-hand cars, wear shabby clothes and prefer to live within the Chinese community. As 'rich' merchants in a foreign land, they avoid flaunting their wealth. Despite such precautions, robbery remains inevitable, adding to the feeling of insecurity among Chinese merchants.

To meet the needs of the majority in Botswana, Chinese merchants have been importing cheap, poor-quality goods ever since the 1990s for a population desperate for affordable goods regardless of quality. Currently, however, despite the fact that the quality of Chinese goods has improved, with increased salaries and more choices in the market, there are even more complaints, particularly concerning quality. 'If you buy clothes or shoes in China shops, then you have to keep on going back again and again. If we had enough money, we would not buy clothes in China shops.' (Pb172 2014) Although the Chinese are criticised for dumping poor quality goods in Botswana, they are still welcomed by those on low incomes.

The problem of poor quality also applies to electronics. I observed that many Chinese merchants repair electronics and cell phones themselves, and when customers come to claim a replacement, they repair them instead. Most Chinese merchants exchange broken goods for their customers if they find their claims reasonable. They accept that their merchandise is not of high quality but assert that it suits local people in need, arguing: 'We sell a TV set at 400 Pula and only earn 20–30 Pula as profit. It's not reasonable to compare the quality of a 400 Pula TV with a 3,000 Pula one.' (CTco23 2013) The Chinese gradually learn to handle false claims, as noted in the following comment:

> When a local customer comes to my shop to claim replacement goods, I will simply exchange them. However, if they talk nonsense, I warn them that I have recorded their actions with a security video camera and will send the recording to the police (CTco116 2013).

Although locals and Chinese migrants meet daily, they are separated into buyers and sellers. Nyíri (2007) is of the opinion that this social relationship serves to deepen hostility rather than overcome it. The locals perceive the migrants not to be members of society but 'a familiar, useful, sometimes exotically interesting, but potentially threatening, alien element'. (Nyíri 2007, pp. 138–139) This attitude strengthens merchants' short-term view of investment, for they feel used rather than welcomed. In the case of South Africa, Park (2009, p. 16) states that, even if the Chinese do find economic success, they will continue to occupy the 'in-between' spaces, wedged between a majority of impoverished local Africans and a narrow elite group. Therefore, the position of the Chinese and the role they play in society tend to determine their fate.

5.2.4. Regulation and Extortion

Chinese merchants are subject to punitive regulations in Botswana, related to labour issues and poor-quality products. The media's use of negative reports leads locals to view the Chinese negatively. Gaotlhobogwe (27 January 2009) published the following news item in the local online newspaper, Mmegionline:

> Botswana's government moved to ban the Chinese trade in clothes. Botswana licensing department issues specialized licenses to protect local traders because the non-citizen investors engage in specialized trade, but the Chinese traders exploited a loophole in the system. ... The Chinese traders were given two years to rearrange their businesses or lose their licenses.

Since then, city council officers and the police have frequently checked China shops. Chinese merchants must continually renew their short-term working permits, as the local government refuses to issue them long-term permits. These practices lead to complaints from many Chinese merchants regarding fault-finding, unfair treatment and extortion. To avoid trouble, some Chinese merchants close their shops if they hear the authorities are coming. However, the local government considers this action suspicious, leading to random checks and increasing anxiety among Chinese merchants.

The relationship between Chinese merchants and Botswana's local authorities is becoming increasingly fraught, as Chinese merchants describe the attitude of officials as one of fault-finding and the officials themselves come to view the Chinese merchants as 'canny'. Escalating competition among Chinese merchants leads some to seek loopholes in order to maintain their profit margins, prompting ever increasing regulation by local government. Newcomers often fall victim to extortion, at least initially:

> The police always come to ask for free gifts from my shop. ... I did not want to raise issues with her when I first arrived, so I gave her some. Now I do not since I am no longer afraid of her (CTcof2 2011).

Comparatively, Chinese merchants with many years of business experience in Botswana are able to swiftly resolve difficulties as a Chinese pioneer shared her story:

> Once a local officer came into my shop saying 'I am hungry'. I said to him: 'I cannot give you money now, since you are officer in a uniform. If I gave money to you, I would be bribing. We will both be caught. If you come to me after I have closed the shop, then we are friends. If you are hungry I can treat you to a meal ...' Then he smiled and left (CTco22 2014).

What make Chinese merchants vulnerable to extortion? The root cause is their uncertainty about whether they have fully followed the local regulations. 'We have every license required ...we are not selling anything that is forbidden. We don't need to be afraid of them.' However, story changes after local government started restricting visas and trading permits; Chinese merchants have to pay a 'fine' to continue their business. During the field research, I did not meet anyone whose visa had expired but met many Chinese who were renewing/extending their trading permits. That kind of ambiguous business status exposes them to many checks and even extortion. Fieldwork conducted in Nigeria and Ghana also describes a similar situation.

In Lagos, small-scale Chinese entrepreneurs are often subjected to unexpected visa and passport checks by Nigerian officials. Officers from the directorate of investigation of the Nigeria

Immigration Service sometimes work undercover. Sometimes the Chinese overstay their visas and are arrested, but Nigerian immigration officials imply that immigrants who have overstayed can be released if they pay a 'fine'. Thus, the primary strategy adopted by the Chinese in order to cope with Nigerian immigration officials is to avoid meeting them, especially during times when immigration controls are stricter. If they are 'unfortunately' inspected by Nigerian immigration officials, the best course of action is to negotiate a price as soon as they are stopped (Xiao 2015, p. 82).

The Chinese in Ghana are increasingly finding themselves targets of extortion by Ghanaian officials. As a result, Chinese business persons in Ghana do regularly give 'tips' (*xiaofei*, extra money) to officials, either upon 'request' from the latter or proactively as an incentive for officials to bypass red tape. Recent arrivals to Ghana reported that they were surprised by the levels of corruption relating to everyday micro-administrative procedures, something they said they experienced less and less over the years in China…Without adequate local knowledge and networks, the new Chinese feel obliged to pay a 'tip' in order to 'oil the wheels' of daily administration (Lam 2015, pp. 17–18).

This kind of corruption is regarded as an everyday phenomenon and a 'culture' in Nigeria (Smith 2007; Xiao 2015) and seen by Chinese as 'local custom' or 'pragmatism to "buy" convenience' in Ghana. Lam (2015) attributes the phenomeon to the vulnerable social status and 'unestablishedness' of some Chinese, because established Chinese are politically protected to a great extent. On the other hand, in Nigeria's case, Xiao argues that the state is both a shadow and real, for 'political authorities grab interests and accumulate wealth through the informal economy; state-sanctioned predation also leaves petty capitalist growth relatively unregulated'. (Xiao 2015, p. 84) However, Botswana has a good reputation as the least corrupt country in Africa (Corruption Perceptions Index 2013). How shall we explain the phenomenon in Botswana? The following factors are thought to account for increasing police extortion in recent years in Botswana. Firstly, the Botswana police are considered to be influenced by scandals and corruption in neighbouring countries (e.g. South Africa). Secondly, Chinese merchants often respond by offering bribes as a short cut to a solution, thereby encouraging corruption. Thirdly, the language barrier increases the likelihood of unfair treatment. In addition, fear and vulnerability lead Chinese merchants to feel that they need to please local authorities in order to run their businesses peacefully, because they know that, as foreigners, disagreements with the local authorities can be dangerous.

5.3. Business Strategies

Involvement in a competitive business environment encourages Chinese retailers to work hard to win customers and to reduce their own living and business costs. When it comes to business strategies, methods of resolving internal challenges include seeking a niche market, improving management practices and taking part in local culture to ease internal tensions. Meanwhile bribes and donations to charities and other causes are used to ease external tensions. My field research shows that business experience and financial status are major influences on business strategies.

5.3.1. Avoiding Competition

As discussed above, competition among Chinese businesses is more severe than between Chinese and local merchants, due largely to the similar products offered. This leads Chinese merchants to source original goods from China in order to avoid direct competition: 'I ordered some classic leather bags from China. ... With these bags I will have my own customers, who are attracted by my bags and when they want to buy bags they will come to me.' (CTco34 2012) Alternative strategies include starting up shops in rural areas where the market has not been saturated.

Chinese merchants are aware that, in doing business in a country with a small population, they will eventually overstay their welcome, and therefore the majority seeks to expand elsewhere. Thanks to Botswana's geographic location, surrounded by three countries[3], the Chinese have the opportunity to move to border towns and neighbouring countries[4] in so far as their networks and financial situation allow them to. Botswana is a landlocked country. McNamee (2012, p. 40) states that in countries like Lesotho and Botswana, Chinese traders have penetrated deep into rural areas as opportunities narrow. Newcomers struggle the most, because they have only recently invested and are yet to receive an adequate return, and newcomers vacillate between staying and going back to China, even though they might fail to catch up with developments when they return home.

A new tendency worth mentioning is that in recent years as the social network Wechat prevails among Chinese users, some Chinese merchants in Botswana start to open online shops to sell African traditional cosmetics, rooibos tea and wine to customers back in China. It may add some additional earnings to their shrinking profits in Botswana, but this trend has not emerged as a main form of business so far.

5.3.2. Improving Management

After a number of years, Chinese merchants' improved language skills, experience and local connections mean that they gain more original ideas for improving their businesses. For instance, to avoid theft, many shops adopt computer registration systems, so that local assistants can handle the cashier machines. In this way, not only do local assistants come to feel trusted but customers are more likely to value the shop. Experience also improves customer relations; although owners may not speak the local language, they can at least call their customers 'my friend' or mosadi ('madam' in Setswana), in order to be positive and show kindness. Some Chinese even try to remember their customers' names and encourage them to become regular customers. Knowing local people like music, many China shops attract customers by playing popular music. To get English-speaking Chinese assistants, some Chinese merchants make connections with universities in China and hire English major graduates to run their shops. In Botswana, the benefits of these strategies are evident, as demonstrated by the following comments:

We hire two university students (who speak good English) from China as employees and an old-time local friend as a manager. Our manager is in charge of everything in the shop. We use a computer register system so that local assistants cannot steal goods. The assistants are able to collect the cash. We think this shows great trust and respect for local people (CTco58 2011).

We are in charge of everything. Our Chinese boss only comes to the shop when he gets new stock. He treats us as friends and trusts us. I am happy with this job (CTbm61 2013).

For most Chinese merchants, building a relationship of trust with local people would seem to be an unrealistic proposition, but there are cases of success as I listed above, which shows that, despite the difficulties, wise management strategies and good interpersonal relations are possible. Some problems arise from the fact that most Chinese in Botswana are not well educated. They have low self-esteem and doubt their business skills, which leads to a reluctance to practise their language skills and to assimilate the language. Labour conflicts appear to result from the attitudes of the Chinese in a foreign situation: they feel vulnerable and give culturally divergent interpretations to identical practices (Giese 2013). In an environment characterised by rejection and hostility, Chinese merchants aim to hire trustworthy employees to limit their perceived vulnerability.

Improving one's management strategies (as outlined above) can help the Chinese to overcome their self-isolation and limit their feelings of vulnerability. Deumert and Mabandla (2013, p. 50) stress that adoption of the local language is a key to achieving local embeddedness and to demonstrate respect. Learning the local culture helps the Chinese to deepen their interpersonal relations and understand both the positive aspects and the limitations of local society, thus promoting tolerance and understanding. It can therefore be concluded that an increased investment in improving management strategies and learning the language will increase the positive experience of living and business.

5.3.3. Bribery and Donation

In order to succeed in a competitive business environment, some Chinese merchants sell forbidden merchandise (e.g. replica clothes and goods that actually require an extra business licence). Despite the risk, bribery is viewed as a universal panacea. Newcomers (who have financial burdens and whose language skills are limited) view selling forbidden merchandise as an option to compete with more established Chinese traders. CTco38 shared his opinion as follows:

> We are bullied here because we do not speak English very well. When the police and officers come to trouble us, even when we know that it is not our fault, we do not know how to explain. In order not to become involved in trouble, we usually choose to pay money so that they will leave. We have neither time nor energy to deal with them (CTco38 2011).

The Chinese merchants tend to stick to the philosophy of 'never trouble trouble, until trouble troubles you'. Most Chinese retailers are rendered 'mute' by language barriers and ignorance of local regulations—they fail to raise their voices in their own defence. If the matter is not considered serious, they do not waste time on going through the legal process or spend money hiring a lawyer. Their limited educational backgrounds mean that they are unable to protect themselves by resorting to legal measures. Dobler (2009) argues that, for Chinese merchants running businesses in a foreign land, on some occasions, giving a gift is more effective than spoken communication, since it overcomes barriers of language and cultural diversity. So in most cases they consider 'bribing' to be the most effective way to resolve disputes with local authorities.

The early comers, having initially benefited from an unsaturated market while learning the ropes of their trade, have a more relaxed attitude towards such challenges. Many answer the Chinese embassy's call to donate towards the financing of housing and goods for needy local people and for orphanages. After running businesses in Botswana for several years, many Chinese merchants like to show their gratitude to local people and are willing to take care of the locals, as the following comment from an early comer indicates:

> I was irritated countless times because of the troubles I have had, but now I have grown up. ... I comfort myself by remembering that I came here empty handed and now I already have enough. I give some goods to local people, which I consider as charity work. I pay a good salary to my local assistants if they work hard for me (CTco22 2012).

The difference between newcomers and early comers is clear from their manner of dealing with issues such as bribery and charitable donations. After years of experience, Chinese merchants finally attain a better understanding of local society and feel more at ease since most of them have gathered some fortune; they also recognise their responsibility to the host society and care for the reputation of the Chinese community as a whole.

5.4. Discussion

By adopting the perspective of the middleman minority, this study has analysed the major business challenges of Chinese merchants in Botswana. Chinese merchants' daily lives are characterised by an isolated lifestyle and strong ethnic cohesion. Due to the rapidly increasing numbers of Chinese merchants and China shops, local markets have become somewhat saturated. Chinese merchants (whether wholesalers or retailers) play a role as middlemen serving subordinate and ethnic groups. This tendency has become increasingly clear in the course of Botswana's development. It is similar to the social position of new Chinese immigrants who run China shops in South Africa, who are in some ways similar to the Indians in Kenya, the Lebanese in West Africa and the Asian Americans in the US (Park and Chen 2009, p. 39).

The position of the Chinese as middlemen leads to a feeling of vulnerability, of being judged negatively by the local people and of being unwelcome. The twin handicaps of the language barrier and lack of knowledge of local regulation mean that Chinese merchants are not in a position to protect their rights. Chinese businesses are limited by local regulations, and merchants experience rejection by local assistants and customers, along with hostility on part of the local authorities.

To survive in a highly competitive market and ease local hostility, Chinese merchants have adopted a number of business strategies, according to their experience and financial situation. Those Chinese who have been in Botswana longest have sufficient language ability and business experience to act more effectively than newcomers. However, when confronted by tightening regulations, neither the early comers nor the newcomers are keen to continue doing business in Gaborone. They see their best option as seeking out a niche market or transferring to a more promising locality.

According to McNamee (2012, p. 42), the lives of many Chinese merchants are dominated by acute fear, anxiety and distrust. Many despair at the quality of life in Africa, and nearly all long for the day they can return to China. So even if the Chinese are able to gain economic success, they will be unable to make longer-term commitments in Africa as long as anti-China and anti-Chinese sentiments continue, in so far as they cannot change their social position as middlemen. To some extent, their middleman position determines their business circumstances, which leads them to undertake short-term investments, along with other limitations that hinder their businesses.

This chapter argues that Chinese merchants' self-isolation and feelings of vulnerability influence their attitudes and direct their decision making, along with their responses to rejection and hostility from the host society. However, the self-isolation and feelings of vulnerability are deeply rooted in their social position as middlemen serving subordinate groups and ethnic groups (e.g. Indians, Chinese, Zimbabweans, etc.). Consequently, they feel used and disrespected by local people. Similar to many Chinese merchants in Africa, the Chinese migrants' perception of their 'vulnerable' status runs contrary to the widely publicised image of a 'powerful China in Africa', which has been a representation common in international and African media reports and political discourse since the 2000s (Lam 2015, p. 10).

In this case, when we see China shops as contact zones for Chinese merchants and the Batswana to interact and negotiate with each other, the disadvantage of language and culture barriers are inherent in Chinese merchants. However, their self-isolation and feelings of vulnerability are newborn characteristics specific to the 'contact zone' through their interaction with local people. These can be considered as the particular 'Chineseness' of the Chinese merchants in Botswana. Taylor (1994, p. 25) also argues that our identity is partly shaped by recognition or its absence, often by the misrecognition of others, and so a person or group of people can suffer real damage, real distortion, if the people or society around them mirror back to them a confining or demeaning or contemptible picture of themselves. When the shortcomings of the Chinese are exposed, the Chinese merchants are mostly devaluated rather than encouraged to conquer the shortcomings, which leads to their feeling of vulnerability. In other words, the 'alienness' and obvious language and culture ignorance place Chinese merchants in a subordinate position in Botswana society. The subordinate position of Chinese merchants limits the development of Chinese businesses, restricts the social network to be within the Chinese community, hinders their ambition as investors rather than pretty traders and shapes the image of China in Botswana presented by the China shop. Furthermore, the business strategies adopted by Chinese merchants are also closely related to their self-image and identity shaping.

However, despite these difficult circumstances, Chinese merchants remain in the country, since they still expect to obtain some profit before leaving. Moreover, Botswana's appeal is increased by its unique geographical position between three further potential markets in neighbouring countries. At the same time, regardless those that succeed make charitable donations for the benefit of local people – evidence of a social responsibility that to a certain extent repairs their relationship with local society, or those that are still struggling to make a profit by bribing local authorities – they maximise profits by seeking shortcuts; their actions are determined by their economic status and their self-image. Both donation and bribery are responses from the Chinese merchants who are shaped by local society, but at different stages. According to Park's (1950) contact perspective, both donation and bribery can be considered as a method to reach a compromise between the two groups if we locate the whole situation in a circle of competition, conflict and accommodation.

Notes

[1] This chapter is a revised version of a published paper of mine. See reference (Zi 2015b).

[2] Original statement: 挣着卖白菜的钱，操着卖白粉的心。

[3] Zambia and Zimbabwe do not issue working permits to Chinese retailers so many people living near the border come to Botswana to buy goods from China shops.

[4] Six Chinese families were planning to move from Botswana to Namibia in 2013 for business reasons.

Chapter 6

Fong Kong Goods and Related Relations in China Shops[1]

10 years ago, local people would say 'hi my Chinese friend', but now they say 'mma China,[2] fong kong!' – Chinese merchant

Nowadays Asians are being grouped with difongkong. They call them difongkong, pertaining to cheap goods, perceived as fake from Hong Kong, despised along with those who consume them. … But the fongkong thing is just playing to appearance, as most of those who are critical also buy things – and they may be of good quality – from Chinese shops. You even find that those supposedly high class South African shops are buying wholesale from the Chinese and retailing in their shops. So you find that the kind of attitudes they have towards Africans and Chinese is very different from the attitudes they have towards whites. – Nyamnjoh, Intimate Strangers 2010, p. 84

Made-in-China goods have received widespread criticism in Africa for their poor quality and negative effects on the local marketplace. They are termed *fong kong* (Barrett 2007), and in Southern Africa including Botswana, are regarded as cheap copies or fakes (Park 2013a, 2013b). In Botswana, *fong kong* goods are linked to Chinese merchants, bringing a negative image to Chinese businesses and triggering governmental restrictions on Chinese businesses. However, surprisingly, *fong kong* goods continue to be sold in the local market.

This chapter aims to address the relationship between Chinese merchants, Botswana local customers and retailers (see Figure 4), as well as local government with *fong kong* goods as a medium. This study mainly explores two questions. First, why are *fong kong* goods prevalent in Botswana society despite of the quality and legal issues, as well as the government regulations? Second, what is the social and economic influence of *fong kong* goods? In the first part of the chapter I will give a brief introduction to the arrival of *fong kong* goods, the push and pull factors on them as well as the local government's attitudes towards them. In the second part, I discuss the influence of *fong kong* goods on local industry and retailers, the local demand for various types of *fong kong* goods, and the related tactics of governmental regulation of China shops.

6.1. *Fong Kong* Goods

Recently, quality issues relating to Chinese merchandise have gathered much local attention, as China is frequently blamed for dumping its low quality products in Africa (Park 2008). These issues are frequently identified by local people and the local media (Gaotlhobogwe 27 January 2009, 9 April 2012; Anonymous 21 June 2010). Chinese goods exported to Africa were usually low in price but also low in quality – especially in the 1990s when pioneer Chinese merchants arrived in Botswana – since the goods were chosen to match the consumer profile in African countries. Chinese merchants brought so called 'leftovers' to Africa that were usually old-fashioned or sale remnants gathered from factories closed down in China. Local people call them 'fong kong'. The term originated in South Africa and Zimbabwe to describe products from Asia (especially China), which are commonly believed to be shoddy and cheap (Barrett 2007). These days 'leftovers' can seldom be found in Botswana. However, local people unaware of this background are in the habit of joking about Chinese goods, and continue to call them 'fong kong goods' (Anonymous 21 June 2010). Some argue that 'fong kong goods' is a concoction of African governments and business people who are attempting to dent the reputation of Chinese traders because they cannot compete with them (McNamee et al. 2012, p. 40). However, although the quality of Chinese merchandise in Botswana has improved greatly in recent years, many local people still keep this bias towards Chinese goods and the name 'fong kong goods' prevails to represent almost all goods that are sold in China shops. In fact, not all goods in China shops would qualify as 'fong kong goods' based on its original definition. Small items sold in China shops such as tools, accessories and cosmetics have never been a problem for customers.

6.1.1. Literature on Counterfeit Goods

'Fong kong' is a term referring to something that is very obviously fake, plastic or inauthentic. This connotes poor quality and implies the products being sold are cheap copies or fakes (Park 2013a, 2013b). It is also important to clarify that a copy is an imitation or reproduction of an original work using the original brand name; this differs from a knockoff, which is a copy of a designer product sold under a different name (Mathews and Yang 2012). In this chapter, the phrase 'counterfeit goods' refers to both copies and knock-offs. Since the 1990s, soaring numbers of Chinese merchants have migrated on a global scale in response to the influence of globalisation and changes to the immigration policy in China, and its increasing role in the production of consumer goods. Chinese shopkeepers are now found worldwide. Such entrepreneurial migration is reflected by the opening of wholesale centres in Africa to supply both Chinese and native retailers (Ma Mung 2008, pp. 648–649). In many African countries, Chinese merchants are involved in the trade of *fong kong* goods. For the majority of the Africans who cannot afford an authentic brand, *fong kong* goods sold at an acceptable price and of good quality are an ideal choice. Despite this, local media, branded companies and local government officials have denigrated these products (Gaotlhobogwe 27 January 2009, 9 April 2012; Anonymous 21 June 2010).

Thus far, research on *fong kong* goods has been scarce. To date, key research has been done by Park (2013a, 2013b), who discussed this issue in the context of African countries' de-industrialisation. Most of the related research done in African countries portrays Chinese merchants as 'dumping' cheap China-made products, and discuss their socio-economic influence on local society (Carling and Haugen 2004; Haugen and Carling 2005; Dobler 2009; Laribee 2008; Tanga 2009). Research focusing on made-in-China goods mainly discusses manufacture and distribution systems, the process of counterfeiting in China, their negative influence on copyright brands and global society, and the importance of intellectual property rights (Chow 2003; Lin 2011; Swike, Thompson and Vasquez 2008). Besides, due to the harm of counterfeit medicines

(Wertheimer and Norris 2009; Nayyar, Breman, Newton and Herrington 2012) and the relation of counterfeit trading with criminal activities (Hardouin and Weichhardt 2006), researchers suggest that dissuading consumers from purchasing counterfeits might focus on educating consumers about the adverse consequences of their purchases, i.e., criminal activity including drug trafficking, child labour and terrorism is supported through the sale of counterfeits (Lee 2008). However, this tendency sees only the negative influence of *fong kong* goods, while it neglects considerations of convenience and benefits to people living in developing countries. In most research to date, judgements have been based on the values of outsiders and the values of developed countries; therefore, the local perspective is lacking. Thus, questions arise concerning whether there is a distinct difference between the views of outsiders and those of involved merchants and local customers and why the *fong kong* goods still thrive.

6.1.2. The Nature and Supply Chain of Fong Kong Goods

As stated in Chapter 4, China shops in Botswana supply almost every daily need. The majority are stocked by Chinese merchants from wholesale markets in China and South Africa. From the Chinese wholesale market, Oriental Plaza, in Botswana merchandise is distributed to cities and towns across the country, through retail trading activities conducted by both Chinese and local retailers. The majority of local merchants and street hawkers prefer to buy clothes and shoes from Chinese wholesalers; however, a handful of them travel to South Africa and China to purchase unique goods in order to avoid direct competition with the Chinese merchants.

The distinguishable *fong kong* goods sold in the China shops are goods like knockoffs and copies of brand-named goods. Poor quality goods are particularly notorious. The counterfeits found in China shops are usually of a high quality and have a contemporary design (this is particularly true of clothes and shoes), and so they attract many local customers. When regulations concerning counterfeits are at their strictest, few knockoffs and copies are available in China shops. This results in local street hawkers travelling to neighbouring South Africa to buy knockoff sports shoes from Indian and Pakistan traders instead of sourcing from China shops. Usually the same knockoff product is sold by street hawkers at a price two or three times higher than that offered by Chinese retailers. Even though many local customers think the sneakers sold in China shops are fake and those sold on the street are authentic, in both cases the shoes are likely to be fakes. Nowadays, very poor quality textiles (expected to last only a few weeks) are gradually disappearing from the wares in China shops, particularly in the big cities, because the locals have higher salaries and can choose to buy better products. As Mathews and Vega (2012, p. 12) state, poor quality Chinese goods are imported to Africa largely because the Chinese merchants in Africa focus on price as the primary determinant when purchasing. People tend to judge quality of made-in-China goods as a whole, while in fact China produces goods of different qualities and creates a space for every customer according to their buying power.

Since the majority of *fong kong* goods are manufactured in China, the counterfeit manufacturing environment there must be understood when considering the supply chain of *fong kong* goods. Lin (2011) maintains that the country's counterfeiting culture was fuelled by waves of Post-Fordism[3] and other trends in the global economy, such as consumerism, the culture of Chinese migrant workers and the entrepreneurial spirit that arose in countless small apartments in various cities around China. However, much of the counterfeiting can be attributed to China's emergence as a world economic power. To date, counterfeit manufacturing in China has been the target of considerable criticism and pressure globally, especially from developed countries (Swike et al. 2008; Chow 2003). However, counterfeit manufacturing has survived and even thrived in China over the years for a number of reasons. 'Local protectionism' is considered one of its root causes; some government officials in China see counterfeiting as an opportunity to innovate, or view it as a product of democracy and popular culture and thus support it (Lin 2011, p. 23). Furthermore, campaigns against countfeiting usually deliver short-term results with raids carried out against individual counterfeiters and distributors to seize counterfeit products, ignoring the manufacturers (Chow 2003).

Thus, Chinese merchants initiated the business of *fong kong* goods in Botswana, and they have become partners with Botswana local traders in the supply chain of *fong kong* goods over the years. In the current climate, *fong kong* goods will neither disappear from the manufacturing industry in China nor from the Botswana market. However, this trend should not be seen merely as a cause of high supply of Chinese goods, but also a result of demand exerted by African consumers.

6.1.3. Push and Pull Perspective

Since the last decade, Chinese merchants have migrated on a global scale in conjunction with China's rising production of consumer goods (Kuang 2008, pp. 648–649). Thus the soaring numbers of Chinese merchants pave the way for Chinese merchandise when the force of merchandise fosters strong pushing power domestically and have to seek international market.

However, on the other hand, local demand is a force that pulls *fong kong* goods, even problematic ones, into Botswana market. Nowadays, the problematic *fong kong* goods that stir up major issues are poor quality clothes, fake brand clothes and shoes, as well as pirated DVDs and CDs. They fulfil different demands but also cause complaints. According to Chinese merchants, low-income people, including local people, Zimbabweans and Zambians, rely on cheap Chinese goods despite their limited quality. The medium income population and college students, mostly Tswana people, are the major consumers of the fake brands. Pirated DVDs seem to obtain favour across all income levels and ethnic groups; even people originally from Europe have been observed buying pirated DVDs. The Botswana government seizes the opportunity of removing counterfeits to control the spread of China shops. On government initiatives like 'Clean Sweep Counterfeits', even the Chinese government has offered some help (Gaotlhobogwe 4 June 2012; Motlogelwa 2 May 2007).

According to local news, it is evident that the sale of counterfeit merchandise has been a long-term problem in Botswana, which has yet not been extirpated despite the efforts of the government. The phenomenon of counterfeiting has caused Chinese merchants to be subjected to punitive measures and has prompted stricter regulation of their goods and China shops. Furthermore, as a result of this situation, all China shops now tend to be considered as hubs of counterfeiting, and all goods made in China are discredited as *fong kong* goods. Despite this, in recent years Chinese goods have increased in both number and variety and even attracted customers from neighbouring countries (Botswana Press Agency 2014; Chube 13 January 2014).

Supply chain management is often defined as fitting into 'push' or 'pull' categories (Harrison et al. 2003). It is not difficult to discover that there are two powers taking control of the supply chain of *fong kong* goods: the pushing power from China, the country of origin and the pulling power of Botswana, the country of destination. To date, research has focused on the stereotyped pushing power of *fong kong* goods, such as hindering development of local industry, bringing competition to local retailers and disturbing the local market (Cissé 2013; Makungu 2013; Mohan and Tan-Mullins 2009), etc. What is missing from this research is an analysis of the pulling power, an exploration of who is taking stock of the balance of the two powers as well as how the power is balanced. This chapter aims to contribute by applying the existing theory on push and pull factors and using a field work approach to explore the role of local governmental regulation on import control. The research question this chapter aims to address is that of why *fong kong* goods prevail despite of the quality and legal issues, as well as the governmental regulation they have encountered.

6.2. *Fong Kong* Goods' Influence on Local Industry

China joined the World Trade Organization (WTO) in 2001 and consequently its market grew globally. Botswana welcomed China as a crucial investor, expecting that its financial aid and capital investment would benefit Botswana's development (Gabotlale 8 May 2006); on the other hand, it also considered China's growth and momentum as potential threats, especially with regard to the increasing volume of Chinese textile imports. As Gabotlale (27 May 2005) states:

Botswana companies in the textile industry may be affected by the surge in Chinese textile imports, which have skyrocketed since the abolition of export quotas at the beginning of the year. It has long been feared that the scrapping of export quotas would expose Third World countries in particular to a battering from Chinese textile exports.

Already, the US and the EU are complaining that Chinese imports are distorting their markets and have started acting but Third World countries do not have the capacity to do the same ...

Deputy Permanent Secretary in the Ministry of Trade Gaylard Kombani said Botswana might not be able to take safeguard measures against the likes of the US who are bigger markets. He said if Botswana were to retaliate they would have to be careful because China may take actions that could put them at a great disadvantage.

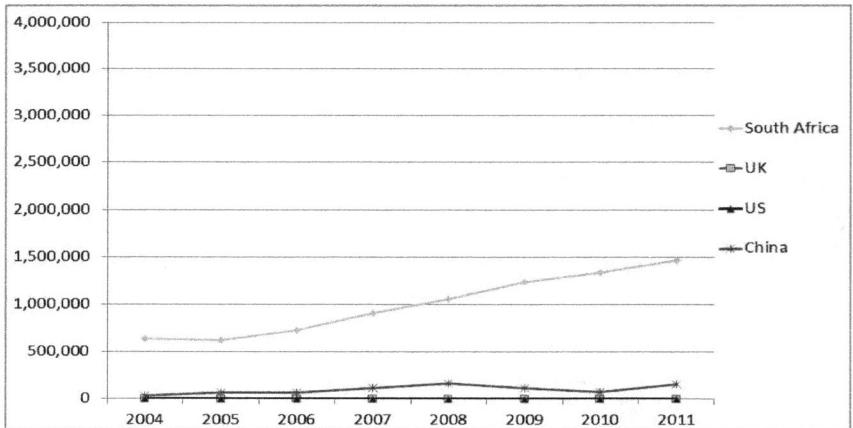

Figure 13. Principal Imports of Textiles and Footwear by Partner (Pula '000)

Source: Central Statistics Office (CSO) of Botswana, see Zi (2014, p. 264)

In reference to the concerns expressed by Botswana and its partners, the related statistics showed no convincing evidence to prove a significant relationship between the import of Chinese

126

goods and any changes to Botswana's trade figures. According to the statistics on Principal Imports of Textiles and Footwear, it is clear that Botswana's textile imports came mainly from South Africa, and that even after Chinese goods became available, Botswana's imports from South Africa increased significantly.[4] Conversely, imports from the UK and US remained at a comparatively low level. Imports from China, although showing growth over the years, have not surpassed one fifth of the quantities imported from South Africa (Figure 13). Furthermore, the volume of textiles exported to South Africa has grown through the years. By contrast, the export of textiles to both the UK and the US reached a peak in 2007 and declined thereafter, and has remained at a low level since 2009 (Figure 14). Meanwhile exports to China have remained at a low level since the beginning (Figure 14). In fact, as can be seen from the statistics on Principal Import Items from China, the import of machinery and electrical equipment has been escalating since 2007 and has become the most important item in the China–Botswana trade relationship (Figure 15).

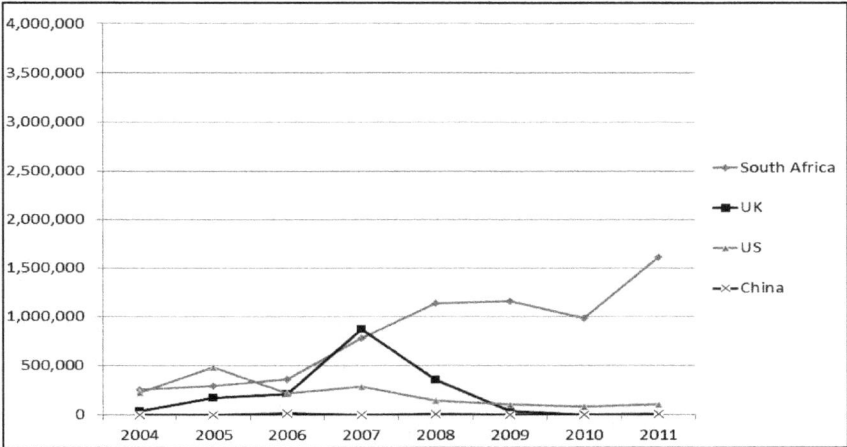

Figure 14. Principal Exports of Textiles and Footwear by Partner (Pula '000)

Source: CSO of Botswana, see Zi (2014, p. 265)

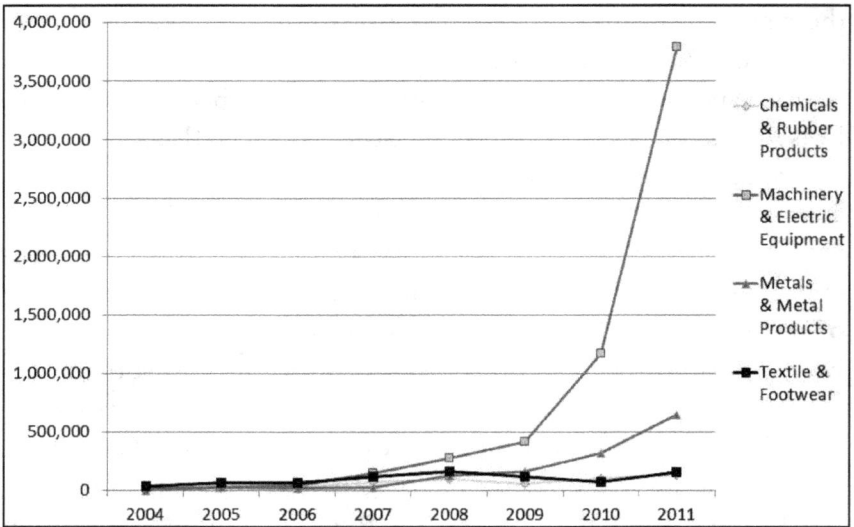

Figure 15. Principal Import Items from China (Pula '000)
Source: CSO of Botswana, see Zi (2014, p. 265)

According to Mogapi (2006, p. 26) the fastest growing export commodities to SADC[5] are fabrics and textiles. The Botswana government has invested substantially in the development of an export-oriented textile hub, which explains the continually increasing volume of exports to South Africa. The tiny boom in textile exports to the US, however, is mainly due to AGOA,[6] which was in place from 2000 to 2008, and provided duty-free access for over 6,500 products from sub-Saharan Africa to enter the American market (Mogape 2005, p. 21). After the arrival of Chinese goods in Africa, some small local mills did manage to supply the local market and survive the competition, benefiting from their large volume and low value. However, Botswana's population is too small to host significant textile mills (Tang 2014). If it were not for agreements such as AGOA and the SADC Trade Protocol, it would be difficult for Botswana to export textiles. The import and export statistics show no solid evidence that Chinese textiles directly influence the import or export of Botswana textiles; however, the reliance of the country on Chinese machinery and electrical equipment has evidently grown over the years. Due to Botswana's initial weak industry, the role played by Chinese imports can be seen as helping to meet the needs of local people, rather than as hindering the development of local industry.

6.3. *Fong Kong* Goods' Influence on Local Retailers

Aside from the worries over the extent to which *fong kong* goods harm the local textile industry, their influence on local markets, especially with regard to competition with local retailers is also a source of tension. Surprisingly, the results show that along with the arrival of *fong kong* goods, competition among Chinese merchants has grown fiercer (Zi 2014, 2015a), while local merchants and street vendors have benefited from rich resources instead of being squeezed out of business. To explain this, let us start by looking in detail at how *fong kong* goods are supplied to retailers and consumers and who the competitors of China shops exactly are in Botswana.

As stated above, the problematic *fong kong* goods flooding to Botswana mainly consist of counterfeit and low-price goods. Counterfeit goods find their way out of China and into foreign cities via sea, air and the internet (Lin 2011). Every year large amounts of counterfeit goods are confiscated by airport authorities. To avoid investigation, counterfeiting operations are increasingly conducted over the internet, with use being made of online auction sites or spam mails, which are designed to complicate the detection of trademark violations and the enforcement of intellectual property rights. That is how fake brand T-shirts, sneakers and pirated DVDs and CDs come to Botswana. On the other hand, in order to obtain lower priced clothing some Chinese entrepreneurs, in days of old would go to closing factories and seek out sale goods. Currently they order clothing from Chinese factories which are similar looking to fashion clothing, however, made with inferior material and sewing skills. The China shops in Botswana target the low-income population, thus ensuring that only a relatively few South African chain shops can be their direct competitors, since locally-owned shops tend to target customers with stronger purchasing power (Table 3). According to my observation of several low-income Botswana families, they only visit local shops before Christmas or after receiving a bonus, while most of the time comparing prices between China shops to hunt for the most economical choices of the goods they desire. Hence, competition between Chinese merchants themselves and that with large South African chains is far fiercer than their competition with local retailers.

Table 3. Prices of Textiles and Footwear in Retail Shops in Gaborone (Pula)

Item/Type	China shop	South African chain shop	Local shop
General feature	ordinary, low price	ordinary, stand price, ex. Jet & PEP[7]	gorgeous, fashionable
Men's T-shirt	30–100	70–120	120–205
Men's socks	5–15	10–30	20–30
Men's Jeans	40–100	110–150	100–300
Ladies' pumps	20–60	60–120	120–300
Sunglasses	20–35	40–60	100–500

Source: based on researcher's field work in 2013 and estimation, see Zi (2014, p. 267)

As mentioned earlier, Chinese merchants originally operated a shuttle trade which involved selling goods brought from China in a market or on the street and then returning to China for the next consignment. This arrangement rapidly developed into a network of larger or smaller 'Chinese markets' (Nyíri 2011, p. 146). Since 'Chinese markets' were founded in Botswana, many traders from Botswana and even neighbouring countries have taken to buying imported Chinese merchandise from China shops and Oriental Plaza outlets and then distributing them in rural towns and neighbouring countries.[8] According to a Chinese retailer, 'Local shops sell the same Chinese goods as ours. However, local people trust their own people, considering their goods are not *fong kong* goods but in a good quality (Interview September 2013)'. A street vendor reveals, 'I usually get these shoes (fake brand shoes, such as Adidas, Puma, etc.) from China shops, but they cannot sell them now. So I go to South Africa every month to restock (Interview September 2013)'. Therefore, many *fong kong* goods are distributed by local merchants who effectively behave as parasites to Chinese merchants. And even when Chinese merchants are forbidden to sell counterfeits, they still continue the business as one the Chinese initiated and sustained.

Furthermore, in recent years many African traders have copied the example of earlier Chinese merchants by going to China as 'suitcase traders'. They represent 'globalisation from below,' which can be defined as the informal transnational flow of people and goods involving relatively small amounts of capital (Mathews 2011). Interviews carried out by this researcher have revealed that there are a number of Botswana local traders who travel to China several times every year to restock their shops with Chinese goods. Moreover, the latest tightening of regulations affecting Chinese merchants (Gaotlhobogwe 27 January 2009) and government financial support for local entrepreneurs has made it easier for locals to start in business by themselves. The Citizen Entrepreneurial Development Agency[9] provides a holistic approach to the development and promotion of viable and sustainable citizen-owned enterprises, which is done through financial assistance in the form of loans at subsidised interest rates and business training services to enhance the sustainability of these enterprises. This situation has led to a widespread belief amongst Chinese merchants that the government is trying to ban retail China shops altogether. As one interviewee puts it, 'Local government tells local merchants that once Chinese are driven out, everything belongs to them'. One Chinese pioneer merchant reveals:

> According to local law, foreigners are forbidden to operate retail businesses selling clothes and shoes. However, the local government did not ban China shops when the Chinese were selling clothes and shoes in their retail shops due to the market need at that time and the job opportunities that came along with China shops. Once local people obtain the ability and capital to run retail shops by themselves, retail China shops will be swept out without doubt (Interview November 2013).

This to some extent explains why the local government has aimed the regulation at retail China shops in recent years under the pretext of sweeping counterfeits from the shelves. In practice, however, local merchants are encouraged to start businesses by themselves, whilst enjoying the benefits and convenience brought by the Chinese.

6.4. Local Demand for *Fong Kong* Goods

6.4.1. Low-quality Cheap Goods

In the 1990s, on the arrival of pioneering Chinese merchants in Botswana, Chinese exports to Africa were typically low in price and low in quality, in order to match the local buying power. As a pioneering Chinese merchant said:

> Most local people went barefoot in those days. A pair of shoes could cost 300 Pula (1 Pula = 0.5 US dollars in those days) in white people's and Indian's shops, and local people's salary was around 200 Pula per month. The quality of Chinese goods was lower, because most were leftovers from factories, but at least local people could buy a pair of shoes for 10 or 20 Pula, even if they only lasted one month. Poor people would never spend 300 Pula on a pair of shoes, no matter how good the quality (CEco158 2014).

Therefore, although the quality of the textiles was poor, they effectively clothed local people, especially the needy on limited incomes. However, with respect to low-quality electronics the scenario is more complicated. During one interview, a Chinese merchant described replacing a TV set for a local customer who had bought it the previous day:

> The TV worked well when we tested it here yesterday, but today it doesn't work. ... Most of the TV sets sold in China shops are second-hand inside, with new cases outside. Otherwise, how could it be so cheap! It is sold at 600 Pula (62 US dollars). Nobody uses this kind of TV set in China any more. I assume some small factory managed to gather the old equipment together to generate business (CTco23 2014).

132

Most Chinese merchants do not want to deal with electronics because the profit is low and no warrantee of quality is offered by the factories in China. However, in response to the need in Botswana, the merchants do sell them despite the low profit and high risk. 'Local people cannot afford a TV set that costs several thousand', commented a Chinese respondent.

Chinese merchants argue that they sell low-quality goods to match the buying power of the majority. However, this preference is the reason for the poor reputation of made-in-China goods in Africa (Mathews and Vega 2012, p. 12). 'Since Botswana is greatly influenced by Western media, local people believe that goods from western are good quality but from China are bad', said a professor at University of Botswana. In response to recent changes in China shops, opinions concerning quality and price in China shops have split:

> Now when local customers come to buy a cell phone or a TV, they want to open the back of the case to check them! What do they want to see? Even if we sold high quality goods at our shops local people would not trust us. However, if the same goods are sold in a white person's shop, they would pay a lot of money to buy them and believe they are high quality (Chinese merchant, CTco34 2013).

> We are so thankful for the China shops. Because of them we have a TV to watch, and clothes to wear. Although some people say that Chinese clothes are smelly, not all of them are bad quality. ... I think they are kind people and they sell goods of good quality as well (Local customer, Pb178, 2012).

> The goods here are almost the same quality as in the China shops, but they are cheaper at the China shops. However, China shops do not display goods properly. Some goods in China shops are of good quality if you know how to choose (Manager of large South African chains, FTbm102, 2014).

To keep pace with the development of Botswana's society, the majority of goods have improved in quality in tandem with price rises in China shops. However, the image of China shops remains the same: cheap, low quality and disorganised. Besides, the failure of several Chinese construction projects also contributed to damaging the reputation of the whole Chinese community. This annoys some Chinese merchants and their anger has a racial component: 'They call our goods *fong kong* because we are Chinese. The goods sold in South African chain shops are also made in China! The Chinese construction company did implicate us in blaming.' The infamy of China shops not only limits their business, but also opens up a loophole for local consumers, who claim replacement goods stating that the goods were of poor quality, even if they were at fault:

> One customer brought a satellite dish but did not know how to set it up. Then he brought the dish back to us and swore: 'Chinese bad quality.' Then one of our local assistants set it up for him. I was angry and did not want to sell to him, but he insisted that he wanted it. Where else could he find a dish at such a low price? (CTco22 2014)

Thus, while low-quality goods have brought business to Chinese merchants, they have also contributed to improving the quality of life of low-income people in local societies. However, the increased presence of Chinese construction workers and shop owners after 2000 created tensions in community relations, which attracted negative media coverage (Youngman 2013, p. 6). Local people are aware of the limited quality of the low-quality goods, however, some rely on them due to their limited buying power.

6.4.2. Counterfeit Goods

Along with the arrival of China-made goods, competition among Chinese merchants grew fiercer as China shops boomed. Meanwhile, local merchants and street vendors also benefited from the rich resources brought by Chinese merchants as we stated above. To survive in the competitive business environment, some Chinese merchants brought counterfeit goods to attract local customers. The common counterfeit sold in China shops are branded shoes, branded toys for children and branded T-shirts. Usually the counterfeits are of a better quality than usual goods and are sold at a comparative price and thus have become popular since their arrival. Some Chinese merchants reveal:

> These days, local authorities check China shops very often, so we do not dare to sell counterfeits. The penalty for selling counterfeits is extraordinarily high once caught. But many local people come to look for branded shoes. The shoes really look better with a brand mark.

Regardless of tightened regulations, counterfeit goods continue to play a crucial role in Botswana's society. In recent years, given the increasing influence of television, considerable numbers of local people developed a taste for elite culture, aspiring towards a higher social status. In response to the fashion influences of neighbouring South Africa, branded textiles are available in almost every shopping mall, stimulating consumers' desire to buy. However, many local people are unable to discriminate between counterfeit and genuine merchandise; the majority identify the quality of goods by looking at their prices. In fact, many locals do not care whether they are wearing a genuine brand or a fake one, as long as the quality is fine and the brand confers the social status they desire. Counterfeit goods are mass-produced to supply lower class consumers; the knowledge of luxury goods increases the referential value of both the counterfeit goods and the brand names (Lin 2011). Counterfeits, despite the criticism, are products that answer lower-income and medium-income customers' needs and desires.

6.4.3. Novelty Goods

The variety of *fong kong* goods has increased quietly over time. Local government shows limited interest beyond counterfeit textiles and pirated DVDs; most likely because they are comparably easy to distinguish from genuine items. In response to the growing needs of local society, Chinese merchants have introduced novelty goods to the market, challenging the existing image of *fong kong* goods, since most of these novelty goods are of good quality. They are called *fong kong* good only because they are sold in China shops.

Chinese merchants themselves also call China shops 'baihuo dian' (shops with assorted goods) in Botswana and other African countries (Haugen and Carling 2005). Some China shops sell as many as 1,000 product lines. When there is a requirement for a special item, local people ask the Chinese merchants for help. In some suit shops, customers can even order bespoke suits from China through the Chinese merchants. The demand for goods in Botswana has risen, and therefore the huge and varied market in China has become increasingly attractive to locals. In addition, Chinese merchants' willingness to help their local customers also contributes to the fascination of China shops.

Regardless of the various restrictions imposed on *fong kong* goods, novelty *fong kong* goods have survived and gathered popularity among local customers. In 2009, when the government tried to drive out China shops, some local people raised their voices in protest, arguing that China shops were a benefit to ordinary people:

> China shops cater for the masses. ... Batswana women are able to watch their favourite South African soap opera, 'Generations', thanks to the Chinese who provide the Philibao decoders, which 'unblock' SABC (South African Broadcasting Corporation) channels (Anonymous 21 June 2010).

Fong kong goods, therefore, counter the rights of the SABC, as people are supposed to pay several hundred Pula every month for the service. However, the local government did not take this threat as seriously as fake branded shoes. Some Chinese merchants were warned regarding the practice by the government, however, it was too difficult for them to refuse their customers who were optimistic.

Besides the needs of locals, *fong kong* goods stimulated creativity and cultural awareness of Chinese merchants. In 2012, Chinese pioneers made baseball caps with the Botswana flag printed on them and football T-shirts for the Botswana team, expecting these products would be popular during the World Cup, which was to be held in neighbouring South Africa. As anticipated, the goods attracted many local people and even foreigners visiting Botswana. However, when the goods were circulated in the country, they were instantly forbidden by the local government, which claimed that the Chinese merchants had used the logo of Botswana without its permission. The goods were quickly removed from the China shops, but the local street hawkers who had sourced them from the Chinese wholesale market were still selling them. Although the Chinese did not benefit, the cultural awareness and creativity of the Chinese had a huge impact on local society.

In order to make clothes that fit local fashion tastes, the Chinese not only import copies and knockoffs of brands but also seek out ideas from local fashion shops. According to an owner of a fashion shop, some Chinese merchants observed the clothes and styles in her shop:

> We travel to Asian countries every year to find uniquely designed clothes that may be popular in Botswana. … The Chinese come to spy on our clothes. One Chinese lady was caught taking a picture of our clothes in the fitting room. … We were told by customers that in China shops there were dresses with the same design as ours but sold at a much lower price with greatly inferior material (BTbo69 2013).

A Chinese pioneer who sells formal suits and shoes states:

> I observe what designs local people prefer, and order similar designs from factories in China. My goods are of the same standard as those sold in white people's shops (representing good quality) regarding design and quality but at a cheaper price. If they sell the same goods as me, they are like an advertisement for me. Since the materials of mine are even better than theirs, I manage to keep regular customers (CTco104 2014).

That local merchandise is being copied by Chinese merchants does not necessarily mean that China shops are in direct competition with local shops. The richest customers will visit branded shops to buy authentic goods, while medium earners and the poor will buy the products sold in China shops. Sometimes, copied goods can increase the popularity of fashion goods (Lin 2011). On the other hand, Chinese merchants consider copying local fashions important to prove that they have been integrated into the local Botswana marketplace. In addition, by moving from a *fong kong* goods distribution role to creators of goods, they may even have the opportunity to take a leading role in local business.

6.5. Local Government's Practical Control of *Fong Kong* Goods

On a practical level 'fong kong goods' is an expression often used by the media to attract local attention and referred to by the local government as a public condemnation to threaten China shops. As McNamee et al. (2012) argues, it is a concoction of African governments and business people who are attempting to dent the reputation of Chinese traders. *Fong kong* goods, although they have received much criticism, are products that answer to lower-income customers' needs and desires. Therefore, the government tries to balance their activities by being strict on some of the *fong kong* goods on the one hand but also turning a blind eye to the majority of them. As mentioned before, according to the law, although foreigners are forbidden to operate retail clothes businesses, the local government did not ban China shops in the beginning, but only regulated them when the necessity arose, such as negotiating more job opportunities or higher salaries for locals, encouraging industrial investment, etc. This tendency has become more obvious since 2008 when Botswana was influenced by the global economic crisis. Many Chinese merchants emphasise: 'Poor people here need our goods, government here needs us' and 'my business provides many job opportunities to the locals'. So far, the government's 'Clean Sweep' activities have concentrated on counterfeits. Furthermore, their actions are usually taken as a result of pressure from 'outsiders', such as the US and South Africa, as the following news item shows:

> The Chinese Embassy in Gaborone has offered to help Botswana to curb software piracy ... The US had threatened to go to court over rampant Chinese piracy. China has the biggest market for US movie companies and IT corporations such as Microsoft. Reports in

Botswana indicate that among the biggest traders of counterfeit movies and software are people of Asian origin, especially Chinese (Motlogelwa 2 May 2007).

In September 2013, a Chinese shop owner who was interviewed stated: 'These days, people from South Africa clothes factory (international brand representatives) are accompanying the Batswana officers to check China shops. Once counterfeit branded clothes are found, people will be fined and the goods will be confiscated.' Due to the fact that most of the counterfeit clothes and DVDs are copies of US and South African brands, it is not surprising that these two governments would devote considerable energy and attention to the problem. Although the Botswana government's attitude towards counterfeit merchandise is clear, it seems that its activity is closely regulated by pressures from outside.

Faced with strict regulations and frequent checks carried out by the government, many strategies are adopted by Chinese merchants to avoid legal penalties. Firstly, the Chinese community tends to close ranks when the government conducts 'Clean Sweep' operations. When officials come to check retail shops in one shopping mall, the information will be spread to other malls through family and other contacts, which tends to invalidate the inspection. Also it has been observed that some Chinese merchants do not put counterfeits in their shop windows. Furthermore, some merchants only show photos of pirated DVDs in albums before the customers decide what they want. Simply, various ways have been adopted to keep the counterfeits from the eyes of local officials. Generally speaking, however, the Botswana government tends to turn a blind eye to attempts to find loopholes in order to avoid social turbulence; provided that Chinese merchants pay their taxes and help solve local unemployment.

6.6. Discussion

'Globalization and lower trade barriers' (Chaudhry and Zimmerman 2009) can be counted as the most influential factors in triggering the phenomenon of *fong kong* goods in Botswana. Due to the frequent media interest in the issue of *fong kong* goods in Botswana, and related governmental regulation, it is easy to concentrate our attention on the push factors from China, and to ignore the pull factors in Botswana society. It has been a puzzle to the observer that, despite tightening of regulations and 'Clean Sweep' activities in Botswana, *fong kong* goods have continued over the years to hold their share of the market. Field research has shown that *fong kong* goods do not bring a negative influence to bear on the local textile industry or local retailers, as had been assumed. Surprisingly enough, their contribution is not limited to feeding the demands of local customers of different income levels, but also creates benefits for local merchants and street vendors. Although they are widely criticised and have damaged China's reputation, *fong kong* goods are still useful to Botswana society. Due to their ambiguous function, the government faces a dilemma when dealing with the challenge of striking a balance between, on the one hand, the complaints of the public and pressures from outsiders, and on the other hand, the advantages gained by local vendors and low-income consumers. Ultimately the government employs delaying tactics, putting China shops under stricter regulatory control when necessity calls whilst training its own entrepreneurs to compete more effectively in the future with Chinese businesses. This tactic helps the government to control the number and scale of Chinese businesses, whilst balancing the pushing and pulling powers macroscopically.

Fong kong goods, especially counterfeits, raise legal and moral issues. However, the boundary between legal and illegal can be vague, depending on one's perspective. Mathews and Vega (2012, p. 9) argue that it is fair to say that legality is nothing more than something designated as such by the agents of globalisation from above (i.e. customs and copyright offices). Making copies of brands is a morally ambiguous activity, particularly when both buyer and seller are aware that an item is a fake. In Botswana, the streams of 'globalisation from above' and 'globalisation from below' conflict at both the social and individual level. Local society propounds, and the media are broadcasting, a forecast of 'high technology' and a 'gorgeous life style'. On the other hand, issues such as poverty eradication, currency devaluation and growing youth unemployment need to be addressed domestically. At the individual level, on a monthly income that can barely feed a family, some people expect to enjoy meals at the Hilton and drive Mercedes Benz cars or Land Rovers. These aspirations, to some extent, increase people's appetites, and create a market, for *fong kong* goods. Therefore, as Mathews and Vega (2012, pp. 9–10) emphasise, morality needs to be debated beyond the perspective of globalisation from above alone. *Fong kong* goods can be beneficial, in that they provide the poor of the world with a taste of the goods bought by the rich, and enable hundreds of millions of people across the globe to make a living.

The Botswana government politically uses Chinese merchants to satisfy the local demands for goods and job opportunities; and regulate Chinese business step by step, according to the time and timing. One thing is certain, however, no matter how the situation develops, local people on low incomes are the greatest beneficiaries, in that their quality of lifestyle has been significantly improved since the arrival of *fong kong* goods in Botswana. The definition of *fong kong* in Botswana has been renewed over the years, for it has departed from the quality of goods to the image that it presents. Now *fong kong* goods equal any goods sold by Chinese merchants regardless of their quality or source. However, *fong kong* goods, despite their bad reputation, will not disappear from Botswana as long as they continue to meet local needs even if Chinese merchants are eventually replaced by local traders. These *fong kong* goods will still be sold by Batswana merchants and vendors but perhaps they will no longer be named 'fong kong' at that time.

Fong kong goods can be seen as a product of the 'contact zone' in Botswana. On the one hand, they are the goods chosen by Chinese merchants after researching the local preferences and affordability; on the other hand, the name 'fong kong' is the valuation and expression given by local people. Labelling Chinese merchandise as 'fong kong goods' generalises an image of 'made-in-China' goods to be fraudulent and of poor in quality, despite the fact that there are varieties in the quality of Chinese goods sold in Botswana. It does not matter that the Chinese merchandise is called *fong kong* or other names as it does not make much difference to the local low-income customers who rely on low-cost Chinese merchandise daily. However, its larger impact may be in undermining image of China, and business development of Chinese corporations. Nowadays, even selling the same product, the price in China shop cannot surpass that in local shops or South African big chains. 'How can the goods in China shop be so expensive?' is a regular complaint among local people. A tacit understanding is that despite the actual quality of goods, as far as the goods are sold in China shops, they are probably in bad quality and should be the cheapest in the market. Many Batswana like *fong kong* goods despite their negative attitude towards China shops; they are even addicted to the convenience brought by China shops while maintaining their discrimination. Therefore, even though the Chinese goods that are labelled in a negative way, they are not necessarily rejected. This label by local people may be a tactic to limit the price rise of the popular Chinese goods. It is common to find customers fake their expressions and evaluation to manipulate the seller to give a discount. However, on the other hand, the local discrimination towards China shops is not without reason. As I will discuss in Chapter 8, the image of China shops is also shaped by other factors that go beyond the China shop business.

Notes

[1] This chapter is a revised version of two published papers of mine. See reference Zi (2014) and Zi (2015a).

[2] 'Mma China' in Setswana means 'Chinese people'.

[3] The idea that modern industrial production has moved away from mass production in huge factories, as pioneered by Henry Ford, towards specialised markets based on small flexible manufacturing units.

[4] It includes the goods that are produced in the Chinese textiles and footwear factories in South Africa.

[5] The Southern African Development Community has 14 members with an estimated population of approximately 208-million people (2001 estimate). One of SADC's principal aims is to co-ordinate and harmonise

the socio-economic policies and plans of its member states to ensure sustainable economic development and growth in the southern African region.

[6] The African Growth and Opportunity Act: the main purpose is to improve trade and economic co-operation between the US and eligible sub-Saharan African (SSA) countries.

[7] Jet and PEP are large South African retail chains. Their chain shops can be found in almost every shopping mall in the big cities of Botswana http://www.jetonline.co.za/ and http://www.pepstores.com/.

[8] Zambian and Zimbabwe traders come to Botswana to ship Chinese goods back to their country, due to the fact that in their countries' goods in retail China shops are more expensive (interview November 2011) and Chinese merchants are not allowed to operate retail shops.

[9] Website of Government of Botswana. Citizen Entrepreneurial Development Agency (CEDA). Retrieved 9 August 2012, from http://www.gov.bw/en/Business/Sub-audiences/Small--Medium-Businesses/Support-for-Existing-Small--Medium/

Chapter 7

Employer–Employee Relations in China Shops

My assistants are lazy and stupid, only become clever when they are stealing. –
Chinese merchant
My boss is so moody. We have to walk on shells when the business is not good. –
Botswana assistant
Chinese shall use a proper process to fire their local labour. – Botswana policeman

In this chapter I present information on the employer–employee relationships between the Chinese Merchants and Batswana employees that was obtained by seeking the opinions of both parties. After investigating recruitment processes, daily employer–employee conflicts, treatments and work attitudes were analysed taking into account the social status of the Chinese merchants and Batswana employees. I found that from the perspective of organisational psychology there is little respect and a low level of interpersonal trust between Chinese merchants and local employees, mainly due to local employees' poor work ethics. On the other hand, Chinese merchants' frugality and exploitative image results in a failure to fulfil the personal needs of local employees, which stirs up complaints and creates a bad reputation.

7.1. Employer–Employee Relations between Chinese and Africans

Since the 1990s, Chinese trading companies have mushroomed in Africa. The number of Chinese merchants in urban African settings has increased exponentially, and the embeddedness of their activities within the local socio-economic fabric greatly influences the local society. The potentially conflictive employer–employee relations in Chinese trading companies may have a much greater impact on the local setting than labour conflicts in large-scale projects operating with few links to the local society (Giese and

145

Thiel 2014, p. 1101). Conflicts arising between local employees and Chinese employers challenge the economic and social integration of Chinese merchants and their businesses (ibid.). So far, most of the research concerning labour conflicts between Chinese employers and local employees has focused on large enterprises within the construction or mineral extraction industries (Brooks 2010; Chen et al. 2009; Cottle 2014; Eifert et al. 2008; Huang and Ren 2013; Lee 2009; Sautman and Yan 2014). Labour relations within small-scale trade and services businesses have been largely neglected. The little research on small-scale trade is limited to Ghana and Uganda (Codrin 2014; Giese 2013; Giese and Thiel 2012, 2014).

From existing research emotional issues, cultural understanding, work performance expectation, as well as work ethics have been highlighted as key issues in these labour conflicts. Giese (2013) analysed labour conflicts in Chinese trade businesses in Ghana. He argues that mutual unawareness of culturally grounded reciprocity expectations lead to dissatisfaction on both sides. The Chinese try to educate the employee through their own example of diligence and the acceptance of hardships in the expectation of future profits, in terms of material security beyond wages as the responsibility of the family. Furthermore, Chinese traders operate from a position of weakness and perceived vulnerability, rather than basing their employment practices on cold-blooded calculations of how best to exploit cheap African labour. Related research done by Giese and Thiel (2012), analyses Chinese–Ghanaian employment relations from the perspectives of psychological contract, cross-cultural equity expectations and foreignness. It emphasises that central to the frictions of mutual equity expectations is the feeling of existential vulnerability that is shared by both Chinese migrant employers taking high financial risks in an unfamiliar and potentially hostile environment and their local employees recruited almost exclusively from economically marginalised groups. Giesea and Thiel (2014) then discussed how Ghanaian employees perceive their psychological contract as a violated attempt to restore equity by means of voice, silence, retreat or destruction. This often fails due to lack of mutual cultural understanding between employers and employees. They concluded that most employment relations, though defective, are perpetuated.

On the other hand, by exploring the locally embedded cultural, social and economic notion of work and labour, in Uganda, Codrin (2014) revealed how relations between Chinese employers and Ugandan employees are shaped by the former's knowledge and acceptance of this practice. The paper explored and deconstructed the context in which Chinese store owners and their local employees interact and sometimes even find common ground, despite markedly different economic, social, cultural, racial and linguistic backgrounds. What all those stories have in common is that the Ugandan employees either acted in ways their Chinese bosses judged to be suspicious or failed to do what they were asked. Over the years, all employees learned the different styles and idiosyncrasies of their bosses and began to adjust their behaviour accordingly (ibid., pp. 153–154). Cordrin further argued that locally grounded economic-cultural categories are not the only areas causing tensions in Sino-African work interactions. The Chinese employers in the study seem to share, along with previous colonial officials and other foreigners in the country, a lack of interest in how local systems of meaning unfold and are expressed on a daily basis in Uganda. They do not speak the indigenous language, they have a very limited understanding of local manners and 'proper' social interactions, and they engage in unacceptable practices, such as verbal and physical abuse (ibid., p. 155).

Lee (2009, pp. 7–9) who conducted research on mining in Zambian and the Tanzania–China Friendship Mills in Dar es Salaam argues that more profound than the communication barrier is the gap between what managers called 'work ethics', but assailed by workers as 'exploitation'. Work ethics, understood to be a devotion to work, a willingness to make sacrifices without concomitant demands for rights, rewards or privileges, is invoked by these managers to explain China's recent economic development and to justify their demands on workers. The Chinese use the phrase 'eating bitterness' to convey their willingness to endure hardship, postpone gratification, submit to company discipline, save and reinvest for personal and corporate development (Lee 2014, p.

54). According to Chinese managers, however, African workers do not see that the Chinese make sacrifices for progress. The Zambian workers think because this is a Chinese owned factory, that they have come to assist the Chinese so it is natural that the Chinese should feed and pay them every day. The Zambian workers do not have any ambition or motivation to improve themselves or work hard (Lee 2009. p. 9).

According to existing research, the employment issues between Chinese employers and African employees vary in different dimensions. However, lack of trust between the two sides – African employees' lack of commitment to the business and Chinese employers' exploitative image – is common.

7.2. Economic and Social Background of Botswana

In Botswana, Makgala (2013, p. 46) pointed out that popular discourse in recent decades paints a picture of Batswana as having appallingly lax work ethics, while acknowledging that they worked hard traditionally. In paid work, however, Batswana are said to lack the necessary discipline to work industriously. Even the former President of Botswana articulated a big difference in work ethics between China and Botswana as quoted below:

> The issue of work style and work habits is at the core of the problem [that Botswana unions have with the behavior Chinese firm]. ....The Chinese wait for the sun to rise and the minute it does they get out there and work and they don't raise their heads up again until it sets. By contrast, Batswana start later, take any number of breaks in between, and then quit work at 4: 30 pm sharp. The Chinese will work until there is no light at all; they arrive in the dark and they leave in the dark (Mogae 2009, p. 23).

In Botswana, China shops have been expanding from cities into the rural areas since 1990s. The boom of China shops created jobs and provided cheaper products for the daily needs of the local people. However, the shops are criticised for saturating the local market and have recently faced strict regulation in an increasingly hostile business climate (Kalusopa 2009). In spite of four decades of rapid economic growth, the Botswana economy continues to be less diversified and driven by diamonds, copper, nickel and beef as the primary products. In addition, the country's import bill has been very high over the last five years (Ministry of Trade and Industry 2011). Therefore, as I mentioned in 1.4.3, the government of Botswana initiated the EDD (Economic Diversification Drive) to reduce the import bill, and develop an entrepreneurship culture for business growth and enhanced citizen participation in the economy in the long run. In order to empower the entrepreneurs, the Botswana Government has started schemes such as the CEDA (Citizen Entrepreneurial Development Agency) and the e-YEP (e-innovation Youth Empowerment Program) (Mwobobia 2012). As a result, Chinese merchants are considered as a threat more than an opportunity for local people, because they are running businesses that the Batswana can do by themselves. As the Chinese merchants have face-to-face contact with local people daily, frictions between the two sides at the micro level may have existed from the beginning. However, in recent years, the frictions are increasing along with the social criticism of China shops. Local media reports show that Chinese merchants face numerous challenges with regard to local people in employer–employee relations as well as in respect of service issues (Anonymous 21 June 2010; Bule 13 November 2009), which trigger government reaction and create a bad reputation for the Chinese business environment as a whole.

The relationship with China is an increasingly important aspect of Botswana's economy, politics and society. At this point in time, there is lack of empirical information that can provide a reliable guide to those who wish to enhance the relationship (Youngman 2013, p. 14). This chapter aims to bridge the gap by providing information from the study that used an anthropological approach to investigate the employer–employee relations between Chinese merchants and Batswana employees in the China shops. The research focused on recruitment processes, daily employer–employee conflicts, treatment and employees' work attitude. Considering the social status of Chinese merchants and local employees, this chapter analyses the reasons for employer–

employee conflicts from the perspective of occupational psychology.

7.3. Perspective of Occupation Psychology

In research on the quality of working life, the variables of trust, organisational commitment and the fulfilment of personal needs play an important part. Cook and Wall (1980) introduced new measures of these variables, each of which has a number of subscales. These measures are: (a) interpersonal trust at work, (b) organisational commitment, and (c) personal need non-fulfilment. All the scales have been developed primarily for use with UK blue-collar employees, and for that reason have been kept fairly brief, with the content of items easily understood (ibid., p. 39). The detailed scales are listed as below:

Interpersonal trust at work: express opinions that people might hold regarding the confidence and trust that can be placed in others at work, both fellow workers and management.
Faith in intentions of: Peers and Management
Confidence in actions of: Peers and Management

Organisational commitment: what people might feel regarding themselves as members of their organisation.
Organisational identification
Organisational involvement
Organisational loyalty

Personal need non-fulfilment: in what they need and expect to get from different areas of their lives.
Social need non-fulfilment
Self-esteem need non-fulfilment
Autonomy need non-fulfilment
Self-actualisation need non-fulfilment (ibid., p. 43)

According to the adaption of Occupation Psychology, in Botswana, China shops can be considered as organisations and

Batswana employees as blue-collar employees. Therefore, the scales used in Cook and Wall measure serve as a guideline to measure the quality of working life in China shops for Batswana employees. In this research, from an occupational psychological perspective, I analysed daily interactions between Chinese merchants and Botswana employees to investigate the root of the conflicts, and also to expose the difference in Chinese and Botswana work ethics.

7.4. Recruitment Process and Background of Botswana Employees

In African countries, it is widely known that the Chinese prefer hiring Chinese employees rather than the local people. In Botswana the same tendency was seen years ago. However, due to recent governmental regulations, every China shop is required to hire Batswana employees in order to contribute to the reduction of local unemployment (CEco158 2014). Compared to South African chain shops (e.g. Ackermans, PEP, etc.) the recruitment process in China shops is less strict. The former usually send out recruitment information and then screen candidates' documents and hold interviews to screen employees (FTbm73 2014). While the latter, usually put job information on the door to attract interviewees (CTco12 2013; CTco20 2013). In the past, to save procedure fees, some Chinese employers even hired local employees without signing any contract with them (CTco74 2011; CTbe79 2011); however, these days with stricter regulation by the local government, most China shops follow the required legal process on recruitment (CTco74 2014). Some Chinese even go through middlemen in the recruitment companies that provide the service of introducing workers, so that when employee theft is found or Chinese employers are not happy with employee's work, they can ask the company to change the person at once without paying extra fees[1] (CTco23 2011).

The average monthly salary in China shops was between 800 and 1,200 Pula (80–120 US dollars) (8–8.5 hours per day; 4–6 days off in a month) in 2014, while in 2009 it was 600 Pula (90 US dollars)[2] (CTco12 2013). The majority of the Chinese merchants only offer a salary that is a little above the minimum (4.32 Pula per hour) regulated by government. Only few shops pay salaries as high as 2,000–3,000 Pula (200–300 US dollars) according to the employers' financial situation and employees' working experiences in the shop. Salaries in large South African retail chain stores in Botswana are usually higher than in China shops reaching 1,400–3,000 Pula (140–300 US dollars). Comparably, salaries in China shops are not attractive at all so most local employees suffer financially. Since Gaborone is a city that grows based on migration from the rest of Botswana, most of the local employees have moved from their home village to Gaborone, and they have to rent house around Gaborone. Due to a rising living cost in Gaborone, many Batswana employees who work for China shops complain about the low salary.

7.5. Conflicts between Chinese and Local Employees

According to my observation, in Chinese businesses, Chinese employers spend most of their time with their local employees. Through interviews with both sides, I found that both Chinese employers and local employees are uncomfortable in their daily interaction and recognise that there are some gaps between them that are difficult to bridge. This section will depict the typical conflicts between Chinese employers and Batswana employees from their respective perspectives. The discussions are in three parts relevant to occupational psychology namely: (a) interpersonal trust at work, (b) organisational commitment, and (c) personal need fulfilment.

7.5.1. Interpersonal Trust at Work

Chinese merchants are employers in China shops. However, as foreigners who can seldom speak the English Language correctly and usually appear shabby in the opinion of the local people, it has been difficult for them to gain respect from their Batswana employees. Although most Chinese merchants are not intentionally racist, it takes time, sometimes a long time, for them to overcome the cultural barriers to accept some habits and values of local people. As a result, it is relatively easy to observe that Chinese employers and Botswana employees have little mutual respect in their daily interactions. Furthermore, the habit of stealing from the shop that is common among the local Batswana employees worsens lack of trust and respect in daily interactions between Chinese merchants and local employees.

1. Faith in Intentions of Management

Usually local employees can have four days off every month except weekends; they choose the dates and tell their boss (CTbe66 2013). In my observations, the majority of the shops are run on a small scale with fewer than 10 local employees in each shop. Chinese employers only make a list stating the work schedule for their employees, instead of adopting a time card system. Shops are always lacking veteran workers due to the frequent turnover of employees. Some veteran employees are required to work beyond the standard time, particularly during busy seasons, which triggers many complaints as the following case indicates:

> Last Saturday, we were supposed to close the shop at 6 pm but my boss was talking to somebody on the phone until 6:20 pm. When we closed the shop, she drove away by herself, without thinking of dropping us at the station, although it was raining. I said she was selfish, and she got angry. The next day we did not talk to each other. I work so many days in a month, when do I have time to do my laundry?! (CTbe10 2013).

> We are not allowed to sit down, even when there are no customers. Our boss knows how to keep us busy. She tells us to unpack this and iron that. When customers come we feel tired and they ask why we have such a reluctant attitude. I wake up at 5:30 am. and then cook breakfast for the family. I arrive at shop at 8:00 am and knock off around 6:30 pm. When I get to bus station I have to wait as there is a long queue (CTbe11 2013).

CTbe10 has been working in the same shop for seven years. Although she does not enjoy the job, she has to work to feed the family back in her hometown. She stays because the salary in the shop is above average. Although the overworking situation in China shops has been greatly lessened in recent years, there are still some Chinese employers who count on employees to work long hours to meet the needs of the shops. On the other hand, some Chinese merchants still evaluate Batswana employees by comparing them to Chinese employees. As CTbe10's boss CTco8 states: 'People here are not like the Chinese who would be thankful for the job opportunity. Even now, I need to beg her (CTbe10) to do things for me, although she has been working for me for seven years' (CTco8 2013).

In this case, CTbe10 expects her boss to give her more rest since she has been working hard for the shop for so many years while her boss was expecting her to be more committed due to the long working experience in the shop. Therefore, although local employees consider their job as a means to live on, Chinese merchants expect them to work for the shop as though they were working in their own business, which indicates an expectation gap between the two parties.

Many local employees feel that they are overworked by the Chinese employers who try to take advantage of them. The local employees are suspicious of the intentions of their Chinese employers and feel they are unfairly treated particularly regarding rules, such as standing in the shop the whole day irrespective of whether there are customers in the shop or not, etc.

2. Confidence in Actions of Management

The quality and ability of Chinese employers are often questioned by the local employees. 'We are looked down upon by our local employee, because we don't speak good English. When they find that you can speak English, they do not dare to touch you, otherwise they will gossip about you for a long time.' said CTcof7 (2013) when I met her in the shop. 'They judge us by local standards. They think we cannot speak English because we are not educated' (CTco22 2014). CTco43 (2012) who has been in Botswana for more than 10 years shared her earlier experience:

I suffered a lot because I was neither able to understand English nor any local language in the beginning. I cried and even threw away the English dictionary when I was not able to understand what my local employees were talking about. Sometimes I became very irritated when local people laughed and talked about me….Most local employees who worked for me were fine. The worst one I met was when I had just arrived in Botswana. She knew my English was poor and would pretend that she did not understand my English when I asked her to do things.

One of CTco43's local employees even gossips about her boss with other Chinese merchants. CTcof39, who opened a shop in the same shopping mall with CTco43 shared with me:

CTco43's local employee always comes to chat with me during her lunch break, saying her boss's English is still so poor despite her long stay in Botswana and that she always wears clothes that are out of fashion and looks so shabby.

As foreign bosses, most Chinese merchants experience instances of being ignored and embarrassed when they commence business. This also has something to do with the poor image that is portrayed of the Chinese in African countries through negative media reports, since Chinese are known as people who eat dogs and snakes (Sb171 2014). As time goes by, the local employees gradually understand their Chinese employers and get used to their broken English (CTcof21 2013), but it may take a longer time to accept their Chinese employers' culture and respect them despite their shabby appearance and Chinese customs. Furthermore, once there is a negative report on the Chinese, sensitivity also increases at the interpersonal level between the two sides. In 2013 Ghana deported thousands in a crackdown on illegal Chinese goldminers,[3] which became big news. Even the Batswana tend to see Chinese people as homogenous; unsurprisingly, the Ghana case brought a bad reputation to all the Chinese in Botswana. At domestic level, in 2013 Botswana suffered a power shortage and had to apply rolling blackouts for several months due to the failure of a Chinese company to complete the power station project successfully. Besides negative media reports, the case stirred up popular complaints and blames towards Chinese companies. Commonplace phrases such as 'Chinese people come to Africa to get benefit from us and destroy us' has become very popular ever since.

In this section, the lack of mutual respect and overworking of local employees have been discussed. It is clear that local employees have little confidence in the actions of their Chinese employers because of their shabbiness and inability to speak English fluently, as well as their perceived intention to exploit local labour force through long working hours. Furthermore, the failure of big projects in the country and even negative news concerning China or the Chinese internationally adds to the suspicion among local people and contributes to an overall worsening Chinese reputation in Botswana. Generally speaking, although not many issues have been raised concerning the trust among the peers, interpersonal trust at work between local employees and Chinese employers is very limited.

7.5.2. Organisational Commitment

When it comes to work attitudes, almost every Chinese employer complains about their employees. The phrase, 'You have to be lucky enough to find a good local employee', is used by many Chinese interviewees. 'Laziness', 'no commitment', 'betrayal' are the shortcomings of local employees from the perspective of the Chinese merchants.

1. Organisational Identification

Most of the Botswana employees have completed junior or senior high school and do not take the jobs in China shops seriously, considering them to be 'better than nothing'. Based on the interviews, most of them expected a job that could transfer skills or with better treatment (CTbe3 2013; CTbe4 2013). Leaving jobs is very frequent in China shops; it is rare to find employees who work in the same China shop for more than three years, particularly those in their 20s. Many employees work in the shops while seeking other jobs or applying for school; working in a China shop is like a bottom line to the employees so that once they find a better choice they will quit it (CTbe3 2013). A Botswana woman in her 40s who had been working in a China wholesale shop for eight years shared her opinion of the recruitment issue in China shops as quoted below:

> The Batswana employees hired in the China shops are usually young ladies who lack maturity. They do not take the job seriously. Besides, people in Botswana do not think working in a China shop is a job that they can be proud of. Many local people think 'As the merchandise in China shops is cheap, people who work there are also cheap' (CTbe139 2014).

Besides this, interviews with Chinese employers revealed that theft and unexpected pregnancy are some of the reasons for the frequent change of Batswana employees in China shops (CTco74 2014b). Due to Botswana employee's poor work ethics, they are dismissed by Chinese merchants very often. And many of them sue their Chinese employers if they are dismissed without receiving an extra one month's salary (CTco1 2011; CTcof2 2014; CTco74 2011). Therefore, Chinese merchants usually only sign temporary short-term working contracts (less than three months) with them, so that they can dismiss the employees whenever they find him or her performing poorly (CTcof2 2014). Almost none of the local people I interviewed felt proud of working in China shops. In fact many expressed that it is shameful to do so. Many who stay do so because they have not found better jobs. Of course, there are a few local employees who would like to make a career of working in China shops.

2. Organisational Involvement

Many Chinese complained to me that local people do not have passion for work, and neither do they have the sense of working not just for themselves but for their company. If it were not for local regulations, they would not like to hire so many local employees. The following two cases are gathered from pioneer

Chinese merchants who have been in Botswana for more than 10 years:

> They are very lazy. Even if you tell them to do something, up to two or three hours later they still have not done it. I brought new stock into the shop, but once the goods on the shelf are sold, they tell customers there are none left. They are too lazy to move the goods from store to the shelf. These days, if I want them to do something, I have to open the box and put everything in front of them and beg them to do the work. Local government encourages us to employ local people, instead of employing Chinese assistants. If local people work hard we will not need to bring Chinese employees to work for us, since we have to invest more money in bringing the Chinese to Botswana. But locals cannot do one-tenth of the job that a Chinese employee can (CTco22 2014).

> The local assistants do not do work properly, especially the new one who talks a lot during work, even when nobody is talking to her. She does not know how to work. She only becomes clever when it comes to money. I would like to fire her at the end of this month (CTco42 2011).

Chinese merchants complain about Batswana employees' laziness and ineffectiveness, which makes them irritable when communicating with their employees. Although the Chinese do not expect the Batswana employees to be as skilful as the Chinese employees, they expect them to contribute more to their business.

As stated above, local employees are not passionate about work. To them, the only exciting day in the month is salary day. In busy seasons, like at the end of the month or the Christmas season, many local employees are very relaxed, and they would like to escape from the work in the China shop and have fun at the first opportunity. The following comments from Chinese employers provide some insight into the situation:

> In the first year when I opened this shop, we organised a Christmas party for the local employees. They ate and drank and took

home with them whatever was left over. The next day was very busy in the shop, but nobody came to work. I called them and they said they had headaches. Since that year, I have never held any party for them (CTco22 2014).

One of my local employees wanted to leave work earlier on payday to spend time with friends. When I asked her to work until 6:00 pm, she took her bag and said 'I will not work for you until 6:00 pm today' and left. Her attitude was so unbridled and arrogant. The next day, she came very early and started to mop the floor and clean things, working harder than ever before. I told her that she did not need to work since she had been fired and then I called the security company to take her away (CTco46 2014).

They do not remember your kindness. After many years, I still find that it is only on payday that all of my employees come to work (CTco22 2014).

Generally, truancy happens in every shop and almost every Chinese merchant complains about it. Many Chinese are puzzled by the local people's lack of a sense of dedication as Chinese have, because absenteeism takes place among not only new employees but also the old ones who are expected to help manage the shop. There are also devoted employees, yet they are very few according to Chinese employers' reports. CTcof93 (2015) with 10 years of business experience in Botswana concludes: 'For 10 years, I met only one local employee who was really devoted. Once she found a thief in the shop, and she just grabbed a knife to chase after the thief. Later she went back to school. I really miss her.' Chinese employers argue that local employees' little professional dedication is universal. However, despite of the overwhelming negative reputation of local employees, it is the few good stories that give Chinese employers hope, so that they would like to try their luck again when they recruit new employees.

3. Organisational Loyalty

'Everyone here steals no matter whether they are rich or poor' – this is a widespread comment on local people by Chinese merchants. In the field research so far, almost every China shop owner complained about theft by the employees. There are security cameras in every China shop, and they are not only for shoplifters from outside, but also for proof of employee theft. When it comes to theft every Chinese merchant has countless stories to share:

> My cell phone disappeared during my nap time. I woke up and asked who took away my cell phone but nobody responded to me. I became serious and watched the video recorder to find out who had removed my cell phone. Although they (my local assistants) knew, none of them told me. And when I found out, they just laughed and treated it as a joke. I was at my wit's end, not knowing how to deal with them. I called police, but later one of the employees lied to the police. Back then my English was poor and, although I was angry with the employee, I did not know how to make the truth known to the policeman (CTce44 2011).

> When I caught an employee stealing I would call the security guards and have them write down what and why she stole, so that I had evidence. Sometimes, they even help customers to steal (CTco74 2011).

> When local employees are too lazy to work and steal things I call the security company to remove them at once. If my local assistants steal things I warn them three times before dismissing them. I have told them that if they want something but do not have money, I can give the goods to them and consider it is as donation in support of local people. But if they steal my things, it will be an absolutely different story. I warn them in advance: 'I know that you will call your friends to come to steal; I have been here for 10 years and know your tricks very well. Be honest with me.' I give them chances before dismissing them because I know if I hire a new assistant, she will steal more than the old one. The old one has stolen whatever she wanted,

but new ones still have many unfulfilled needs, which increases the possibility that they would steal (CTco22 2012).

The majority of Chinese merchants have experienced being 'betrayed' by their local employees. Since theft takes place in various ways, few Chinese merchants trust their local employees. CTco74 (2011) said that she even asks her local employees to wait outside and she locks the shop when she goes to the bathroom. Because of employee theft many Chinese merchants are disappointed with the whole local community; they are even curious about why local people do not feel ashamed of theft (CTco12 2012; CTco43 2011; CTco145 2014). However, through interviews with the managers of large South African retail chains (e.g. Ackermans, Style, etc.), I realised that the salaries in those shops were much higher than in China shops and local employees in those shops treasure their jobs more than those in the China shops. One of the interviewees says: 'Salary for the employees is not enough, but they do not steal much for they don't want to lose the job, Botswana is a small country with few job opportunities (BTbm101 2014)'. Some Chinese have been badly hurt emotionally in former employment relationships: 'Although I paid them good salary and bonus, they still sued me in the Department of Labour Affairs. They thought once they sue me they would get more money' (CTco182 2015). Many Chinese people have experienced being sued by their own employees due to salary issues. Some cases are due to their illegal means of dismissing employees, others are because local employees wonder if they are paid less than they deserve. Therefore, Chinese merchants may need to review their treatment of local employees instead of complaining about employee theft and accusing them.

People tend to think that Batswana employees have a poor work attitude because they work for Chinese people. The limited management skills and business experience of Chinese merchants also contribute towards Batswana employees' work attitude. However, we observed that the poor work ethics in Botswana has been widely recognised even by the people of Botswana themselves. Makgala (2013, p. 45) cited what Daniel Kwelagobe said in 1980: 'The work ethic which in Botswana was portrayed in euphemistic expressions such as, "those who do not work hard will subsist on crumbs from their comrades' table" have most unfortunately been virtually swept into limbo'. The 2010–2011 Global Competitiveness Report (compiled by the World Economic Forum) noted that 'poor work ethics tops the list of 15 factors identified as the most problematic for doing business in Botswana' (Schwab 2010, p. 104). Makgala (2013) emphasised the importance of the analysis of discourses of work ethic for Botswana given the current government's large but unsuccessful investment in attempts to make the country globally competitive, including its all-important but elusive goal to diversify the economy away from over-dependence on diamonds (ibid., pp. 45-46). Therefore, Batswana employees' poor work performance is more likely to be influenced by the prevalent poor work ethics than racial issues.

In this section, local employees' 'frequent turnover,' 'laziness,' and 'lack of dedication at work' has been discussed mainly relying on the voices of Chinese employers. Needless to say, local employees' commitment to China shops is very low. Their involvement with the job is mostly due to the need to work that was motivated by salary, while not linked to their interest in the job itself. The employees' frequent tendency to quit their jobs and poor performance in China shops are obvious evidence of their lack of identification with China shops. In summary, there is very limited organisational commitment among local employees working in China shops.

7.5.3. Personal Need

Based on the field research, it is obvious that there are many conflicts between Chinese merchants and local employees in daily operations. Chinese merchants are described negatively as people who 'talk rudely' and 'shout in the shop' by local employees during my interview. On the other hand, there are also considerable numbers of local employees who report that their Chinese employers are fine. Local media, however, generally report more negative news on Chinese merchants than positive (Rasina 20 June 2013). As the old saying goes 'bad news travels fast' and the negative image created by the media, particularly the exploitive

162

image of Chinese employers seems more acceptable to local employees. Overtime working, low pay and strict working rules are the things that are unacceptable to the majority of the Batswana employees.

1. Social Need

Local employees are free to make friends with their peers and they enjoy that the most in their jobs. Many local employees enjoy chatting with each other while working, but sometimes that is only possible during the absence of their Chinese employers. If employees are lucky to get a kind Chinese employer then they can chat and joke together during work. There are some local employees who claim that jobs in China shops could be tough and boring and if it were not for the fellowship enjoyed with good peers, they could barely continue working in the shops. Generally speaking, local employees usually enjoy good relationships with each other, while their relationship with their Chinese employer differs from case to case.

2. Self-esteem Need

Many local employees reveal that their Chinese employers are rude to them, due to the way they talk. Others complain of the moodiness of their bosses; that sometimes they feel that they have to 'walk on eggshells' when working together with their Chinese employers.

When our boss comes in the evening to count cash, she says, 'Why so little, why don't you encourage customers to buy'. But she doesn't know that when we suggest to the customers that they buy more goods, they ask: 'How much commission do the Chinese give you that you want me to buy so much?' However, when my boss suggests clothes to customers, they are happy and would like to try them on (CTbe10 2013).

When our boss is here, we do not dare to talk. We have good relations with each other (among local assistants) though. When our boss is in a good mood she smiles and talks. However, it can be very tough sometimes too (CTbe66 2013).

Based on the communication with Chinese merchants, it is not difficult to assume the pressure on the Chinese which makes them moody. And sometimes they even transfer their pressure to their local employees, making them afraid of their boss, especially on a bad business day. Basically, the local employees are often scolded but seldom recognised for their achievements by their Chinese employers. Of course, it does not necessarily mean that the employees perform poorly in China shops, but Chinese employers withhold their praise of the employees on purpose. 'If you praise them, they will forget who they are and do not listen to you afterwards' comment Chinese merchants.

Chinese merchants' so called 'rude talking' links closely to their language ability and cultural consciousness. Many local employees report that their Chinese boss would embarrass them in front of customers. 'Our boss talked us to tears, 'Do this ... do that. Why don't you ...' (CTbe66 2013). Based on my observation, usually China shops are big (some even bigger than 100 m^2). Since Chinese merchants are usually the ones who are in charge of the cash machine, they remain behind the machine, standing on a footstool. When they talk to their employees and give commands, they usually speak loudly so that their employees can hear them from anywhere in the shop. Some Chinese even have to speak louder than the background music they play in the shop. To their local employees their Chinese bosses' loud voices sound like shouting. What is worse is that once local employees do things wrong, most Chinese would not walk down to talk to them if they can simply direct them by talking to them from where they stand. Few Chinese choose to correct their employees later, because they usually fail to explain the situation or totally forget about it due to their limited English or hectic schedule. Therefore, they have to catch their employees when they are doing wrong and correct them immediately, regardless of the presence or absence of customers in the shop. To local employees, being corrected by the Chinese boss is embarrassing, especially when their bosses do not talk kindly

(CTbe139 2014). CTbe179 (2014) said: 'We feel ashamed when being scolded by Chinese in front of our own people (customers)'. However, the majority of the Chinese people, particularly newcomers, do not have that cultural consciousness. After years of experience, Chinese merchants realise that local people have pride and are easily hurt; some do not realise the problem until their local employee talks to them and then they speak in a more acceptable way (CTco34 2011; CTco35f 2011; CTco38 2011; CTco73 2014).

Due to the reputation of China shops, working in China shops can hardly be considered as a source of pride in the social lives of the local employees. Furthermore, the stressed Chinese merchants tend to rule over their employees and judge them according to Chinese standards rather than totally allowing them to manage or encourage them towards further achievement. Therefore, to local employees, their self-esteem actualisation needs can seldom be fulfilled through jobs in China shops.

3.   Autonomy Need

Many Chinese report that their local employees are good at first for several months before they have mastered every job in the shop, but they become more and more cunning and disobedient as time goes by (CTcof21 2013; CTco55 2014). When the situation becomes unbearable for Chinese merchants, they fire their local employees. This, to some extent, explains why the majority of local employees fail to work more than two years in China shops. Two cases were observed when I was visiting CTco145's and CTce85's shops:

> One female employee wrote a receipt for a customer after receiving cash. However, after the customer left, CTco145 realised that the employee had written on a wrong page and was trying to correct the employee. So he called the employee and talked to her, using gestures due to his limited English. Obviously the employee understood what CTco145 meant, but she showed no regret, instead she slapped her hands on the desk pretended she was angry and then left with laugh. CTco145 sighed and said: 'None of the local

employees are afraid of me. They are blasé, and also joke with me' (Observed at CTco145's shop in November 2014).

This employee was told not to send text messages during working hours but she did not listen to me. We Chinese would feel ashamed if we got warnings, but they don't feel things in that way. And sometimes when you tell them not to do so, they talk back. We are Chinese, and their view is that this is their country (CTco104 2014).

Chinese merchants usually have hectic days, particularly when they are running big shops. They expect their local employees to be active and helpful. But unfortunately, most of the time, trouble is more likely initiated by local employees than anyone else (CTco8 2013; CTce85 2013). Therefore, many Chinese are stressed by their relationship with their local employees because they feel that local people are not as submissive as Chinese employees. Many 'early comer' merchants who have worked in Botswana for a while gradually acquire strategies to deal with this issue based on experience. 'We do not treat them too kind at the beginning, otherwise they would become "bosses" in my shop' (CTco22 2014). 'I change local employees very often, usually every half year; once I sense that they do not respect me, I will fire them at once' (CTco74 2011).

Local employees working in China shops work under constant supervision and even during the employers' absence video cameras in the shop record them from different angles. The situation is similar to the *kan dian* system used in Southeast Asia (Yao 2002), which was argued by Yao as a sign of the general lack of trust in employees, in their work and honesty (ibid., p. 94). 'Questioning or discussing instructions' are not welcomed in China shops, as many Chinese employers call it 'talking back' and 'disobedience'. Of course, Chinese employers' language ability should be taken into consideration. It could be an embarrassing for Chinese employers when they fail to answer the questions asked by their employees. Therefore, instead of facing the risk of being embarrassed by their local employees, it is better to discourage them from asking questions. 'Why do you have so many questions? Just do what I told you to do.' is a phrase that Chinese merchants use. In addition, due to their vulnerability as foreigners, Chinese merchants are afraid that their authority as the boss of the shop will be challenged by the questions of their local employees. When local employees negotiate the work load, Chinese merchants consider the employee as disobedient and maybe also as having a negative influence on other employees. In this kind of situation, dismissing the employees who ask a lot of questions is considered as a 'management' and 'control' strategy in the business. Generally, local employees are hired to assist the Chinese merchants but not to give advice, so their question and discussion on the instructions of the Chinese will only threaten the Chinese authority in the shop and remind the Chinese of their shortcomings in business and vulnerability as foreigners. For these reasons, local employees cannot enjoy autonomy in the China shops, unless they gain the trust of the Chinese employers and be trusted as local managers.

4. Self-actualisation Need

As I have stated earlier, the majority of the Chinese employers offer a salary just slightly above the minimum wage. When asked why they give such a low salary, many Chinese employers respond as follows: 'We give salary according to local labour law', 'All China shops give this sum of money and 'Indian shops give even less'. Narrow profit margins, the bad business situation, employee theft and the high cost of living are the reasons behind Chinese employers' stinginess. Given the rising cost of living in Gaborone, life is difficult according to local employee CTbe11 (2013), who is an orphan and single mother:

> I receive 800 Pula every month, but spend 14 Pula on transport every day. I have to find jobs near the station to save money on transport. The Botswana Government only financially supports orphans who are under 18 and since I am not, I do not have support from the government. Now, I have to feed the whole family (son, grandmother, aunt). I budget for everything I spend. I spend 500 Pula on food every month. I look for discount information from supermarkets then buy sorghum, maize, rice, etc., once I get my

salary. Since eggs are expensive I only buy one box every month (1 dozen). The good thing is I live in a house of my own so do not need to pay rent.

Most of the Chinese do admit the salary they offer is not good, but they are reluctant to raise salaries particularly to the new workers. It is easy to consider paying higher salaries to stop employees' theft. However, most Chinese do not think so. 'There is a certain amount of goods that are stolen at our shop every month. But even when we raise the salary, we still find them stealing. Theft is their hobby' (CTco22 2012). There is even a voice like this: 'When they have money they wear good clothes and invite many guys to the shop to chat with them during working time' (CTcof35 2011). When CTco34 (2013) complained about the rising cost of living, she said: 'We have to raise salary for our employee next week. She has been with us for seven years. With such a high food price how can she make a life?' Before the holiday season CTco74 and CTcof75 (2014) discussed when they should send some potatoes and food to their employees so that they could enjoy holiday with their families. Therefore, these Chinese merchants do show some propensity to be generous. Perhaps the low wage is determined not simply because the Chinese are intentionally exploitative, but because they live frugally. In China shops, it is common to find the Chinese bringing homemade lunch boxes to the shop, while Batswana employees eat fried chicken and coca cola from the supermarket. However, it is comparably true that Chinese merchants are busy with their own families and businesses and usually neglect the living situations of their employees who are worn out by the long working hours and never-ending chores back home. Therefore, China shops usually fail to offer the salaries that can satisfy local employees.

Furthermore, many people expect to learn new skills and business strategies by working in China shops. Whereas, the skill transformation and employees' steps towards further careers seem to be hindered in reality. 'You can learn nothing by working in China shops, after several years of working you will even forget all what you learned in the school' (CTbe139 2014). Some local employees even dreamed of being business partners with Chinese merchants. It seems that even after years of working together, there are still some barriers that prevent them from being business partners. Through an in-depth interview with CTbe139, an employee who had worked for a China wholesale shop for eight years, I would like to highlight the potential reasons for this barrier. CTbe139 worked for a South African company before joining the Chinese wholesale shop. She taught her boss English and gave much constructive advice over the years on management and selling. She and her boss have a good relationship, using her words 'We treat each other like family'. However, when asked if she thought they would be business partners in the future she stated as below:

> I wanted to cooperate with my boss in a business venture, but she took that lightly. I wish she could share some stock with me. Even now I do not have much money, I can start by getting a loan from the government (as long as we are serious in wanting to do business, the government will provide a loan of up to two million). Three years ago the government wanted to help the Batswana to start businesses by asking the Chinese to share 49/51 with locals (Chinese partners take 49 per cent and locals take 51 per cent), but they were not prepared to accept the arrangement. Even in the shops, they do the accounting themselves. There are many things with which we can help them, but they just keep 'secrets' to themselves. There is a limit to trust. Since the regulation of Chinese businesses has been tightened, we have a chance to run our own businesses. We can even ask our government to buy the goods for us from China (even if we cannot go to China very often by ourselves), and then we can buy from our government (CTbe139 2014).

From the Chinese merchants' side, opinions were gathered from those who had long-term business experience in Botswana. Through their assessment of their Batswana employees, we find that there is little trust by the Chinese of the locals. Many Chinese tried to be nice and trust local people until they were betrayed and sued by their own employees. In Chinese merchants' minds, the unhappy memories of experiences with employees are generalised to create a negative bias towards Batswana. Many Chinese merchants draw a line with Batswana: in their minds, it is clear what locals can and cannot be trusted with. This might provide some explanation as to why many Chinese employers keep the accounting and business situation to themselves. Furthermore, due to the recently founded projects, Economic Diversification Drive (EDD) and Citizen Entrepreneurial Development Agency (CEDA), many Chinese presume that the local government is ready to drive them out and give the China shop types of business opportunities to the local people. As foreign merchants in Botswana, Chinese people are prudent in their business dealings, because they know they are not of this land and once they are betrayed by their Batswana employees they could lose every investment in Botswana. Additionally, the difference in values is also a hurdle to overcome, as one Chinese revealed: 'We tried but failed to cooperate with local people. We Chinese plan investment for long term, but people here want to get money back as soon as possible. They would think that 10 year later "who knows where I will be!"' In summary, factors such as the negative image towards Batswana people, trading policy changes, as well as value differences all hinder the cooperation between Chinese merchants and local people.

To balance my view, I would like to emphasise that CTbe139's case does in some extent show the barriers between Chinese merchants and local assistants to become business partners. However, it should not be understood in a totally negative context, as CTbe139 has contributed considerably to the business of her Chinese boss and they have established a strong relationship that could allow them to consider being business partners in the future. According to the statement of CTbe139 (2014towar), her contribution to the business is obvious and she is totally trusted as the local manager of the shop:

> I am happy with this job and feel I am the boss of this shop …
> At beginning I taught my boss how to read and pronounce English correctly. When she did not understand the labour law, I told her not to ask people but to go to the labour office to get an official

document. And I explained everything on the paper to her. I think it took two years for us to build a good trusting relationship with each other. Now we can go out to spend some time together and when I have difficulties at home, she also helps me.

I train the other employees, teaching them to treasure job opportunities in China shops and not to have negative attitudes towards China shops no matter what outsiders say. I told my boss to talk to employees nicely and not to shout or point out their faults in front of other people when they make mistakes.

I told my boss not to sit there the whole day and use her cell phone, while asking local assistants to deal with the customers. I told her that she should say 'dumela (hello)' and talk to the customers so that they will correct her if she makes language mistakes. By doing this, she can improve her English. When employees see her deal with customers they will also follow her example.

I also taught my boss that when she treats all customers well, they will come back to her shop. When they need something they will think 'let me buy it at my friend's place' and as some of the customers are from the government, once they buy stationary they buy a lot … Some customers will also give her ideas of what to stock next time she goes to China; otherwise she only sources what she thinks will be popular here.

Through the contribution of CTbe139, not only her Chinese boss but also the other local assistants benefited from good training in business skills and customer service. This case could be used as an encouraging message to both Chinese merchants and local assistants. It shows the potential possibility of the China shop serving to foster mutually beneficial ties between Chinese merchants and local people. Furthermore, it reminds them of the importance of a positive attitude and sincerity in employment relations.

In this section (7.5), most of the voices were gathered from local employees concerning their opinions and feelings towards Chinese employers. According to the local employees, there are very few skills that can be obtained from jobs in China shops and, besides, they earned a minimum salary. The majority of the interviewed employees report that they enjoy the relations with other colleagues and some even like their Chinese employers, so the work may help them to fulfil their social needs to some extent. However, long working hours and few transferable skills make the job like drudgery (particularly for those who have to commute to work every day), which explains why the majority of the local people consider the job as no more than a part-time job. Moreover, although good employment relations do exist in China shops, due to the prudent attitudes of Chinese merchants, a business partnership relationship between Chinese merchants and local people has not been found so far. This disappoints some veteran local assistants. However, this is not an issue that can be solved through individual efforts, but requires the Botswana government to secure a stable business environment to encourage the cooperation at grass-roots level. Therefore, generally speaking, the local employees' personal needs can be partly fulfilled by the jobs in China shops but there is still much more room for improvement.

7.6. Recruitment Process and Background of Chinese Employees

Before 2013, the Chinese were often criticised for not contributing enough to local unemployment as they preferred to hire Chinese as shop assistants instead of local people. However, since 2013 local regulations have restricted working visas for the Chinese and therefore many Chinese merchants had to hire more local people as assistants in their shops. So far research has revealed little about the relationship between Chinese employers and their Chinese employees. As a result, many African people guess that Chinese are nicer to their own people and somehow look down upon African local assistants. However, my argument here is that Chinese employers' treatment of local assistants is no different from their treatment of Chinese employers. The differences revealed in the treatment of the two groups are mainly due to work performance and not ethnic or race issues. In fact, Chinese employers are even stricter with and have higher expectations of their Chinese employees.

Back in 2013, because of the severe competition, more qualified service and management skills were in demand to win customers. During the recruiting process, priority was given to 'single' Chinese employees, considering they would be more dedicated compared to married people who would face more challenges and complicated family issues after coming to Botswana. Because the valid term of a work permit was three years, to make a full use of it, most Chinese employees were required to sign a three-year contract with their Chinese employers. However, even if some of the employees ended up quitting the job before fulfilling their contracts, no compensation was required from their employers in reality. The similar family chain phenomenon is also found in Cape Verde (Haugen and Carling 2005), South Africa (Laribee 2008) and in the 1980s' Indonesian market (Omohundro 1981). However, the family chain system recorded in Indonesia is more like an apprenticeship than an employer–employee relationship.

During the employees' stay in Botswana, most of them live in their employers' houses with other co-workers. Food, clothes and daily use of facilities were also provided by the employers. According to the interviews, it was common that employers buy food and employees in turn cook and do chores. CTce79, a Fujianese lady, who had been in Botswana looking after a shop for her cousin for two years said in the interview:

> My cousin gives me 2,000 Pula for one month. He does not pay my salary every month, but promises to give me the money when I go back to China or send it to my parents. During my stay here, I eat and use daily necessities freely. They also paid for the tickets for my flight (CTce79 2011).

Although money is mostly paid into a bank account, employees are still given pocket money. 'My employer says that we are free to take the money from cashier to buy food if we are hungry during work time,' said CTce84, an employee from Jiangxi Province, who was working for her aunt. However, due to the different relationships between employers and employees, the ways of using pocket money are different. Although most of the shop owners allow their employees to use the money in the cash register without reporting it, not every employee dares to use it as freely as CTce84 did. For instance, another employee said that she never took money from the cash register. As one case shows:

> My cousin is a good employer, but his wife is stingy. Once she complained to my cousin about me when we were shopping together, only because I spent 10 Pula (1.3 US dollars) to buy an ice-cream. And since then, even if my cousin allows me to use money freely, I never use it (CTce79 2011).

This issue presents the trusting relationship between employers and employees. If the shop owner does not trust the employees, s/he does not give permission for using money freely. However, there are also owners who pretend to be generous. Fortunately, it seems most employees are clever enough to find out if their employers really mean what they say, and manage to make peace with their employers no matter how generous they are or are not.

It appears that Chinese employees complain more about the work itself than the treatment, because watching the shop is such a boring job, particularly during the days that there are very few customers. There are Chinese employees who read novels or play cell phone games to kill time; however, it is considered as negligence hence most of them hesitate to do so, although they desire to. In comparison employers are freer to do what they want, because they are the bosses. Some of them even bring laptops to the shop to read downloaded novels or chat with their neighbours when there are no customers in their shops (CTco74 2011; CTce84 2011). Besides, Chinese employees are usually in charge of some local assistants working in the shops, so they are supposed to be good role models in the absence of their employers. Thus, many of them hesitate to play cell phone games, read novels or wander around the shops. Furthermore, some Chinese employees are under pressure, as they have to report on the business situation every day during dinner time. If the business is not good, s/he has to bear with the 'long face' of their employers (CTce79 2011). Some Chinese employees also face competition with other Chinese employees who work for the same Chinese employer. If they watch different shops for the same Chinese employer, they tend to see each other as rivals when they give their business reports every evening (CTco64 2012; CTco71 2012). There are also few Chinese employees who do not perform well or do not obey their Chinese employers. According to my informants, those employees usually are encouraged to go back to China before their contract period expires. The majority of the Chinese employers do not want to create conflict with their Chinese employees, who are usually relatives, in a foreign land. On the one hand, it creates a bad reputation for the family and becomes material for other Chinese to gossip about. Furthermore, the Chinese employers feel that it is their responsibility to take care of their employees during their stay in Botswana, since the employees go to Botswana because of the employers. However, the reality is, no one can assure that every Chinese employee came from China is hard working and will go well with the employers and other Chinese employees.

Generally speaking, Chinese employees do not have much cultural or language barriers with their Chinese employers, which is beneficial to developing a trusting relationship with their employers. However, on the other hand, they have to work longer both at shop and home with the supervision of their Chinese employers despite better pay. Furthermore, they usually have to share business pressure with their Chinese bosses to a greater or lesser extent.

7.7. Discussion

This chapter mainly analysed the employer–employee relations between Chinese merchants and Batswana employees. I looked at the background of Chinese merchants and Batswana employees as well as the recruitment process in China shops. Neither Chinese employers nor Batswana employees have high social status in the local community; one as foreigners and the other as a low-income group who are threatened by unemployment. Due to cultural and language barriers, there is little respect, and interactions between Chinese employers and Batswana employees are usually stressful. Batswana employees' complaints and negotiations for better treatment are often perceived by Chinese merchants as 'laziness' 'no commitment to work' and 'betrayal'; while Chinese employers' frugality and prudence are seen as exploitative and incredulous. The difference in ethics has been the biggest barrier to the building of a trusting relationship between the Chinese and Batswana (Lee 2009; Giese and Thiel 2014) resulting in their inability to become business partners. The findings are common in cross-cultural businesses and are not necessarily due to racial issues. However, racial comments are sometimes still made by Chinese merchants for them to release their stress and incomprehension. Concerning the exploitativeness and incredulousness of the merchants, without a comparative study, it is difficult to say if the traits can be considered as the cultural heritage, the 'Chineseness', of the Chinese merchants in Botswana or universal characteristics of all merchants.

Although Batswana employees usually have good relationships with each other, the mutual trust and confidence between Chinese employers and Batswana employees are lacking. Few Batswana are proud of working at China shops, since they only consider it as a transition or stepping stone to a better job. They get involved in the work in the China shops mostly due to financial obligations, and few are enthusiastic about working there. Their poor performance is the most convincing proof of their lack of loyalty to the workplace. The amount of salary offered may help to fulfil basic financial and social needs to some extent, but generally does not meet employee expectations. Local people comment that what China shops can provide, other jobs can provide as well or even better. The difficulty encountered in becoming a business partner with Chinese merchants has disappointed many committed local employees, making them lose the enthusiasm to work in China shops. On the other hand, due to the fact that China shops can only offer limited skills transfer, it fails to bring spill over effects that would in the long run boost the indigenous business sector and benefit the local population. The criticism of Chinese migrants for providing only limited skills and development opportunities for the local population is common in African countries (Dobler 2009; Hanisch 2013; Haugen and Carling 2005; Giese and Thiel 2012; Park 2009). Hanisch (2013) argues that potential for skills development of an employee in wholesale and retail sector is limited by its nature, regardless of whether in Chinese or Indian or local businesses.

The marginal position of local assistants in the retail business partly shows the distrust of the Chinese and partly reflects the fact that local assistants are regarded as 'low-to-medium-qualified personnel' even in local society (Hanisch 2013, p. 92). Many people misunderstand this point and criticise the Chinese as racist when it comes to employment issues. However, as Sautman and Yan (2015, p. 2152) argued 'Chinese racialisation rests on the concept of "quality" or *suzhi*, conceived in terms of discipline, honesty, industriousness and skill'. Compared to Westerners, most Chinese have far less of a cultural overlap with Africans, yet do not generally display the aloofness that scholars of racialisation of labour note in enterprises in developed country in the Global South. Those Chinese who go further than Westerners in interacting with Africans may have more modest economic positions or a different sense of 'race', which may be due to China's socialist legacy or to a sense that China is a developing country (Sautman and Yan 2016, p. 2160).

Frequent and close interactions between Chinese and local people in China shops may be the reason for increasing numbers of problems concerning Botswana–China business relations. Chinese employers and local employees have the most face-to-face interactions, among all the social interactions that occur between Chinese employers and local people in China shops. To some extent, on a ground level in Botswana, Chinese employers read Batswana society through their employees, and Batswana learn about Chinese culture through their Chinese employers. In Chapter 6 I focused on the relationship between Chinese employers and local customers. The relationship between local people and Chinese merchants is greatly influenced by local media and the Chinese reputation in widespread, regardless of the type of interactions. Nevertheless, a direct touch of 'made-in-China' merchandise and the face-to-face interaction with Chinese merchants are the sole evidence for local people to judge China. When it comes to employment relations, the more interaction the more they clash, and the closer interaction the fiercer the clash is. In this context, employment relations in China shops, which sound the worst of all the interactions, may be only due to the frequent and close interaction of the two parties. When comparing the interaction experience between established and newcomer Chinese merchants, it seems a natural cycle of conflict, and accommodation exist which to some extent proves Robert Park's (1950) contact perspective.

Power relations are different between the original 'contact zone' context and the case in China shops. In the original contact zone, the two sides that interact are often within radically asymmetrical relations of power (Pratt 1992, p. 7). However, in the case of China shops we can find a level pegging relationship: Chinese employers are the bosses of the China shops, while local employees are in the submissive position; on the other hand, Chinese employers are the foreigners in Botswana, while the local employees are native to the host country. Due to Chinese merchants' failure to speak English and the local language fluently, on many occasions, they assume a submissive position and are even considered uneducated by local employees. Because of the intervention of the Botswana government and their programmes to 'protect the rights of local people' and 'support local entrepreneurship,' the power of the government rules over China shop management. Local employees who work in China shops are given the right to sue their Chinese bosses if they question the low salary they receive or they feel they are bullied or exploited by their employers. To the Chinese, however, with their limited language abilities and rights, they can just about handle the employment issues with their local employees. Furthermore, their business would suffer greatly once local employees seek refuge with the local authorities and threaten to sue them. Even if the Chinese have done nothing wrong, they often do not have the confidence or the energy to argue with the authorities. As mentioned in Chapter 5, paying bribes and dismissing local employees are strategies that can be seen as signs of the Chinese merchants' attempt to escape from the clash, and take a break from the energy-consuming 'contact zone' before playing another round of the 'game'. After all, although there are many conflicts in the 'sharpening process', the mutual understanding between the

Chinese and the local people has made great progress as one Chinese merchant revealed: 'When we just came to Africa, we would use lighter to sterilise the forks local people handed to us before eating. Now we have no problem working together.' Therefore, both the Chinese and Batswana need to be more patient with the 'sharpening process' and, most importantly, stand the heat without fleeing.

Notes

[1] According to local law, the employer has to warn the employee three times before dismissing him/her, and pay an extra one month's salary.

[2] The US dollar to Pula rate has been changing over the years.

[3] http://www.theguardian.com/world/2013/jul/15/ghana-deports-chinese-goldminers.

Chapter 8

China–Botswana Relations beyond China Shops

Chinese reputation suffered a loss this time because of the electricity factory, glass factory and the construction of the airport. – Chinese merchant

In this chapter, I would like to share some information concerning Chinese business that is 'hidden' from the public scene (Lam 2015), like construction companies and factories that do not own shops in the visible commodity market in Botswana. I discussed the influence of *fong kong* in Chapter 6. However, this chapter answers the remaining question in Chapter 6 regarding why local customers in Botswana have negative attitudes towards Chinese goods despite the fact that their quality has improved. My main argument is that local customers' negative attitudes towards Chinese goods are mainly influenced by the failure of Chinese mega-projects, local negative media reports and their own economic vulnerability. Furthermore, I discovered that China shops play a lens role by indicating the macro-level China–Botswana relationship by portraying micro-level interactions and perceptions in society. This chapter first introduces the recent tensions surrounding Chinese mega-projects in Botswana and subsequent responses from both governments. Secondly, the social environment surrounding Botswana customers and their status will also be introduced. Thirdly, the interactions between Chinese merchants and local customers will be analysed against the background of a deteriorating Chinese reputation in Botswana.

8.1. Overview of Local Media Reporting on Chinese Projects

Given the crucial role that the media plays in China–Botswana relations, some media reports about the failure of Chinese mega-projects in Botswana will be introduced as a background to the 'recent conflicts' in China–Botswana relations. The failure of four mega-projects garnered the most local attention will be highlighted. The media is considered a very important source of data in research on Africa–China relations due to its role in communication and actively shaping perceptions and views of readers on a wide range of topics (Moahi 2015, p. 61). Additionally, when it comes to diplomatic relations and mega-projects, media sources are usually the only means for local society to obtain insight on developing news. Moahi (2015) assessed how Botswana–China relations are portrayed in the Botswana print media. The findings showed that the coverage of the Botswana–China relations cannot be neatly categorised as either positive or negative, but as a complex collection of contrasting views, depending on the topic covered. The local press presents some aspects of this relationship in a positive way, but inconsistently (ibid. 2015, p. 61). However, research shows that local print media reports negatively on both Chinese mega-construction projects and Chinese goods (Moahi 2015, p. 69–71).

A brief summary of the history of China–Botswana economic relations follows. The China Civil Engineering Construction Company (CCECC) was the first Chinese company to work in Botswana. It came to the country in 1985 to rehabilitate the railway line as an aid project funded by the Chinese government (Chen 2009). According to Chen (2009), the statistics of the Chinese Embassy showed that sixteen Chinese SOEs were operating in Botswana, thirteen of which were top construction companies. Besides the Chinese SOEs, about ten to twenty private Chinese companies run by Chinese who live abroad were operating in Botswana. Setting aside some individual problems, the overall benefit of the Chinese engagement in this sector to Botswana was to substantially lower the cost of infrastructure projects and create new employment opportunities for the local people (Chen 2009, p. 8). However, tensions emerged between Botswana's government and Chinese businesses over high-profile projects as the country geared up for elections in October 2012 (Nadalet 27 July 2012). Some candidates claimed that Chinese investments caused local contractors to lose business opportunities by offering cheap prices for sub-standard work. On the other hand, Chinese business leaders insisted that teething troubles on some major initiatives should not be used as a weapon with which to attack growing economic ties between the two countries (ibid.). Tensions surfaced in July 2013 when the Botswana–Chinese General Chamber of Commerce (BCGCC) complained that Chinese businesses were all 'being painted with the same brush' by local critics portraying them as a 'like-minded monolith' (ibid.). Since then, it seems that local media reports concerning Chinese mega-projects in general continue to be of a negative nature. Batswana people often use the term 'quality from fong kong' to describe substandard Chinese products or Chinese work (Chen 2009, p. 14). Since the quality of Chinese construction work is not a key issue in this research, in order to explain the notoriety of Chinese work, Chinese mega-projects in Botswana will be introduced using local media reports as examples.[1]

1. Airport
    In 2012, Botswana's government dismissed Sinohydro Botswana (a Chinese state construction firm), the contractor on the Khama International airport expansion, over delays and other setbacks. The airport is prominent on a list of projects highlighted by critics who accuse the Chinese of shoddy work (Nadalet 27 July 2012). Sinohydro's submission was the lowest tender. However, that did not necessarily guarantee quality. The Chinese state-owned company, Sinohydro Botswana finally relocated from Botswana to China. In March 2012, Mmegi reported that the company was saddled with five unfinished projects, deteriorating performance and a heavy workload (Mosikare 19 July 2013). President Ian Khama was reported to have said that Botswana would in the future be careful in assessing any Chinese company seeking to provide construction services in Botswana, due to the bad experiences with Chinese companies (Moeng 11 March 2013).

2. Glass Factory
    Shanghai Fengyue Glass Company based in Palapye[2] ran into problems before it could mould a single glass, which cost Botswana dearly and ruined job hopes and strained ties (Nadalet 27 July 2012). The glass manufacturing project was a 500 million Pula (56 million

US dollars) joint venture between the official Botswana Development Corporation (BDC) and the Shanghai Fengyue Glass Company. The court papers revealed that the BDC funded 75 per cent of the project but it had equity control of only 47 per cent whilst Shanghai Fengyue had 53 per cent equity control for its 25 per cent contribution. At inception in 2007, it was envisaged that the project would cost 539 million Pula. However, in 2013 it estimated that the project would require a further 765 million Pula for completion, an astonishing cost of 1.3 billion Pula (Fengyue Glass Manufacturing liquidated 2013). In 2016, the controversial glass project that cost the BDC over 500 million Pula was finally auctioned (Piet 16 February 2016).

3. Power Station

Not far from the Palapye glass factory, the Morupule B Power Plant has been the focus of involvement by a Chinese company since 2008. The contract value was 970 million US dollars. The successful signing of this project marked a break into the power market in Botswana by Chinese enterprises. It was also the largest power plant project in Botswana, attracting great attention from the Government of Botswana (Correspondent 2009). The Morupule B Power Plant boilers were manufactured by a Chinese company named Wuxi Huaguang Boiler Company (WHBC) and were developed using technology and designs licensed by international organisations. Andritz Energy and Environment (AE&E) Lentjies, a German company, designed the boilers while the American Society of Mechanical Engineers (ASME) set the standards (Seretse 28 March 2014). Many people wondered how this project could fail with the support of billions of Pula and the involvement of many specialised players (Seretse 28 March 2014). Although the Chinese company was responsible for only part of the project, the blame for its failure was still shifted on to the Chinese company.

So far, limited research has been undertaken on the reasons and factors behind the failure of these mega-projects. The media including newspapers, were the only way to gain information on and insight of these projects. According to Youngman (2013), economic relations and their impact on community relations gained the most press attention in the Batswana print media. The recent focus in the media was on the Chinese role in the construction industry and the retail sector, bringing into sharp relief the difficulties arising out of these activities. Moahi (2015) showed that person-to-person cultural and technical exchange activities were positive. However, there was some scepticism expressed in certain quarters, and certain aspects of the Chinese people's conduct in business and economic areas were viewed negatively. The latter tended to spill over into other dimensions such as the political, diplomatic and community relations (Moahi 2015, p. 72). Therefore, the media ended up playing a role in extending the negative image of China since successful Chinese projects are seldom reported in the media (Mogalakwe 2015). The reports regarding the failure of several mega-projects impacted directly on the Botswana government's policy towards Chinese investments in Botswana. Not only Chinese construction companies but also Chinese trading businesses were influenced and this will be discussed in the next section.

8.2. The Botswana Government's Response to Chinese Mega-projects and their Restriction

The failure of Chinese mega-projects in Botswana not only produced cracks in China–Botswana cooperation, but also triggered tension in diplomatic and trading relations. After a series of bad investment experiences with Chinese firms, Botswana's president, Ian Khama, stated that Botswana may no longer award government contracts to China. At the very least, Gaborone would be much more selective in granting infrastructure projects, especially those on which Chinese companies had placed bids (Botswana Says 'No' to China 2013). Furthermore, concerning the power plant case, Khama said that, if not for delays and problems with Chinese-constructed power plants, Botswana would be totally self-sufficient (ibid.). The Chinese embassy in Gaborone did not respond to a request for a response to those recent allegations. It is important to note that in 2009 when Khama became president, relations with

China were strong and China was involved in eighteen construction projects in the country (ibid.).

President Ian Khama's visit to South Korea in 2015 could be the latest indication of a turbulent relationship between the government of Botswana and the People's Republic of China. What could be a further sign of strain was the fact that Botswana has reportedly rejected Chinese soft loans (Masokola 9 November 2015). President Khama's visit to South Korea resulted in a lot of undertakings that could spell uncertainty for the China–Botswana relationship going forward. Masokola (9 November 2015) also indicated that Khama offered the South Korean government 2.6 billion US dollars (equivalent to 27.4 billion Pula) to solve the power crisis affecting the country and threatening the economy. Khama was also reported to have offered the South Koreans an opportunity to partner with the Botswana government in development of other public infrastructure as part of 27.4 billion Pula's worth of projects. Khama's gesture towards South Koreans indicated that Botswana was extending an opportunity to Korea at the expense of long term partner in infrastructure development, China (ibid.).

Since Botswana and China established diplomatic relations, bilateral trade between the two countries has now reached over 300 million Pula. The relationship between the two countries began to decline in the last five years, following the failure by the Chinese construction companies to complete projects on time, and on budget. Of the projects in question, the Morupule B, the 11-billion-Pula World Bank and the African Development Bank funded projects and the Palapye Glass Project was the most contentious. In 2013, Khama told the South African publication, Business Day, that Botswana had bad experiences with Chinese companies and going forward Botswana would be looking very carefully at any company that originates in China and which provides construction services of any nature (Masokola 9 November 2015). However, Khama recently defended the Chinese and other foreign-owned companies to those who called on them to be compelled to partner with local companies in order to be awarded government tenders. Khama said he did not want a situation where citizens rode on the back of the

Chinese and remarked that the Chinese were welcome as long as they hired Botswana citizens (ibid.). The Chinese government recently made offers of soft loans to Botswana in the form of interest-free or low-interest concessional loans. It was reported that the Botswana government showed little interest in taking up the offer to develop the country's infrastructure (ibid.). Therefore, due to several failures within the construction mega-projects, the brand of China was tarnished in Botswana.

Although there was no clear declaration concerning the restriction of Chinese investment, it was not difficult to observe that the failures of mega-projects to some extent intensified the restrictions on Chinese investment as a whole. Since the mega-projects became problematic, China–Botswana diplomatic relations and trading relations have deteriorated accordingly. Many Chinese experienced rejections in extending work permits and visa applications, while China shops received more frequent checks from local officials.

8.2.1. *Visa and Residence Permit Issues*

Chinese merchants experienced rejection of visa applications and reluctance in renewing residence permits. Complaints both from the Government of Botswana and from the Chinese in recent years created a diplomatic strain between the two countries. Botswana was not happy with the quality of construction work by some Chinese companies (Masokola 9 November 2015). On the other hand, what emerged as the biggest concern for the Chinese government was the continued rejection of their citizens when they applied for residence permits and Botswana visas. It emerged that on average China offers 3,500 visas to Botswana citizens annually with a turnaround time of two days. However, Botswana issues less than 100 annually, and the Chinese may wait for months to receive visa approval (ibid.). The Chinese were confused as they were never certain if they were guaranteed a future in Botswana, and potential Chinese investors were limited due to the current situation with visas and permits (ibid.).

However, the Chinese were not the only group disappointed about immigration matters as some Indian investors were also rejected by immigration. Former President, Festus Mogae, suggested that expelling foreign nationals from Botswana was self-defeating, as Botswana needs skilled professionals and foreign investors. On the other hand, foreign investment might be reduced in Botswana due to this uncertainty. It was found that investors were not willing to put their money into a country where they were not certain whether they would have a long-term presence or not (ibid.).

8.2.2. Frequent Checks and Permit Limitation towards China Shops

As I mentioned in 5.2.4., in addition to visa and resident permits, frequent checks by local officers and a difficulty in renewing trading permits also bothered Chinese merchants. Chinese merchants are subjected to punitive regulations in Botswana, relating to labour issues and products of poor quality. According to Chinese merchants, City Council officers and the police frequently check trading permits in China shops. Some of the Chinese whose work permits had expired or were under process of renewal tended to pay some 'fines' to the officers. Therefore, many Chinese merchants consider checking permits as a way for local officials to get 'extra income'. Chinese merchants who are put on a long waiting list for renewing documents have to look for *guanxi* (personal connections) to get quick renewal, so that they can continue to run their business without fear. However, during that time local offices only issued short-term working permits or sometimes issued permits to only the wife or husband of a Chinese couple. These practices further lead to unfair treatment, bribery and extortion issues.

Given the Botswana government's response to the Chinese government and Chinese merchants, there are other side effects to the event. The Botswana government's treatment of Chinese merchants not only increased pressure on Chinese business but also marginalised the presence of China in Botswana, which further affected local people's perception of Chinese business.

8.3. Status of Local People

In order to understand local attitudes to and perspectives on China shops, it is necessary to first understand the social environment surrounding Botswana local people and their status.

8.3.1. Financial Status

Besides the influence of local media and the restriction by local government, financial insecurity also contributes to the perceptions of local customers. According to Benza (2012), almost half of Botswana's population lives on under 2 US dollars per day. People receive financial support from the government, but their income still does not meet their needs. According to my field research people who work for China shops received 800–1,200 Pula per month, which was a standard salary for workers in retail or wholesale shops. Managers working in big South African chain stores received 4,000–8,000 Pula per month. Despite the limited quality of *fong kong* goods, the goods met the economic consumption needs of the local population. In Botswana, people became familiar with a 'high technology' and 'gorgeous life style' through media broadcasting and South African shopping malls (Zi 2015a). 'At the individual level, on a monthly income that can barely feed a family, some people expect to enjoy meals at the Hilton and drive Mercedes Benz cars or Land Rovers. These aspirations, to some extent, increase people's appetites, and create a market, for *fong kong* goods, in particular counterfeits (Zi 2015a, pp. 21–22).' Therefore, despite their bad reputation, *fong kong* goods thrive in the Botswana market. Furthermore, local consumption habits also contribute to their addiction to *fong kong* goods. Many local people squander all of their money before pay day and do not have the habit of 'saving enough to buy the best'. It may also account for their tendency to purchase *fong kong* goods.

8.3.2. Xenophobia

In addition to the demand for cheap high quality goods, the xenophobic attitude of local people is another factor influencing negatively on attitudes towards Chinese goods. Botswana has always

189

been a migrant sending country historically, especially in regard to the South African mines and farms. However, after independence, with a change in its economic prosperity the country became a migrant receiving country. Due to its lack of manpower, the government adopted an open approach to migration policy making unrestricted entry of immigrants possible in Botswana. The consequence of this open door policy was an influx of immigrants resulting in a shift in policy to a more restrictive approach towards immigrants. In the past decade, large numbers of migrants came to Botswana, mostly from Zimbabwe and some other African and Asian countries. (Lesetedi and Moroka 2007, p. 7).

Marr (2012) who analysed the media discourse on Zimbabweans in Botswana concluded that the Batswana is an anxious and xenophobic nation which harbours the fear of unfair competition and of invasion by foreigners. Marr argued that, in an environment of economic uncertainty and ethnic instability, the spectre of the stranger/Zimbabwean is used to reconfigure the content and emphasis of citizenship in Botswana. Nyamnjoh (2006, pp. 18–19) explained the xenophobia phenomenon in Botswana as below:

> There is a hierarchy of citizenship fostered by political, economic, social, and cultural inequalities, such that it makes than others. In addition, like South Africa, the tendency is for competing Botswana nationals to label and scapegoat foreigners, among whom similar hierarchies exist. Black African immigrants, denied a name of their choice just as in South Africa, are given the same Makwerekwere by Botswana nationals. Again, these hierarchies demonstrate not only the paradoxes of the globalization process but also the limits of bounded notions of citizenship and belonging informed by the 'nation-state' and its hierarchies.

In a similar way, it appears that the Botswana media ended up carrying stories encouraging negativity towards China and the Chinese. This could be attributed to the possibility that Batswana people feel threatened by strangers and perceive themselves as a nation under siege from foreigners (Moahi 2015, p. 63).

8.3.3. Governmental Support

Furthermore, the initiation of local entrepreneurial culture into the local government policy also contributes to the attitude of local customers, since the policy indicates that Chinese merchants have occupied a business position that local people can fill themselves. Botswana has so far relied on imports, but in recent years the local government has established new policies to initiate business and manufacturing instead (Ministry of Trade and Industry 2011). The local government, through the Economic Diversification Drive (EDD) and the Citizen Entrepreneurial Development Agency (CEDA), facilitates a holistic approach to the development and promotion of viable sustainable citizen-owned enterprises in order to promote the growth of a vibrant and globally competitive private sector. In this political environment, many Chinese merchants are experiencing difficulties with government officials due to increased inspections targeting sales of counterfeits, tax evasion and other illegal or informal business activities. In 2015 the government of Botswana even made plans to drastically reduce the number of retail licences issued to Chinese people, with the aim of preserving the retail business for Batswana locals (Motsamai 1 July 2015).

Not to mention how many local people managed to initiate their businesses through the EDD project. During my field research, a rumour concerning government loans was circulated. It said that some local people, after receiving a 30,000 Pula loan, first bought a Range Rover car and then dined out at the Gaborone Sun from Christmas to New Year to finish all of the money. 'They have eaten the seed before cultivating the land', as one local person put it.

8.4. Local Attitudes to China Shops under a Deteriorating China Brand

In Chapter 6, I introduced the market for *fong kong* goods. Despite its disrepute, it has been popular among local people so far. However, having a market for *fong kong* goods does not necessarily mean that Chinese merchants have an easy business environment. In reality there are many negotiations and conflicts between Chinese merchants and local customers in the China shops regarding different types of *fong kong* goods. It is almost doubtless the failure of mega-construction projects that tarnished the China brand and added extra pressure to Chinese merchants. The attitudes of local customers can be categorised into three groups, although they overlap to some extent.

8.4.1. Suspicion

Local customers are more suspicious than ever before despite the improvement of *fong kong* goods. As mentioned before, despite the notorious reputation of *fong kong* goods, their quality has greatly improved. However, due to the widespread negative local media reports concerning Chinese mega-projects, local customers became more suspicious about the quality of Chinese goods. Generalisation may be part of human nature, but as soon as Botswana local media reported on the quality issues concerning Chinese construction work and Chinese goods, local customers manifested their suspicious behaviour towards Chinese goods in China shops, as indicated below:

> Now when local customers come to buy a cell phone or a TV, they want to open the back of the case to check them! What do they want to see? Even if we sold high quality goods at our shops local people would not trust us. However, if the same goods were sold in a white person's shop, they would pay a lot of money to buy them and believe they are of high quality (CTco34 October 2013).

> A customer came to buy a MP3 that can be adapted for use in a car. He wished to pay 50 Pula but the cheapest was 60 Pula. He complained about the unfair cost and asked CTco34 to help check if it worked in his car. CTco34 made an excuse saying she was the only one watching the shop and therefore could not leave. After hearing this, the customer left unhappy (Observed at CTco34's shop, September 2014).

CTco34 said that she learnt to be quiet when customers complain or murmur rudely about Chinese goods, so that she would not quarrel with them:

> You need to bear much when you are running a business. Some people here are terrible. They pay little but expect good quality. But I am also thankful for the gentle and kind customers. They differ from case to case. Because of the failure of power station project and the glass factory, we are all under pressure.

Therefore, due to the deteriorating reputation of Chinese goods, particularly those with marginalised financial status, local consumers become more prudent and even suspicious when shopping in China shops. Even if the quality of goods in China shops has improved, it is still a challenge for Chinese merchants to get rid of the notoriety represented by the expression 'fong kong'. The failures of the mega-projects intensified the negative image of Chinese merchandise. Furthermore, the negative attitudes of local customers manifested during their face-to-face interaction with Chinese merchants in China shops.

8.4.2. Anger

Another common attitude of customers is anger towards Chinese merchants, particularly after the failure of mega-projects. CTco104 has been in Botswana for more than 10 years and reads English and even has local friends who work for local government. She expressed her understanding towards local people's reactions. Listed below are some conversations overheard in her shop, concerning the influence on the market as a result of the power station fallout.

> The President of Botswana was angry with a Chinese company, because electricity controls the economy of Botswana. Even the Chinese were angry about the power shortage. We merchants also suffered the consequences of the power station project failure. The business situation was deteriorating and the power station case was like a punch to us. When there is a shortage of power our customers

take their frustration out on us (Interview with CTco104 November 2014).

> Our wish is that the Chinese company can fix the power station as soon as possible. The shortage of power is the cause of much inconvenience in our daily lives. What makes it worse is that I think that if the Chinese company fails to fix it, we cannot stay here any longer. There are many local customers who come into the shop to insult me. They say things like: 'China tsamaya (get out of this country)!' (CTco34 2015).

Due to the circulation of such antagonistic local media reports, Chinese merchants are exposed to negative attitudes from local customers and are sometimes even insulted. This is not a side effect of quality issues of Chinese goods, but is mainly triggered by the tarnished image of China in Botswana.

> More and more customers come to complain, saying that Chinese goods are too expensive. I am angry when local people say: 'These are made in China. How can they be so expensive?' In the old days, people here would say: 'Hi Chinese, my friend', but now they say, 'mma China, fong kong' (Chinese merchant August 2015).

In particular, during the 2014 summer a power shortage greatly impacted people's daily lives. Many Chinese merchants were stressed and nervous once power shifts affected their shops. They believed that if the power station could not be fixed as soon as possible they would all be forced to return home since they could not renew their trading permits as local officials come to check their shop to pick fault frequently.

8.4.3. Taking Advantage

Suspicious attitudes and anger towards Chinese goods among the customers was overwhelming. In addition, there are also some customers who try to take advantage of the negative image of Chinese goods, as a Chinese merchant reported:

Local customers come to claim replacement goods. Some of them do not even remember in which shop they brought the goods. One day a local man bought boots in my shop and the next day he came with a pair of old boots of the same type, claiming replacement. I asked my local assistant to handle the case. She smelled the old boots (boots cannot deteriorate like that in one day!) and checked the size, she found that the boots were size 42 but the boots he bought the day before were size 41. Once she said the boots were not the same size, the man ran away. Even if I knew something was wrong, I would not be able to argue without the help of my local assistant. Years ago, local people would not come to claim at all, even if the shoes they had bought were broken in a week. If the shoe lasted for three months, they said it was a very good one (Interview with CTco116 September 2013).

Some local customers even use the power of local authorities to manipulate Chinese merchants into giving a replacement. During interviews with CTco107, the following case was observed in the shop:

One customer bought a suitcase from the shop and a local assistant helped him to set a code number for the lock and things went well. A few hours later the customer came back with the suitcase, angry, asking the local assistant to help him open the suitcase. The local assistant could not open the case and realised that the code she set together with the customer had been changed. The customer asked for replacement and the Chinese shop owner refused.

Customer: 'You should exchange it for me now! You open the case for me!'
CTco107: 'No! How can I open that for you? Only you know the code.'
Customer: 'You don't follow the law. You know who I am?' (showing his police licence)
CTco107: 'You changed the code. How can I help you?'
Customer: 'Close the shop!' (showing his licence)

(While they were quarrelling, another lady came in. It seemed that she knew the customer.)

Lady: 'You cannot treat customers like this. You shall provide good service so that the customer can come back again. Do you know who he is?'

Customer: 'You don't know the law in this country. I am the police here.'

(Local assistant managed to open the case)

Customer: (taking back the case) '... I am from Maun ...I will bring you fish next time ...' (and left the shop immediately)

(Observed at CTco107's shop 23 September 2014)

After the customer left, CTco107 stated: 'If you don't do what they (local customers) want, they will call the police. Policeman here always shows favouritism to local people.' Facing this kind of customer, Chinese merchants usually can only choose to lose some money and bear with it. They know that they are neither eloquent enough to quarrel with local customers nor have the patience to deal with them. Local customers who must survive with limited economic incomes often sense this vulnerability of Chinese merchants, and explore every possibility to benefit from the Chinese. Therefore, the interaction between Chinese merchants and local customers tends to be problematic, as one tries to maximise business profit and the other tries to increase the benefit they can receive from the China shops.

Some locals, who are sensitive to the business environment and the changes of local policy, look forward to gaining some benefit from Chinese businesses. According to CTco104's report, one day when she forbade a local person from taking a photo of her goods, the customer felt embarrassed and the following conversation ensued:

Customer: '(...) Chinese useless.'

CTco104: 'If you think us useless don't come to buy.'

Customer: 'I will come to buy.'

CTco104: 'In two years, we will all go back home (then you will have no place to buy).'

Customer: 'Then this shop will be mine!'

Since the local government initiated the Economic Diversification Drive (EDD) and Citizen Entrepreneurial Development Agency (CEDA), many local people looked forward to receiving benefits from this kind of policy. Some even wait for a windfall from China shops, as some local people believe that 'once the Chinese go back home, their shops are ours'. It was widely believed among local people that the Botswana government was trying to drive the Chinese away, to retain the local market for local people. However, some local people think that once the Chinese leave, the China shops and all the goods contained in them will be passed on. Therefore, it is clear that local people who are marginalised and, irrespective of economic and social status, expect to receive some benefits from the China shop business.

8.5. Solutions

8.5.1. Defense through Different Media

Functioning as the 'contact zone' between China and Africa, the China shop is the place that first receives rejection once there are any problems in China–Africa relations. The majority of the local people follow the reports of local media and the movements of the local government. Therefore, once there is a negative report regarding China or Chinese company in Botswana, Chinese merchants in China shops are usually the first to suffer the consequences. In 2005 the Chinese Embassy released a press release[3] as reproduced below to encourage more positive reporting because of its concerns about stories (Bolaane 2007, p. 167; Youngman 2013, p. 6);

> Targeting the Chinese people as a whole and their business operation in Botswana, which serve to mislead public opinion and even plant seeds of resentment towards the Chinese community in the mind of local people.

The majority of local people are aware of the differences between China shops and other Chinese companies, however, they tend to target the Chinese as a whole, particularly when they criticise the failure of construction projects operated by Chinese companies. Some Chinese merchants become speechless when facing local condemnation, and covertly join in blaming Chinese companies themselves. Other Chinese merchants argue with local people to protect Chinese companies in order to 'save face' for China, arguing that local construction companies even fare worse.

So far, there have been many negative comments concerning Chinese companies in Botswana. However, in 2015 the past BOCCIM[4] president Mr. Ebrahim wrote a public article (Ebrahim 2015 August 7) named 'Poor state of projects: Who is to blame?' to defend Chinese companies. He argues that the failure of the projects is the responsibility of both the Chinese construction companies and Botswana Government, thus it is not only the construction companies who should be taking the blame.

> Over the past few weeks there have been reports in the media of the negative comments made by Ministers targeting Foreign owned companies and other worrisome 'anti-business' comments. Leading the pack is the litany of complaints against some Chinese companies, particularly in the construction sector for their poor performance in executing some Government projects. Quite rightly we have reasons to complain after all they left behind unfinished projects, shoddy construction works and other failed projects that cost the nation greatly. But I am surprised that we are focusing so much anger and venom only against the construction companies.
>
> It is not only the construction companies who should be taking the blame, as the saying goes 'it takes two to tango'. Why are we not blaming those individuals and companies who oversaw the Government projects or even naming and shaming them.
>
> Has anyone been held responsible for their negligence in carrying out their duties in the oversight of these projects? Why blame only the construction companies without even looking at the failings of our 'employed' professionals who did not or failed to monitor those projects?

8.5.2. Responsibility of Chinese Media in Botswana

Oriental Post, the Chinese newspaper founded by a Chinese entrepreneur, tried to look for a solution for the Chinese community. During an interview at Oriental Post, a staff member emphasised the role of media:

As far as it is called media, we have to post the fact regardless it is good news or bad news. The media plays the role of a bridge, linking the Chinese community with local society. Concerning the case of Power Station, the Chinese government started to check the state owned Chinese company after we exposed the issue on the newspaper. Of course, our intention was not to get Chinese government and Chinese embassy to examine the company. However, the Chinese company tarnished our brand and caused all the Chinese in Botswana to 'lose face'…The company was unhappy with us, but it's the responsibility of the media.

In this case, the Chinese media in Botswana managed to fill the gaps between the Chinese community and the Chinese government. Oriental Post, as introduced in 4.5.2., was initiated to help Chinese merchants to catch up with local news and news concerning the Chinese living in Botswana. However, it also played a role as supervisor of the work of Chinese companies and helped to bridge the gap between the Chinese community and the Chinese government. The local population has a tendency to generalise the Chinese community as a whole, regardless of whether they are Chinese state-owned companies, Chinese private companies or Chinese merchants. Therefore, the social power of Chinese media is considered crucial when there are issues at stake for members of the Chinese community.

8.5.3. Strategy of Chinese Merchants

Facing growing hostility from local customers and further restriction of work permits, many Chinese merchants 'hid' themselves from the public view and became more willing to hire local people as managers of their shops. According to my conversation with Chinese merchants, there were three main reasons that led them to make the decision.

At first, the Chinese failed to obtain work permits to watch their shops. Since 2013 the local government has restricted the number of work permits issued to foreigners in the retail section. Therefore, many Chinese were not allowed to work as cashiers once their work permits expired. Some tried to extend them but the process usually took a long time. As a result, many Chinese had to train local assistants to work as cashiers. They themselves either sit in the storeroom to monitor the work of their assistants through security video cameras or only go to open and close the shops.

Secondly, local managers were considered to present a better image than Chinese owners for local managers are more qualified to deal with troublesome local customers.

Now many China shops let local assistants operate cash machines with the intention of improving business that way. ...

> When local people see Chinese people, they may say something insulting to the Chinese, so now I teach local assistants to tell the people who come to make trouble that the Chinese boss is not around (CTco1 2014).

Without language or cultural barriers, local assistants perform better as managers in the China shops. Many Chinese merchants hesitated to allow local assistants to watch the shops for them in the beginning, because they were concerned about theft issues. However, after they lost their permits to work in the shops, they were, to some extent, compelled to give managing positions to local people. As many of them commented:

> Local assistants steal to a greater or lesser extent, although we have put security cameras everywhere in the shop. As long as we do not lose too much, I will turn a blind eye to it.

Finally, Chinese merchants have more free time to deal with other issues. They also realise that their business of running retail shops may not last long, as the Botswana government has already enacted a local regulation stating that 'general clothing'[5] retail is reserved for Batswana local people only. Therefore, some of them have considered it as an opportunity for them to explore new markets and upgrade their businesses.

8.6. Discussion

The China–Botswana relationship has celebrated its 40th anniversary. Looking back, the relationship has benefited both sides despite the conflicts of recent years. Both governments tend to pay attention to the problems. Sometimes it is more important to find out how the problems arose and how they influenced the different layers of China–Botswana relations. Only by doing so can both sides advance to a higher level of cooperation.

This chapter investigated how the negative reputation of Chinese goods and Chinese construction work impacted the local market and the interactions between Chinese merchants and local customers regarding *fong kong* goods. The research found that the failures of mega-projects tarnished the China brand in Botswana. They not only caused the Botswana government to restrict cooperation with Chinese construction companies but also triggered a restriction on Chinese business overall in Botswana. However, on the other hand, it was linked to the promotion of local labour in Chinese businesses and to some extent encouraged Chinese merchants to look for business opportunities in other sections. This somehow at a macro level proves Park's (1950) theory that intergroup relations move in a natural cycle of competition, conflict and accommodation. After competition over limited job opportunities (between Chinese employees and local assistants), through the power of the local authority, Chinese merchants adjusted their business management from hiring Chinese employees to recruiting local assistants as managers in China shops, which to some extent achieved coexistence.

Local customers who have relied on *fong kong* goods due to their limited buying power and consumption habits hoped to gain an advantage from the China shops when Chinese representation departed. In a globalised society like Botswana, when marginalised citizens cannot beat inequality in the domestic market, their attention and anger tend to focus on strangers (Nyamnjoh 2006).

Therefore, they may try to take advantage of the Chinese in order to counterbalance their unfair treatment in the domestic society. The Botswana government restricted Chinese business while trying to cultivate a local entrepreneur culture. However, many local people mistakenly thought they would receive a windfall once the Chinese left. In this context, local media seems to play a role in increasing the tensions, particularly in regard to mega-construction projects.

We usually distinguish Chinese investment in Botswana as small business versus mega-projects, or private petty trading run by individual Chinese merchants versus government investments, however, they all work together to build the 'image of China'. Herbert Blumer's (1958, p. 5) position theory states that the shaping process of group definition is both at individual level and group level. Through the analysis in this chapter, it is obvious to conclude that the failure of mega-projects played a role as a 'big event' that expresses the negative abstract image of the Chinese and China in Botswana through the circulation of local media. On the other hand, we find the Chinese community also realised the importance of media to seek justice and save the image of China in Botswana. However, regardless of the attack by local media, China shop businesses' managing to survive in the stressful business environment was thanks to the local connections and relationships they have accumulated through years of business experience. In this sense, although the judgement of the abstract image of China was great, we cannot ignore the rooted individual level connections between Chinese merchants and local people.

Petty trading is sometimes neglected as the traders are considered as failing to impact the local economy, as if they only introduce *fong kong* goods to Africa. However, this research indicates a new facet of the story: mega-projects are influential while at the same time risky. The results of mega-projects impact directly on diplomatic relations and also petty trading that has the most interactions with the local community. China shops, however, play a lens role as they receive the most obvious and immediate responses from the local community concerning local opinions towards Chinese investment in Botswana in general. Furthermore, China shops also function as a cushion to absorb local criticism of the entire China.

Notes

[1] Most of the quotations are cited from Mmegionline as it is one of the most accessible online media in Botswana.

[2] One of the largest cities in Botswana.

[3] Economic and Trade Cooperation between China and Botswana (Issued by the Chinese Embassy on 7 July 2005)
http://bw.chineseembassy.org/eng/sgxx/News/P0200509287849606268
68.pdf#search='argeting+the+Chinese+people+as+a+whole+and+their
+business+operation+in+Botswana.

[4] BOCCIM: Botswana Confederation of Commerce Industry and Manpower.

[5] Details have been explained in 4.3.3.

Chapter 9

Movement of Chinese Merchants

The Chinese who have earned money have already left. I think many Chinese will be leaving in two years. – Chinese merchant
Business is like a fortress besieged: those who are outside want to get in, and those who are inside want to get out[1]. – Chinese merchant
The most painful thing for us is seeing the next generation running the same business as we do. – Chinese merchant

This chapter highlights the mobility of Chinese merchants with a bird's-eye view of the development of the China shop business in Botswana. It uses interview data to describe the geographical expansion process of China shops and how China shops grew into the unauthorized 'nation brand' of China in Botswana. This chapter also tries to provide some insights of the struggle that many Chinese merchants experience when facing the issues of going back to China.

9.1. A Snapshot History of China Shops

As discussed in the previous chapters, Chinese merchants were once welcomed by the Batswana and the government. However, recently Chinese merchants seem to have overstayed their welcome. The following table sets out the timeline of the development of China shops and the change of the local attitude towards China shops. Table 4 has been drawn up from interview data gathered from pioneer Chinese merchants.

9.1.1. Embryo

In the 1990s and the very beginning of 2000s, there were very few Chinese merchants in Gaborone. CTco55 stated her early business experience in Gaborone as below:

I sold goods at the free market at BBS shopping mall[2] on weekends from morning to evening; and on weekdays I walked here and there in the city to source goods from those Chinese traders who shipped the goods from China (early stage of wholesalers). In those days I pulled a cart to carry the goods to the market. There were some other Chinese selling Chinese merchandise in the market too (CTco55 2014).

These days in BBS shopping mall, only some local traders are selling second hand clothes and shoes at the free market. All of the Chinese merchants at BBS shopping mall have their own shops now. However, it was said in the old days that the shops were not allowed to be rented to foreigners.

Table 4. The Development and Transition of China Shop Business in Botswana

Time	Development of China shops	Number of Chinese & China shops	Attitude of local government & local people
Starting ~2002	Street stalls set up at shopping malls and rural towns	Around 10 stalls in capital city	• Welcomed Chinese investment • 'Hi, my Chinese friend'
Spreading 2002~2008	• Shops opened in shopping malls • Shop chains developed around the country	Increased and spent in cities and towns	• Encouraged Chinese investment (construction and industry) • Welcomed Chinese and Chinese goods due to their needs
Saturating 2009~2013	• Sought loophole (sold replica; evaded tax) to survive	Around 700–1,000 shops in the country	• Restricted Chinese business and supported local people run business • Started to consider Chinese as rival; negative attitudes increased
Struggling 2013.Feb~ Aug	• Shops handed over to local assistants to manage • Looked for market in other towns (countries)	• No big change in shop numbers, • Number of Chinese decreased	• Stopped extending working permits for Chinese merchants • Looked down on Chinese merchants and China shops
Abandoning 2013.Aug~ 2015.Oct	• Majority were struggling • Very few opened new shops	• Fewer shops • Fewer Chinese merchants	• Fewer working permits were issued • Negative attitude towards China shops increased

9.1.2. Boom

After Chinese merchants were allowed to open shops there was a big boom in China shop businesses and the number of China shop grew rapidly. To avoid competition with other Chinese merchants, some Chinese expanded their businesses from cities to towns. Although at that time, life in the cities was far more convenient than that in the towns, some Chinese sacrificed their quality of life and moved to towns. According to the Chinese employers and employees interviewed during the research, there are both benefits and challenges to run businesses in rural towns.

Concerning the benefits, the profit is higher in rural towns than in cities due to less competition and as one employer stated: 'We try to make a profit by setting higher price in the towns, because customers are fewer compared to cities and transportation costs more' (CTce111 2011). Hanisch (2013, p. 92) who conducted her research in Lesotho also finds that smaller towns and villages are an attractive destination for foreign migrants because the advantages of having fewer competitors outweigh the disadvantages of long-distance supply chains and a smaller customer base. Secondly, regulation is reported to be less strict than in cities. Also due to the limited population, it seems easier to establish a good relationship with local authorities; as another employer said: 'Policemen here know me, and they don't come to check us very often' (CTco112 2013). Sometimes, even the relationship with local assistants is easier to deal with in the rural areas. 'My local assistant has worked at my shop for six years. She does not steal and very helpful to our business. I give Chinese food to her. Even when we cook Chinese buns, we share with her' (CTco116 2013). Thirdly, the shops in the rural towns can be used as a place to sell unpopular clothes. Some Chinese who have chain shops in cities usually ship the goods that failed to meet the fashion demands to rural chain shops (CTce58 2012; CTce59 2012).

On the other hand, negative comments also exist. The most complaints gathered from the Chinese merchants in rural towns are the dullness and isolated lifestyle in the rural areas as the following comments reveal (CTce109 2013; CTce111 2013; CTce113 2013; CTco121 2013; CTce122 2013):

We become dull here, and cannot catch up on any other business in other areas.

We don't socialise with local people or white people, since we don't speak English very well. When the Chinese construction company team was here, I sometimes socialised with them.

Since coming to the shop I have had nobody to talk to, which is very unhealthy ... I really want to learn about local culture and attend a local wedding to see their lives.

I live in a Chinese yard shared with three other Chinese families ... I watch TV and chat with family via *Wechat* at night.

Through these comments, it is not difficult to discover that Chinese people who open shops in rural areas live a more isolated life compared to the ones running businesses in cities. Although they yearn to join in the activities held by Batswana people and would like to know more about the local culture, language and culture barriers, coupled with a busy schedule, hinders their communication with local people and limits interaction to business relations alone.

Moving shops appears to be beneficial to the survival of the business, but it also has a side effect that distracts Chinese merchants from analysing potential problems in their business management and themselves for future improvement. As we explained in the previous chapters, the Botswana government encourages Chinese merchants to invest in industrial and technological fields while opening China shops in rural areas is not actually encouraged. The business environment in rural areas may be more profitable for China shops due to local needs for Chinese goods. However, in the long run, China shops may lose dominance when the market is saturated or living standards are raised.

The China shop is the easiest business for Chinese people to start in Africa, which explains why so many China shops have been opened. Benefiting from many relative connections, an urgent need of cheap merchandise in the market and a manufacturing resource back in China, it has been comparatively easy for Chinese people to open China shops in Africa. However, when the local market becomes gradually saturated, the majority of the Chinese merchants fail to move their businesses to other areas, or develop their small business into medium size or invest in industry.

9.1.3. Greener Land

The mobility of Chinese merchants is not limited in Botswana. Some Chinese merchants moved their businesses to neighbouring countries (Namibia and Zambia) when regulations got more restrictive in Botswana. In this kind of movement, a wide range of family connections are often used, not to mention blood relatives, particularly among the Fujianese who come to Botswana through family connections. Some Chinese merchants even use tourist visas to visit neighbouring countries to do market research. According to the interview research conducted in 2014 in Namibia, when Botswana restricted working permits to the Chinese in 2013 at least six families of Chinese merchants moved from Botswana to Namibia in the same year. Besides, some Chinese merchants in Namibia mentioned their plan to move to Mozambique, because their relatives there told them that the business environment in Mozambique was better. *Wechat*, a social network frequently used by the Chinese, has enabled many Chinese merchants to keep a close link with extended family and exchange business information.

Rural towns by the country's borders could be a sheltered harbour for businesses as well. I visited the border town, Katima Mulilo (Figure 16) in Namibia, which is very near Botswana and Zambia. Although the town is small, there were around 40 China shops in 2014. Some of the Chinese merchants moved there from the Botswana side, others moved from Oshikango, a border town between Namibia and Angola. Many Chinese merchants were in Oshikango and made the small town one of the biggest trading towns in Namibia (Dobler 2009). The town is named 'Dragon City' because of the large Chinese population and the impact of Chinese business. In Katima Mulilo, the Chinese merchants benefit from a looser regulation, plenty of customers from neighbouring countries (Zambia and Zimbabwe)[3] and some extra income through exchanging currency. Listed below are some voices of Chinese merchants in Katima Mulilo about the business opportunities they have:

Many customers, tourists come to exchange currency.

Working permit policy is very strict in Gaborone, but we do not receive much influence.

We have customers from Zambia and Zimbabwe. However, now it becomes difficult for Zimbabweans to come, because the government issues limited permits for crossing border.

When business is not good in Botswana, we rely on customers from neighbouring countries.

We were the first to open a shop here, but now we have many rivals. Some other Chinese also find this town as a good place to develop.

Market saturation, business competition, government restriction and family chains seem unrelated at first glance, but these are the factors that quietly drive the geographic expansion of China shops. It is the expansion of the China shops that creates the impression of the presence of China in Botswana, particularly in rural areas.

Figure 16. Rural Towns in Botswana and Namibia

9.1.4. *Eggs in Various Baskets*

Chinese merchants invest their finances and energy in various areas in order to reduce the financial risk. Some Chinese merchants invest their money in real estate in China. After decorating their house, they usually rent it so that they can get some benefit even when they are not home. There are also some Chinese people who invest in the stock market back in China:

> I watch stock every weekday before going to open my shop. Playing the stock market is a national game in China[4], and it is a legal gamble (CTco104 2015).

Putting money in the bank would be the last choice for these merchants. They believe that money in the bank gradually devalues and therefore they have to invest the money somewhere else. With the internet and *Wechat* the Chinese merchants have easy access to the stock market information back in China.

Education is another area in which many Chinese invest. They send teenage children to international schools to get an English education and then send them to universities in the US, UK, South Africa, etc. As long as their children would like to study, I think no Chinese parents would be reluctant to pay tuition fees. Some Chinese merchants whose children were studying in the US and UK, expressed much satisfaction and hope. Their feelings can be summarised according to what one Chinese lady said:

> I suffered bitterly for decades in Botswana, but when I look at my children I know my hard work paid off. My daughter is studying at a top university in the US and she had a job offer from a US company. I am very happy for her. …. One of my friends in wholesale spent a lot of money to send his son to a European university. However, the son could not get a job after graduation, and a few days ago I saw he was helping the family with their business in the wholesale store. You know, the most painful thing for us is seeing the next generation running the same business as we do (CTco22 2015).

In 2015, a story of a pioneer Chinese merchant couple's returning back to China has been circulated widely among Chinese merchants. The merchant couple managed to invest in some real estate in China with the capital they accumulated over many years of doing business in Botswana. Furthermore, their daughter after being educated in the West has already got a good position in a big bank in China. I observed many young and middle-aged merchants expressing their admiration when they shared the story with me. After sharing the story, they usually added: 'How many more years shall I wait?' What is considered as a 'happy end' to migration life for Chinese merchants in Botswana? The answers may vary. However, I guess having enough money to spend for the rest of one's life and raising a next generation to be proud of is the dream of the majority.

9.1.5. Stay or Leave

Staying or going back is always a difficult choice for Chinese merchants overseas. However, behind their choices there are calculations and discussions, expectations and struggles. In my field research in 2014, I was told that many Chinese merchants had already gone back to China, and even the ones who were still in Botswana were considering going back. Listed below are some voices from the Chinese who were considering going back home:

> Although my husband and I have been here for 10 years, this time they only issued a work permit to me, but my husband's application was rejected. Now he is in China, I have to visit him every half year. The permit system here is ridiculous (CTco181 2015).

> Pula to RMB rate is very bad for our business. Local people's attitudes towards us have been getting worse in recent years. I kill time in the shop every day. Once my daughter graduates and has a job I will go back (CTco43 2012).

Chinese merchants reside in Botswana mostly for business purposes, with little inclination for immigration and their business plans tend to be short term due to the restrictions of regulations and falling profit margins. The worsening of security in Botswana and unfriendly local attitude pressurise Chinese merchants to go back to China. According to interviews, even some pioneer Chinese merchants who have obtained Botswana citizenship are thinking of going back to China, considering that their citizenship can only benefit their current business but not their life plans.

In spite of its small number, it is still worth mentioning that there are also some Chinese merchants who once went back to China, but after business failure they decided to come back to Botswana again. Despite the decreasing profit margin in Botswana, to a person who has neither skills nor a diploma, opening a China shop may be the most ideal means to survive.

There are also a few Chinese who genuinely like Botswana and enjoy their lives there. CTco130 has been in Botswana for more than one decade. He married a Motswana woman and has two children. He told me that he could speak neither English nor Setswana when he just came to Botswana, but later he managed to talk to local people in Setswana and even made some friends in the local government. His business goes smoothly and he manages to help other Chinese merchants with their business. Chinese pioneer CEco156 has been in Botswana for almost two decades. Besides running business, he is very passionate about investing in newspapers and charity. He initiated the Oriental Post, the first and only newspaper published in Chinese in Botswana, which helps countless Chinese merchants to catch up with the local news and market information. He also set up a slogan 'in Botswana for Botswana' to encourage Chinese merchants to donate money and goods to orphanages and needy people in Botswana.

Even among Chinese merchants who arrived recently, some have committed their near future to Botswana despite the competitive environment. 'We have been running shops for years and know the local situation very well. The China shop is only our first step, now we try to start in industry. There are still many opportunities that haven't been explored. Compared to China, establishing a business here is easier' (CTcof 39 2015). There are also some Chinese merchants who love the quiet environment, nature, food and simple social life in Botswana, as the comments below show:

> Botswana has the best beef in the world, and it is much cheaper than that in China.

> I love the simple lifestyle here. Local people sometimes make me angry but most of them are kind and forgiving with pure hearts. Every time I go back to China I feel tired of the complicated social life and tense interpersonal relations.

When Botswana was chosen as the number one place for tourists to visit in 2015, the Chinese in Botswana were very excited about it. Almost every one of them posted the online news on their *Wechat* page. It is also interesting to me that at evening football games, Chinese merchants are big supporters of the Botswana national football team, the Zebras. Most Chinese merchants have an attachment to Botswana after living and running businesses there, although they complain about it sometimes. As many Chinese merchants would say, 'Although we blame them, we still appreciate them.'[5]

9.2. Business Upgrading

The Chinese Embassy considers the long term goal of Chinese merchants in Botswana should be in investment and not trade. At my interview with the China Embassy in Botswana, a Chinese officer told me:

> The China shops do improve local economy but haven't been a big contribution. China shop in rural areas may still provide some help to local people, however, in cities local people expect 'high-end, elegant, and classy'[6] things. The Chinese Embassy has been encouraging Chinese merchants to shift their business to other sections. Some Chinese merchants have changed their business from clothes to car parts and furniture (China Embassy September 2014).

Most of the Chinese merchants attribute the reasons to their failure in business upgrading as below: first, with a low education background, some Chinese people can only handle China shop businesses that require few language or special skills. Secondly, due to the water shortage in Botswana, farming and establishing industries are regarded as difficult by many Chinese. Thirdly, the majority of the Chinese do not believe that the Batswana can be effective factory workers and therefore hesitate to open factories. Fourthly, many Chinese communicate poorly with local people, and thus do not have information on directions for investment. Finally, many Chinese people consider Botswana's trading policy towards foreigners as volatile; therefore they do not dare to invest too much money in the country.

However, the Chinese Embassy does not completely agree with the opinions of the merchants concerning the challenges of upgrading their business portfolios. During my interview in the Chinese Embassy an officer said:

> The business environment in Botswana is very good. However, the majority of the Chinese are still in the early stages of accumulating capital investment in their entrepreneurships. Some of them do not know the local language or culture very well and have a comparatively weak sense of localisation. Some problems are encountered with the local government concerning their execution of the issued policies; however, to a certain extent the investment environment here is even better than in China (Chinese Embassy September 2014).

There have been expectations through the years that Chinese business networks can be important catalysts for Africa local industrialisation (Bräutigam 2003). Facing an increasingly competitive trading market, many Chinese merchants also started to look for new business. Particularly, since 2010 the Botswana government has restricted trading permits (for details see 4.3.3). Investing in industry or manufacturing has a higher possibility of obtaining long-term business permits. For some young merchants, seeking development opportunities in Botswana is more practical than going back to China after years of business experience in

Africa. I would like to introduce one the few cases that successfully upgraded from trading to industry:

A young couple CTco38 and CTcof 39 went to Botswana in 2004 and 2007. After watching shops for their relatives for several years, they opened their own shop after marriage. With years of business experience in Botswana, their shop was well managed. Since 2013 the Botswana government has been restricting trading business. And the couple tried several ways to seek new business opportunities. CTco38 took a trip to neighbouring countries to research the market and also went back to China several times to look for opportunities. Finally in March 2016, they opened a factory for making XX.[7] After years of living in Botswana they realised there is an XX shortage in Gaborone, and considering making XX could be a good business for future. They imported all the equipment from China and learned the skills for making XX and managing marketing and finance by themselves. They have already managed to penetrate the local market with their product. Meanwhile, they still have their China shop open, and have had to work on both sides of the business so far, as they are not sure how far they can go. CTcof 39 once told me: 'It's a totally new business from running a shop; we have so many things to learn. We have to manage everything by ourselves. We need encouragement.'

Many Chinese merchants wish to invest in industry or manufactory, however, the majority are still complaining about the deteriorated business situation while running the same shop year after year. What is hindering them to step out and make a try?

During my field research, I realised that the impediments were: first, short-term business vision that hinders Chinese merchants from moving forward; secondly, the ground level interactions in trading business; and thirdly, the unstable business environment in Botswana. At a micro-level, Chinese merchants spend much time in interaction with their local assistants, local customers and local authorities in the course of their daily business. Those are the people that help them to know Botswana society and culture. That bit of experience at a local level discourages the merchants from staying longer. For instance, many Chinese merchants through years of experience still have not managed to organise their local assistants or had such bad experiences with their assistants that they would never like to own a factory and handle more local labour. On the other hand, bribery, theft and labour relations are issues that almost every Chinese merchant experiences. How they experience their daily interaction with locals to a great degree determines whether they would like to move forward.

Besides, the reasons discussed above, microeconomic policy also contributes to the decision making of Chinese merchants, and this will be discussed in the coming section.

9.3. Vicious Circles

Most Chinese merchants come to Botswana for business, and few intend to settle there forever, despite their attachment to Botswana after years of living and business experience. Consequently, obtaining citizenship is considered nothing more than a business strategy (there are special cases). Therefore, their business strategies have a short-term pattern as they try to keep investment low while maximising profits. Such short-term business plans can be linked to their limited interest in developing language skills, their frugal life style and even their habit of paying the minimum salary to local employees. Furthermore, such motives could direct Chinese merchants to seek loopholes in regulations, extend business hours and even spread shops around the country (Haugen and Carling 2005). Thus, frictions at different levels become apparent in the development of Chinese businesses. Although the Botswana government issued more and more restrictions to control Chinese business, the results did not turn out as expected. Such regulations to some extent cornered Chinese businesses and created an unstable business environment rather than directing them towards a better business model. As seen in the vicious circle (Figure 17), the reasons for frictions are rooted in the short-term vision of Chinese merchants, and government regulations only reinforce such an investment vision, failing to reduce frictions.

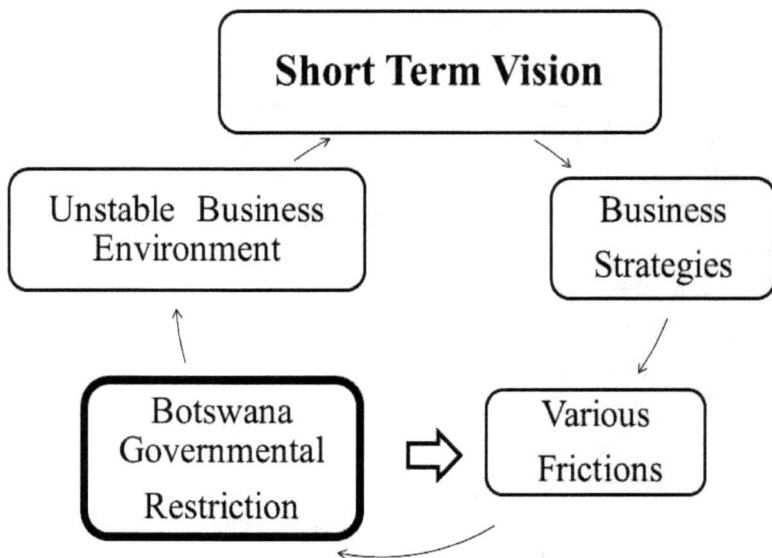

Figure 17. Vicious Circle

The regulations that China shops encounter are not only because of the misbehaviour of China shop business owners, but to some extent China shops are also treated as a scapegoat. In 2013 a Chinese company failed to deliver the power station project in Palapye (for details see Chapter 8). The power shortage influenced the whole country. In those days, many Chinese merchants experienced insults and blame, and during that time the renewing of work permits was the strictest in 'history'. Concerning the negative influence on the China shop business and the uncertain business climate that has been created in Botswana Ebrahim (7 August 2015) stated:

> Now we are talking of closing Chinese shops, after granting them trading licences. What law are we going to use to do that? Very easy, we use tactics like refusing to renew their permits, cancel and withdraw them, or even as is now happening, approve the husband's permit and reject the wife's, or vice versa.
>
> Delay the renewals, I know some who are waiting for over seven months, they have to make the monthly trek to Immigration for a 30 day extension! The effects of rejection and cancellation of permits is

so widespread countrywide that many investors are now thinking of relocating to options elsewhere …

Do we realise that China is now a major player in the world economy? They are part of the grouping called BRICS, (Brazil, Russia, India, China and South Africa). They are regarding to launch a Development Bank like the IMF and World Bank. Should we need development funds in the future will we be comfortable to go begging because of our 'soured' relations with China, a major contributor to this bank? With these anti-foreigner sentiments being expressed against foreign owned businesses we are unwittingly sowing the seeds and beginning to fan the flames of xenophobia and racism. Today it is them, which nationality is next in line? …

What we don't realise is that in the business world when you create uncertainty in the business climate you create a domino effect. This effect ripples throughout the business community as they begin to question their future investments going forward. There is a marked deterioration in business confidence right now and this can translate into negative economic growth. …

Today we are fortunate to have diamonds to drive our economy, but remember that tomorrow, when they are gone, we will have no economy to drive us.

The article is considered to be in defence of Chinese construction companies and merchants in Botswana. Of course, the article does not represent the opinion of all people in Botswana. However, to a great extent, it again emphasised that in a supportive policy environment Asian business networks can be important catalysts for local industrialisation in sub-Saharan Africa, as they were in South-east Asia (Bräutigam 2003, p. 467). On the other hand, we can say that the short-term vision of Chinese merchants is a part of their life plan on running businesses in Africa. The uncertain business climate and the flames of xenophobia and racism are the hidden factors that drive the majority of Chinese merchants in Botswana to make the decision to be a foreign retail entrepreneur forever.

Therefore, daily micro-level interactions and microeconomic policy have a great impact on the decision-making process of

Chinese merchants concerning their investment vision. Since long-term commitment is required for Chinese merchants to invest in industry, helping Chinese merchants to get embedded in Botswana society not only impacts on short-term trading relations but also may contribute to potential industrial development.

9.4. Summary

China shops have been in Botswana for more than 20 years. In different stages of development, there are variations in the circumstances of Chinese merchants, local perceptions and attitudes of the local government. Despite the deteriorating business situation, there are still some newcomers to Botswana who seek business opportunities. Knowing the market in Botswana is too saturated, the newcomers still want to get on the bandwagon; on the other hand, the early comers are either looking forward to going back home to China or looking for new business opportunities in neighbouring African countries.

The short-term investment vision of Chinese merchants could be the factor that causes friction in employment and trade relations. Their vision has influenced business strategies, resulting in a growing bad reputation in recent years. While local governments have enacted regulations to direct and control Chinese businesses, such regulations have created an unstable business environment, consequently reinforcing short-term investment plans. Therefore, in order to encourage the Chinese to invest in industry, both the local government and the Chinese Embassy should first create a stable investment environment and help Chinese merchants to get embedded in local society.

Notes

[1] Originally comes from a famous quotation in a Chinese novel Fortress Besieged: 'Marriage is like a fortress besieged: those who are outside want to get in, and those who are inside want to get out'.

[2] A shopping mall in Gaborone.

[3] I was told that Chinese merchandise was more expensive in Zambia and Zimbabwe than that in Katima Mulilo. There were no China shops in Zimbabwe so many local people sourced Chinese merchandise and ran businesses by themselves.

[4] In Chinese they say: 全民炒股

[5] Original statement: 骂归骂，待了这么多年还是有感情的。

[6] Original statement: 高大上, 高端大气上档次

[7] Since their business is still in the early stage, I decided not to share their business secret.

Chapter 10

Conclusion:
What Next for China–Africa Relations

This chapter presents a summary of the research, findings and conclusions. It begins by summarising the problem and the research questions. It then highlights the main findings of the research and the conclusions drawn from them. This is followed by a comprehensive discussion of the study on the theory and China–Botswana relations. The chapter concludes by suggesting implications of the findings for further research based on the findings.

10.1. Summary of the Research Problem and Study Questions

This book examined how the interactions between Chinese merchants and Batswana people that they meet in the China shops shape the image of China in Botswana, by focusing on the micro-level relations between Chinese merchants and the local customers, local assistants as well as local authorities who represent the local government in the regulation of the legitimacy and management of shops.

The research questions that were examined are:

1. What are the experiences of Chinese merchants when they move to and live in Botswana?

2. What challenges are encountered by Chinese merchants in Botswana? What strategies do they put in place to combat the challenges?

3. How do Chinese merchants interact with the local customers, local employees and local authorities? How does the social interaction with local people shape quality (*suzhi*) of Chinese merchants as well as the quality of Chinese merchandise?

10.2. Summary of the Main Findings of the Study

The key findings of the study are presented below in line with the three research questions examined in this research.

1. What are the experiences of Chinese merchants as they move to and live in Botswana?

Many Chinese merchants started businesses in market stalls. They later built up China shops and Chinese wholesale markets in Botswana. The qualitative findings reveal that Chinese merchants who go to Botswana usually have poor English ability. The majority are Fujianese with a low economic family background; their status as foreign merchants makes them vulnerable to isolation from the local society. The research acknowledges that the experience of Chinese merchants in moving to and living in Botswana closely relates to the business challenges they face in their daily business operations. The majority of the Chinese merchants in this research have come to Botswana through family chains. There are apparent differences between 'early comer' merchants and 'newcomer' merchants relating to their migrant experience, current status and migration plan.

2. What challenges are encountered by Chinese merchants in Botswana? What strategies do they put in place to combat the challenges?

Chinese merchants' daily lives are characterised by an isolated lifestyle and a strong ethnic cohesion. Due to the rapidly increasing number of Chinese merchants and China shops, local markets have become somewhat saturated. Chinese merchants (whether wholesalers or retailers) play a role as middleman minority entrepreneurs (Bonacich 1973). Their characteristics such as 'intending to return to their origin', 'aiming to profit quickly' and 'serving subordinate and ethnic groups' reinforce their status as outsiders. These tendencies have become increasingly clear in the course of Botswana's development. The position of the Chinese as middlemen leads to a feeling of vulnerability, of being judged negatively by the local people and of being unwelcome. The twin handicaps of the language barrier and lack of knowledge of the local law means that Chinese merchants are not in a strategic position to protect their rights. Chinese businesses are limited by local regulations, and merchants experience rejection by local assistants and customers, as well as hostility from the local authorities.

To survive in a highly competitive market and ease local hostility, Chinese merchants have adopted a number of business strategies, according to their experience and financial situation. Those Chinese who have been in Botswana for long time have sufficient language ability and business experience to act more effectively than newcomers. However, when confronted by tightening regulations, neither the early comers nor the newcomers are keen to continue doing business in Gaborone. Since even the majority of the early comers are still at the stage of accumulating capital, they see their best option as seeking out a niche market or transferring to a more promising locality.

Chinese merchants' self-isolation and feelings of vulnerability influence their attitudes towards local people and direct their decision making in business, along with their responses to rejection and hostility from the host society. Furthermore, the self-isolation and feelings of vulnerability are deeply rooted in their social position as middleman minority entrepreneurs serving a subordinate group and ethnic groups (e.g. Indians, Chinese, Zimbabweans, etc.). Consequently, they feel disrespected and betrayed by local people because they feel no obligation to help the locals as the merchants are driven more or less by self-interest. Despite these difficult circumstances, Chinese merchants remain in the country for profit and potential opportunities. Moreover, Botswana's appeal is augmented by its unique geographical position between three potential markets in neighbouring countries further away. At the same time, those who succeed, make charitable donations for the benefit of local people as evidence of a social responsibility that, to a certain extent, repairs their relationship with local society.

3. How do Chinese merchants interact with the local customers, local employees and local authorities? How does the social interaction with local people shape the quality of Chinese merchandise as well as quality (suzhi) of Chinese merchants?

Influenced by the frequent media interest in the issue of *fong kong* goods in Botswana and related governmental regulation, people tend to concentrate attention on the pushing power of China while ignoring the pulling factors in Botswana society. It has been puzzling to observers that, despite the tightening of regulations in Botswana, *fong kong* goods have continued to hold their share of the market over the years. Field research has shown that *fong kong* goods do not negatively influence the local textile industry or local retailers, as had been assumed in the past (Zi 2014). Surprisingly, their contribution is not limited to meeting the demands of local customers at different income levels, but also creates benefits for local merchants and street vendors. Although they are widely criticised, and have to some extent damaged China's reputation, *fong kong* goods are still useful to Botswana society. However, the bad reputation of *fong kong* is deeply rooted in local people's minds and memory despite the improvement in quality through the years. Once the image of China in Botswana is attacked, local people recall their negative thoughts towards *fong kong* and try to take advantage of Chinese business with a xenophobic attitude. Due to its ambiguous position, the government faces the challenge of striking a balance between complying with public complaints as well as outside pressures and enhancing the advantages gained by local vendors and low-income consumers. Ultimately, the government employs delay tactics, putting China shops under stricter regulatory control when necessary whilst training its own entrepreneurs to compete more effectively in the future with Chinese businesses. This tactic helps the government to control the number and scale of Chinese businesses, whilst balancing the push and pull powers.

Regarding the employer–employee relations between Chinese merchants and Batswana employees, I investigated the background of Chinese merchants and Batswana employees as well as the recruitment process in China shops. Neither Chinese employers nor Batswana employees have a high social status in the local community: foreigners and low-income groups who are threatened by unemployment. Due to culture and language barriers, there is little mutual respect in daily interactions between Chinese employers and Batswana employees. Batswana employees' poor work ethics are often cited by Chinese merchants as 'laziness', 'no commitment to work' and 'betrayal,' while Chinese employers' frugality and prudence are seen as exploitative and incredulous. The difference in work ethics has been the biggest barrier for the Chinese and Batswana to build trust (Lee 2009; Giese and Thiel 2014) and business partnerships. Furthermore, similar to the findings of Codrin (2014), the Chinese employers in the study seem to lack interest in how local systems of meaning unfold and are expressed on a daily basis in local culture. They do not speak the indigenous language and have a very limited understanding of local manners and 'proper' social interactions; they are engaged in unacceptable practices, such as verbal and physical abuse (ibid., p. 155). The findings are common in cross-culture businesses, and are not necessarily due to racial issues. However, racial comments are frequently released by Chinese merchants in a bid to release their stressful and puzzling emotions. The Chinese's lack of interest in local culture and language may be rooted in their short-term business vision which is strengthened by the restrictive local regulations.

The interactions between Chinese merchants and local authorities mostly involve the contents of 'Chinese bashing' – Chinese merchants either have issues with local customers or are being reported by local assistants. The authorities go to China shops either to regulate the management of China shops or to respond to the complaints by the local customers or local assistants concerning their relations with Chinese merchants. Chinese merchants believe that local authorities tend to pick fault so as to benefit from the Chinese; the police are unable to catch thieves while always showing partiality towards the local people. The negative bias by the local authorities not only leads Chinese people to be mute when facing trouble or even unfair judgement, but also pushes them to escape the checks of the local authorities and use bribes as a short cut. On the other hand, the local authorities see the Chinese as canny merchants who exploit local people only to enrich themselves. This results in a bad reputation for the Chinese community and hinders the building of trust between China and Botswana traders at large. However, Chinese merchants somehow find a way to achieve coexistence by hiring local people as managers of their shops. This was a compromise after the failure of mega-projects, because the local government further restricted the trading permits issued to Chinese. This proves the theory initiated by Park (1950) that intergroup relations are like a natural cycle of competition, conflict and accommodation.

Fong kong goods, regardless of their character as factory leftovers, counterfeit or novelties, are imported to meet the needs and buying power of Botswana local people. Therefore, the quality of Chinese merchandise in Botswana is shaped and negotiated through the daily interactions between Chinese merchants and local customers in commercial activities. There have been many quarrels concerning quality issues of Chinese merchandise. However, quality itself seems not always be the centre of the conflicts. In the beginning, Chinese merchants offered the worst quality while receiving the best welcome; on the other hand, when the quality was greatly improved just before the failure of mega-projects, Chinese merchandise received the most doubt and criticism. Through several decades of business in Botswana, Chinese merchants have not managed to build a solid local trust, which may be due to their short-term business vision and China's lack of a strong national brand originally.

Suzhi (quality) of Chinese merchants has also been sharpened through their daily contact with local people. 'Suzhi' in the Chinese context usually refers to discipline, honesty, industriousness and skill etc. Through social interaction with local people, their discipline and skills have been obviously improved. Concerning discipline, they pay more attention to their appearance and manner when they were in their shops. They even learned the correct way to talk to local customers and local assistants to share their hospitality and respect respectively. Furthermore, their language skills and understanding of local culture, including taboos and customs also improved through business practice, which helps them to be more localised and embedded in local society. Social interaction in the China shops can also be considered as a learning process for Chinese merchants to be seasoned in a cross-culture environment.

10.3. The Roles of Chinese Merchants, Chinese Merchandise and China Shops

For a long time, people who arrived from Europe and India played a crucial role in Botswana's economy (Best 1970, p. 601). Before the arrival of Chinese retailers in Botswana, shops and stores were mainly concentrated in urban areas selling items which were priced above what most people could afford. According to Bolaane (2007, p. 164), China shops have brought convenience to consumers, particularly those in remote areas, and they play a role in curbing prices. China shops have been helping to alleviate local poverty not only by providing affordable Chinese goods but also by providing job opportunities. Although the jobs offered by China shops have not been well appreciated by the locals through the years due to their limited skill transformation opportunities and 'low salaries' they have contributed to local unemployment reduction in one way or another. Due to the high unemployment rate in Botswana, particularly youth unemployment, jobs in China shops have been sought by young females as a temporary stop on the way to finding an ideal job or returning back to school.

Besides these obvious impacts, China shops have also motivated local people to initiate their own businesses. Chinese merchants have established a supply chain for distributing Chinese goods, which provides Botswana's local merchants with many business ideas. In recent years, there have been more and more local merchants travelling to China as 'suitcase traders'. Mathews (2011) argues that this represents low-end globalisation, a globalisation brought about by individual traders carrying goods in their suitcases back and forth from their home countries. As Mathews and Yang (2012, p. 95) argue: 'one essential economic role China plays today is in manufacturing the cheap, sometimes counterfeit, goods that enable Africa and other developing-world regions to experience globalization; the African traders who come to China help make this possible.' Furthermore, several pioneer Chinese merchants attempt to establish manufacturing industries after spending a number of years obtaining trading experience and resources. Therefore, it is likely that Chinese 'shopkeepers-turned-entrepreneurs' may contribute to the establishment of local industry and manufacturing in the near future.

Despite the benefits brought to Botswana through China shops and Chinese merchants in recent years, the local perception towards them has been generally negative. Regarding the reason for the negative perception, three objective and subjective reasons will be discussed respectively. From an objective perspective, first, due to the increasing South African big chain stores and development of transportation since the last decade, the craving for Chinese goods has decreased, which means that the perceived benefit of having China shops to the local society is not as evident as it once was. Second, the competition that is created by a saturated local market (Haugen and Carling 2005) leads the merchants to apply strategies for survival, which give them a bad reputation. Third, the local government's intention to reduce import and empower the local entrepreneurs makes rivals of the Chinese merchants, particularly retail merchants. From a subjective perspective, the social position of Chinese merchants, the issues surrounding Chinese merchandise *fong kong* and the China shop's function as a 'contact zone' all help to shape the image of China, or better put, they all contribute to shaping the image of China through social interactions in local society. We now look at the three subjective factors in details.

10.3.1. Chinese Merchants

The Chinese merchants were once able to succeed and live peacefully in Botswana, where they kept a low profile, focused on economic activities and tried their best to preserve the reputation of the Chinese community. However, given a small population, the market in Botswana got saturated quickly by the influx of Chinese businesses. Chinese merchants with their limited capital outlay, intensive labour input and small employment faced rising competition from foreign and local entrepreneurs. Despite their contribution to local poverty alleviation, they unavoidably became visible targets of nationalist legislation (Hau 2014). For instance, legislation in Zambia has forced them into a hide-and-seek game with Zambian immigration officials (McNamee et al. 2012); and in Botswana, government plans to drastically reduce the issue of retail licences to Chinese people, with the aim of preserving the retail business for Batswana people (Motsamai 2015 July 1). Their fate at this point seems similar to the Chinese merchants who migrated to Southeast Asia. McNamee (2012, p. 42) reported that the lives of many Chinese merchants are dominated by acute fear, anxiety and distrust. Many despair at the quality of life in Africa, and nearly all long for the day they can return to China. So even if the Chinese are able to gain economic success, they will be unable to make longer-term commitments in Africa as long as anti-China and anti-Chinese sentiments continue, in so far as they cannot change their social position as middlemen (Zi 2015b).

Furthermore, it is also found that the Chinese merchants' social position as middleman minority entrepreneurs who serve subordinate groups and ethnic groups (e.g. Indians, Chinese, Zimbabweans, etc.) contributes to their self-isolation and feelings of vulnerability. Their self-isolation and feelings of vulnerability may be considered as the 'Chineseness' of the Chinese merchants in Botswana who are struggling in an environment engaged in racial and security issues. Their feelings of being disrespected by local people influence their attitudes and direct their decision making, along with their responses to rejection and hostility from the host society. Chinese merchants remain in the country in spite of these difficult circumstances, because they still expect to obtain some profit. Moreover, Botswana's appeal is augmented by its unique geographical position between three potential markets in the neighbouring countries of Namibia, Zimbabwe and Zambia. The majority of the Chinese merchants in Botswana were coping by either transferring their businesses gradually to more skilful and profitable fields (e.g. farming, manufacturing) or seeking greener pastures in the neighbouring countries in order to survive the restrictive regulation. Therefore, due to a saturated market and ethnic frictions between Chinese merchants and the local population, Chinese merchants are mobile and non-acculturated in Botswana with unfathomable futures.

The biggest difference that these Chinese merchants who went to Africa have from those who went to Southeast Asia is that they did so in the background of a rising China. Africa has not only become a continent of economic benefits, but also a continent which desires global knowledge and experience. It has been a place for

Chinese merchants to pursue personal development (Mohan et al. 2014, pp. 72–73). However, this kind of development is not free. On one hand, they benefit from the business opportunities and are shielded by the umbrella of the increasing presence of China in Africa. While on the other hand, they suffer the consequences and conflicts inherent in China–Africa relations, such as social and cultural barriers. In Botswana, the business situation in China shops is affected by the diplomatic relations between the two countries, the reputation of Chinese construction projects and local media reports. The China shop's role as a 'contact zone' allows Batswana to have face-to-face contact with Chinese people. While on the negative side, this also becomes a cause of vulnerability when frictions occur in the top China–Botswana relations.

To Chinese merchants, China shops may be the place where they have the most communication and interactions with the local society. Although most of the Chinese merchants are struggling to interact with the local people, they benefit from the 'unfriendly attitudes' of local people to some extent and develop attachments to their shops. As merchants, it is necessary to strike a balance between 'emotions' and 'profit'. If Chinese merchants had very good relationship with local people, they might have failed to run their businesses for such a long time or perhaps local people might have already succeeded in Chinese businesses. However, their business attitudes and strategies need to be polished in order not to influence the whole Chinese community and the image of China in Botswana negatively. For Batswana people who do not have a comprehensive understanding of China, the Chinese merchants they meet in China shops may be their only reference for their perceptions of China. For Chinese merchants, their business experience in China shops could be a great business foundation if they manage to refine their social and business skills through their daily interaction with the local people. Since no matter whether they invest in industry or in small business, skill to handle person-to-person interactions is unavoidable between the Chinese and Batswana.

10.3.2. Chinese Merchandise – Fong Kong

The middleman position of Chinese merchants, to some extent, determines their business circumstances. Their social position leads them to undertake short-term investments, along with other limitations that hinder their development in Africa. The root cause here may be due to China's lack of a national brand. O'Shaughnessy and O'Shaughnessy (2000, p. 56) emphasised the importance of nation brands:

> Any nation can be viewed as a brand as it can be viewed as a compound of contemporary and historical associations that have relevance for marketing. This is commonly accepted, and the notion of the nation as a brand has an instant and even populist resonance. For some brands, identity is bound up with their national affiliation: brands of Swiss chocolate, French perfume, Italian sports cars, and Japanese electronics are instantly meaningful partly because the sponsor nations do function as a brand – a brand moreover that can signify an entire cultural history.

China is different from Japanese or German nations that have strong brands. China has been increasingly using the soft power of nation branding, such as the Shanghai Expo, Beijing Olympics and the revival of Confucius (Barr 2012, p. 83). In Botswana, the Confucius Institute was founded in 2009, and attracted the attention of the educated population. Furthermore, Chinese merchants reveal that many Batswana were so impressed by the opening ceremony to the Beijing Olympic Games that their attitudes towards Chinese merchants changed after the event. However, the impact of the image campaign that China adopted is somehow limited to a short period of time (Shanghai Expo, Peking Olympic) and some of the campaigns only impact a certain group of people (Confucius Institute). Compared to nation brands like Toyota and Benz that are familiar to a wide range of consumers, China's image campaign is less effective to capture the majority's hearts and minds. Moreover, at the ground level, it is Chinese merchandise – *fong kong* – that impacts the majority in Botswana and represents the image of China. There is a big gap between the China image campaign and the Chinese merchandise on the ground, which makes China suspicious and ambiguous to the Batswana.

Fong kong is accepted by locals economically and practically but rejected emotionally. McNamee et al. (2012, p. 40) argue that *'fong kong* goods' is a concoction made by African governments and business people who are attempting to dent the reputation of Chinese traders because they cannot compete with them. Through my research, it was difficult to trace how the name *fong kong* was coined. However, *fong kong* goods are obviously a reluctant choice to the majority. Some local people who have high social status revealed that they feel ashamed to be found wearing clothes bought from China shops, as the fake and cheap image of *fong kong* tarnishes their reputation. Although low-income people in Botswana rely on made-in-China goods, they still reject them emotionally. 'If I have received more salary, I would not buy from China shop' is the typical answer of the locals. Seeking better quality goods and superior representation of a self-image are common among customers, no matter at which income level while *fong kong* goods fail to meet customer needs in the long run.

Furthermore, the local perception towards *fong kong* goods is negative also due the fact that *fong kong* goods hurts local people emotionally more or less. As a production of 'contact zone', both the quality and price of *fong kong* goods are set through trial and error in the Chinese business to make sure the Chinese merchandise has a market in Botswana. However, most of the local customers do not see it in the same way. They usually ignore their buying power at large while feeling looked down upon by the Chinese when they see Chinese merchants ship 'leftovers' to Botswana, particularly when they know that the made-in-China products sold in the EU and USA are of much better quality. On the other hand, Chinese merchants are frustrated when they are insulted by local people as merchants selling 'leftovers' or from a country producing 'fong kong', only because they bring in the goods that best fit the local market. This explains why local complaints about *fong kong* goods usually stir up anger among the Chinese merchants.

10.3.3. *China Shops as a Self-promoting Brand*

As the most obvious presence – a visible 'face' of China in most African countries – China shops contribute considerably to shape the image of China on the ground. They set a scene where local people can interact with Chinese merchants and Chinese merchandise. The image of China presented by many China shops puzzles African local people: China is rich and with so many business opportunities, why do these Chinese people come to Africa? Why is Chinese merchandise of such a low quality? Ironically, the image that is presented at the ground level in Africa by China shops is usually at odds with the image of the rise of China. Is the so called 'the rise of China' no more than a mirage or image campaign? Are the tangible China shops closer to the reality of China? In the beginning, the majority of the local people were puzzled. They thought all Chinese merchandise was of bad quality but did not understand that the quality of Chinese merchandise sold in Botswana was determined by the local buying power and market. Moreover, many local people thought the poor ability of Chinese people to speak English was due to their low level of education. It takes time for local people to know the reasons behind it. Surprisingly enough, some of them learn the truth through quarrelling with Chinese merchants. 'We have good quality back home, but you guys cannot afford it', 'we did not need to speak English in China, since we have not been colonised by British' are some answers the local people may get from angry Chinese merchants. This kind of quarrel can be considered as clashes in the contact zone China shop. In this way, the China shop reaches the group of local people that the top-down styled image campaign cannot reach, and helps to fill the gaps between Botswana and China, facilitating increased and comprehensive understanding of each other by the two sides.

The shops operated in Botswana are called 'China shops'. Grammatically they should be called Chinese shops, because they are the shops owned by Chinese and selling Chinese merchandise. It is difficult to find out the origin of the name. If the name 'China shop' was given by Chinese merchants, then it is obvious they translated it directly without considering the English grammar. If the name was given by the Batswana, then the name 'China shop' may already indicate the attitude of local people: expecting something that is representative of a rising China, a state power, a donor, which can bring multiple benefits to Africa or with fear and suspiciousness towards the arrival of a nation with the largest population in the world. The Botswana majority only know 'China' through media, until they meet the Chinese merchants in their China shops. The Batswana only knew China as a rising economic and political power, but did not know that the rise of China is founded on the diligence and even frugality of Chinese people. They did not know that in China there is furious business competition that pushes many Chinese out to seek dreams in Africa in order to catch up with the rising cost of living in China. Therefore, the China shop helps Batswana people to recognise a vivid image of China by a narrow demography of people and a collection of low-price and poor-quality merchandise through exchanges of impressions and evaluations with Chinese people. In this context, the name 'China shop' is like a self-promoting brand name, although unauthorized, that is not built through nation branding or an image campaign but is coined on the ground through the daily social interactions between Chinese merchants and Batswana local people.

10.4. Image of China in Botswana

In Botswana's situation, the image of China is mainly shaped through complex interactions as well as through the abstract group image of the Chinese. During the daily interaction between local people and Chinese merchants, *suzhi* (quality) of Chinese merchants became familiar to the locals through observation, communication and negotiation. At the same time the business relationship via *fong kong* goods also shapes local perception towards China. Blumer (1958, p. 5) argues that a sense of group position is clearly formed by a running process in which the dominant racial group is led to define and redefine the subordinate racial group and the relations between them. However, I argue that in Botswana, the defining and redefining of 'Chinese in Botswana' is more through the interaction between the Chinese and Batswana rather than the exchange ideas among Batswana locals alone. The quality of both Chinese merchants and *fong kong* goods were improved and localised through the interaction process. We tend to assume that the image of China would become more positive accordingly. However, to our surprise, in Botswana's case, it turned negatively instead. To explain this point we have to also look at the process of group definition in the abstract image of the Chinese in Botswana. Blumer (1958, pp. 5–6) lists 'public area', 'big event', 'leader of subordinate group' and 'strong interest groups' as implications. In the case of the Chinese in Botswana, the Chinese embassy and Oriental Post can be regarded as the voices that represent Chinese/China to the public. Furthermore, many Chinese merchants who are active in making donations can also be seen in local and Chinese newspapers. However, since local press media feature more negative than positive news about China, a less positive image of China is shaped. Apart from that, the Chinese Spring Festival and cultural exchange programmes organised by the Confucius Institute, to some extent, are central to the formation of collective images of China, but their influence is usually limited to the well-educated locals. Finally, I would consider that the failure of several mega-projects plays a negative role of the 'big event' in Botswana which has greatly tarnished the image of the Chinese and China that was built up through the other approach.

After examining the issues of the group position theory, I would like to examine them with some intergroup theories. First, the economic threat of being out-competed in the labour market and business market (Bonacich 1973; Zhou et al. 2016) is a key reason that provokes fear and anxiety among local Batswana individuals. However, negative attitudes are mainly shaped by media and local government propaganda. Rather than squeezing local merchants out of the market, Chinese merchants play a role as middleman minority that offers a niche service to the local merchants. Also, when the two groups compete directly in the job market, it was due to lack of qualifications that local assistants failed to manage the shop as well as Chinese employees did and failed to win the trust of Chinese employers. However, this issue was somehow overcome through government regulation and restricted working permits.

Secondly, symbolic threat constitutes another key exclusionary mechanism according to the existing literature. Negative attitudes can stem from a collective fear or anxiety of being overpowered or infected by a foreign 'deviant' or inferior culture (Blumer 1958). This mechanism seems to be pervasive in the case of Chinese merchants' encounter with the local Batswana. The Chinese in China shops and Chinese construction companies treat the locals as an exotic foreign cultural group. However, cultural conflict exists and materialises in certain situations, such as negative media reporting about lifestyle differences, and social problems. Botswana's xenophobic tendency increased their fear of the Chinese who are even more alien that their Zimbabwean neighbours.

Third, the effects of contact are not uniform, but are conditioned by the types and levels of contact as well as by the contexts in which intergroup encounters occur. My findings partly confirm Allport's argument (1954) that common goals, intergroup cooperation, and the support of authorities set optimal conditions for successful intergroup contact. However, in the case of Chinese merchants in Botswana, the equal status did not help them to engage with each other. Particularly between Chinese merchants and local assistants, their status is difficult to compare. Chinese merchants are bosses although foreigners; on the other hand, local assistants are employees although comfortable in their native land. The lack of support by the authorities appears to negatively affect intergroup relations on the ground to a large extent. Language barriers and foreignness seem to put the Batswana natives of higher socioeconomic status together with Chinese of lower socioeconomic status in the same business and labour markets, a condition that, in the short run, seems to modify intergroup tensions. Whether local protection will lead to increased hostility between groups in the long run remains an empirical question.

Chinese–African encounters are paradoxical which is very similar to what Zhou et al. (2016) described in their research on African merchants in China. At the institutional level, lack of official endorsement and working permit restrictions put the Chinese in a vicious cycle of exclusion. They are misrepresented by the mainstream local media and official discourse as foreigners who come to take business and job opportunities away from the local. They are negatively perceived by local authorities and local people in general. At the micro level, however, greater contact reduces social distance, which in turn facilitates greater cooperation and nurtures closer relations, leading to a virtuous cycle of inclusion (Zhou et al.

2016, p. 158). Therefore, the image of China at a macro level is shaped by local media and official discourse, negatively if there is necessity. On the other hand, at a micro level, the image of China is built up through daily social interaction that sharpens both Chinese merchants and local people to accept each other and cooperate.

In spite of the trivial looking nature of the China shop business, it has its own advantages in contributing to the image of China in Africa. First, most of the China shops have been operated in the same area for more than five years, which is longer than any construction project and even longer than one term of an ambassador. The China shops, therefore, are given opportunities to build solid local networks. Secondly, since China shops are deeply integrated into local people's lives; it has its own unique stability. Even facing xenophobia, Chinese merchants are indispensable in local people's lives, since they provide a service that meets the desperate needs of African local people. Third, the China shop is a good 'training centre' to develop social and business skills. China shops have helped Chinese merchants to obtain practical skills for running businesses in Botswana while, on the other hand, facilitated Batswana to comprehend the way of Chinese business. The same frictions that happen in China shops also happen in big projects. Due to the complexity of the system and the difficulty to observe a project *in operando*, it is difficult to find the root cause of a problem once issues appear. In this context, the China shop has helped a large number of Chinese and Batswana people to develop social and negotiation skills through a simple and detailed version of issues on a daily basis.

After all, the importance of the China shop as a self-promoting brand of China is undeniable. Its continuity, wide network, grounded service as well as practical use have not been paid enough attention. While China is busy building her nation's image through soft powers, it should also make full use of the way that has been paved. Despite the vulnerability and limitation of the China shop, it is worth exploring its potential with patience.

10.5. China–Botswana Relations

The findings of this research agree with Giese (2015, p. 4) that in many ways the activities and practices of Chinese entrepreneurs in Africa do not differ from those of other local and foreign actors, that they usually benefit local populations or at least certain groups and strata thereof, and that relationships of cooperation and conviviality have developed despite widespread mutual distrust. The Embassy of China admits that most of the Chinese nationals in Botswana are playing their active part in strengthening the friendship and understanding between the two countries while some unpleasant behavioural problems have been encountered by certain Chinese individuals living in Botswana (Liu 2010). The Embassy also has promised not to tolerate such problems and has appealed to every Chinese citizen in Botswana to behave properly at all times and to live harmoniously with the local people (ibid.). Managing Chinese merchants in a foreign land is not easy due to its business model and wide geographic coverage. However, if Chinese government can pay more attention to educate and assist the Chinese merchants concerning local business regulations and local language, less friction will occur at grass-roots level. Furthermore, grass-roots level cultural exchange programmes can also be expected to build a strong tie between Chinese and local people. Additionally, a private Chinese media broadcasting in English or a local language is necessary to balance the negative image of China created by local and Western media. Last but not least, Chinese merchants should be encouraged to get involved in long-term investments in industry and the high-technology realm in order to change the negative local perception towards Chinese merchants as 'coming to take advantage of the local people'. Along with the development of Botswana, China shop businesses may offer less and less to the local society, as one day the Batswana will be able to take the businesses for themselves.

In this research the China shop has been regarded as a 'contact zone' where Chinese merchants meet local people face-to-face to interact. In spite of the fact that the term 'contact zone' was initially used to refer to interactions in colonial relationships and 'West and Rest' relations, my research highlights contact between non-Westerners, in the context of rising China and its growing economy, in the realm of petty trade. In the relationship between Chinese merchants and the Batswana, there is no clear border between dominant and subordinate, superior and inferior. The relationship between Chinese merchants and the Batswana is more like in a tug-of-war. As Chinese people try to obtain respect and economic success from the locals, the locals also try to receive respect and convenience from the Chinese. They become close friends when they are in a mutually beneficial relationship and they struggle and start to negotiate when either side's need is unfulfilled. In this tug-of-war there has been no landslide victory so far and, therefore, the game is still on.

A popular view holds that there are increasing problems regarding trading relations and that the China–Botswana honeymoon is over. On this point, I agree with Professor Li Anshan who stated that, 'The more problems the better. Because if there was no or minimal contact, there would be no problems. When relations become wider and deeper, more problems naturally occur. With an equal relationship and mutual respect, China and Africa can sit down to discuss their problems and together find solutions. Once the problem is solved, relations will get closer still' (Li 2015). All these frictions and problems should be considered as a learning process for both Chinese and African people, following the old saying: 'iron sharpens iron; so one person sharpens another.'[1] How China–Botswana relations develop in the future also depends on how the two sides sharpen each other. As the process of globalisation permeates the everyday lives of people, each individual is empowered to be an 'ambassador' in shaping international relations.

10.6. Suggestions to Policy Makers

In order for the Chinese merchants to get out of the vicious circle, both the Botswana and Chinese governments need to take action. The Botswana government, as Ebrahim (7 August 2015) suggested, needs to stop creating an unstable business environment. Since foreign entrepreneurs are encouraged to invest in industry, even small-scale foreign investors should be issued with a middle-term to long-term working permit. Secondly, a business travel visa application process should be simplified for foreign entrepreneurs to research the Botswana market. Thirdly, business and trade policies need to be made more stable and transparent, as the frequent change of trading policies has frustrated many Chinese merchants. The Chinese embassy in Botswana has been working on the mutual beneficial relationship between the two countries for years. In recent years, the Chinese Embassy has been paying more and more attention to the Chinese retail trading section in Botswana. I suggest that the Chinese Embassy gets involved in restricting the retail business before the Botswana government takes action. By doing this, on the one hand, it can facilitate Chinese merchants' understanding of local regulation and, on the other hand, can avoid negative influence on the Chinese reputation.

I would like to encourage more cultural and language exchanges between the Chinese and Batswana on different levels. A research done by Wang and Lemmer (2015) stated that Batswana students were limited to the classroom contexts of their native institutions, without access to a broader learning environment where they could learn the Chinese language. It has been a 'lonely' language learning experience in which they feel isolated in spite of their intense interest in Chinese. I think it will be beneficial for the both sides if the Chinese embassy or a Chinese organisation could offer more opportunities to help local people to engage with the Chinese in Botswana, not limited to the Chinese leaders.

Finally, I would like to encourage the Botswana government and 'Think Tanks' to consider a more practical environment for the young generation. We know that the unemployment rate is very high in Botswana. However, it is neither because there is no job to do nor because the young generation are not skilled. Pride may be one of the reasons that hinder the Botswana young generation from finding jobs. I discovered through my field research that the Botswana young generation cannot bite the bullet nor do they want to take any risks. Some of them look down on a job in a China shop despite their failure to get a full-time job anywhere else. I have seen a Zimbabwean young lady managing six shops back in her home town and she comes to Francistown every week to restock on Chinese shoes. I have seen a young Chinese lady who graduated from university and then came to Botswana to work from morning to night in a small shop. The young generation in Botswana should be encouraged to work harder before being offerred a choice of jobs. On the other hand, the Botswana government and ministry of education may need to think about how to help the young generation to choose their major subjects and careers. I have met so many university students in Botswana who majored in business, finance and engineering but cannot get a job after graduation. Ferguson (2015, p. 37) states: 'Teaching a man to fish in these times, may be just a good way of creating an unemployed fisherman, or, at best a marginal hanger-on in an already oversaturated competitive field. It is not obvious that being trained for a non-existent job would benefit the man in any way, and it is certainly nonsense to suppose that he would, by virtue of that training, be fed for a lifetime.'

10.7. Rethinking Intergroup Relations and International Relations

In this last section I would like to list some of my ideas for future research. In 2012, I met a Chinese merchant whose business has been very successful in both Botswana and South Africa. We spent hours chatting about the business environment, his business experience and how successful he is. What he obtained is what the Chinese merchants in Botswana yearn for. I thought he must be satisfied. However, he ended up our conversation with sigh. He told me: 'Sometimes when I drive on the desert I feel so lonely. I want to cry. Yes, people think I have everything. But they cannot understand how empty and lonely I feel'.

I could not totally understand that kind of feeling, because I have not been in his shoes. However, this kind of sigh is not alien to Chinese merchants. Some Chinese laugh at themselves saying: 'We are so poor that we only have money.' Many Chinese say that their life experience in Botswana makes them realise there is something wrong with their values and lifestyle.

> We see local people face so much stress but they are happy every day. They don't worry about tomorrow. But we Chinese always worry about tomorrow. We also worry about our next generation.

Some even joke that local people were more pure and kind before the Chinese came. Now they also learn from the Chinese how to take advantages from other people:

> When I came to Botswana 10 years ago, people here were nice. If your car was broken on the road, local people would come to help you to fix it. But now they either ignore your needs or they will ask for money from you.

In this research I have tried to focus on interpersonal relations, intergroup relations as well as provide some light on international relations. However, with an anthropological method there is no way of exploring people's hearts. I had no way of researching on their relationships with themselves. However, as the old saying goes: 'The heart of every problem is the problem of the heart.' To understand the problem between Chinese merchants and Botswana people well, I may need to explore more of their inner selves.

A notable British theologian and author, Clive Staples Lewis in his classic *Mere Christianity* (1952), points out that there are two ways in which the human machine goes wrong:

> One is when human individuals drift apart from one another, or else collide with one another and do one another damage, by cheating or bullying. The other is when things go wrong inside the individual – when the different parts of him (his different faculties and desires and so on) either drift apart or interfere with one another. You can get the idea plain if you think of us as a fleet of ships sailing in formation. The voyage will be a success only, in the first place, if the ships do not collide and get in one another's way; and, secondly, if each ship is seaworthy and has her engines in good order. As a matter of fact, you cannot have either of these two things without the other. If the ships keep on having collisions they will not remain seaworthy very long. On the other hand, if their steering gears are out of order they will not be able to avoid collisions. Or, if you like, think of humanity as a band playing a tune. To get a good result, you need two things. Each player's individual instrument must be in tune and also each must come in at the right moment so as to combine with all the others.

But there is one thing we have not yet taken into account. We have not asked where the fleet is trying to get to, or what piece of music the band is trying to play. The instruments might be all in tune and might all come in at the right moment, but even so the performance would not be a success if they had been engaged to provide dance music and actually played nothing but Dead Marches. And however well the fleet sailed, its voyage would be a failure if it were meant to reach New York and actually arrived at Calcutta.

Therefore, according to Lewis (1952) morality is concerned with three things. Firstly, it requires harmony between individuals. Secondly, it needs harmony inside each individual. Thirdly, with the general purpose of human life as a whole; what man was made for; what course the whole fleet ought to be on. However, we academics nearly always think about the first thing and forget the other two. Without harmony inside each Batswana and Chinese individual, how can we find harmony in their interactions? After overcoming language and cultural barriers what is the next barrier waiting for them? In a resource-limited globe how can countries maintain harmony if there is no morality beyond competition and profit?

Notes

[1] Bible, Proverbs 27:17 (New International Version)

References

Achberger, J. (2010) 'The Dragon Has Not Just Arrived: The Historical Study of Africa's Relations with China', *History Compass*, Vol. 8, No. 5, pp. 368–376.

Akhidenor, A.E. (2013) 'Code-switching in the Conversations of the Chinese Trading Community in Africa: The Case of Botswana', *English Today,* Vol. 29, No. 4, pp. 30–36.

Barr, M. (2012) 'Nation Branding as Nation Building: China's Image Campaign', *East Asia*, No. 29, pp. 81–94.

Barrett, G. (2007) 'Fong Kong', *A Way with Words*, online: <http://www.waywordradio.org/fong_kong_1/.> (15 October 2007).

Benza, B. (2012). *Gross Poverty Despite Botswana's High per Capita,* online: <http://www.mmegi.bw/index.php?sid=4&aid=.> (9 October 2012).

Best, A. C. (1970) 'General Trading in Botswana', *Economic Geography*, Vol. 46, No. 4, pp. 598–611.

Blumer, H. (1958) 'Race Prejudice as a Sense of Group Position', *The Pacific Sociological Review*, Vol. 1, No. 1, pp. 3–7.

Bodomo, A. (2015) 'Africans in China: Guangzhou and Beyond – Issues and Reviews', *The Journal of Pan African Studies*, Vol. 7, No. 10, pp. 1–9.

Bodomo, A., and Pajancic, C. (2015) 'Counting Beans: Some Empirical and Methodological Problems for Calibrating the African Presence in Greater China', *The Journal of Pan African Studies*, Vol. 7, No. 10, pp. 126–143.

Bolaane, M. (2007) 'China's Relations with Botswana: An Historical Perspective', in K.K. Prah (ed.), *Afro-Chinese Relations: Past, Present & Future*, CASAS, pp. 142–174.

Bonacich, E. (1973) 'A Theory of Middleman Minorities', *American Sociological Review,* Vol. 38, No. 5, pp. 583–594.

Bräutigam, D. (2003) 'Close Encounters Chinese Business Networks as Industrial Catalysts in Sub-Saharan Africa', *African Affairs,* No. 102, pp. 447–467.

----------(2009). *The Dragon's Gift: A Real Story of China in Africa,* Oxford: Oxford University Press.

Brooks, A. (2010) 'Spinning and Weaving Discontent: Labour Relations and the Production of Meaning at Zambia-China Mulungushi Textiles', *Journal of Southern African Studies,* Vol. 36, No. 1, pp. 113–132.

Carling, J., and Haugen, H.Ø. (2004) 'How an African Outpost Is Filled with Chinese Shops', *Paper presented at the Fifth International Conference of the International Society for the Study of Chinese Overseas (ISSCO).*

Chaudhry, P., and Zimmerman, A. (2009) *The Economics of Counterfeit Trade: Governments, Consumers, Pirates and Intellectual Property Rights,* Springer-Verlag: Berlin Heidelberg.

Chen, A.Y. (2009) 'China's Role in Infrastructure Development in Botswana', *SAIIA Occasional Paper,* No. 44, online: <http://www.saiia.org.za/occasional-papers/chinas-role-in-infrastructure-development-in-botswana> (6 May 2016).

Chen, C., Goldstein, A., and Orr, R.J. (2009) 'Local Operations of Chinese Construction Firms in Africa: An Empirical Survey', *The International Journal of Construction Management,* Vol. 9, No. 2, pp. 75–89.

Chow, D.C. (2003) 'Organized Crime, Local Protectionism, and the Trade in Counterfeit Goods in China', *China Economic Review,* Vol. 14, No. 4, pp. 473–484.

Cissé, D. (2013) 'South-South Migration and Sino-African Small Traders: A Comparative Study of Chinese in Senegal and

Africans in China', *African Review of Economics and Finance,* Vol. 5, No. 1, pp. 17–28 .

----------(2014) 'Hypocrisy and Hysteria in Western Criticism of China's Engagement in Africa', Centre for Chinese Studies, Stellenbosch University, *CCS Commentary,* pp. 1–2.

---------- (2015) 'African Traders in Yiwu: Their Trade Networks and Their Role in the Distribution of "Made in China" Products in Africa', *The Journal of Pan African Studies,* Vol. 7, No. 10, pp. 44–64.

Codrin, A. (2014) 'Chinese Employers and Their Ugandan Workers: Tensions, Frictions and Cooperation in an African City', *Journal of Current Chinese Affairs,* Vol. 43, No. 1, pp. 139–176.

Cook, J., and Wall, T. (1980) 'New Work Attitude Measures of Trust, Organizational Commitment and Personal Need Non-fulfilment', *Journal of Occupational Psychology,* No. 53, pp. 39–52.

Cottle, E. (2014) *Chinese Construction Companies in Africa: A Challenge for Trade Unions.* Global Labour Column, online: <http://column.global-labour-niversity.org/2014/07/chinese-construction-companies-in.html> (6 May 2016)

Denbow, J., and Thebe, P.C. (2006) *Culture and Customs of Botswana.* Westport, Connectict and London: Greenwood Press.

Deumert, A., and Mabandla, N. (2013) 'Every Day a Newshop Pops Up' – South Africa's 'New' Chinese Diaspora and the Multilingual Transformation of Rural Towns', *English Today,* Vol. 29, No. 1, pp. 44–52.

Dobler, G. (2009) 'Chinese Shops and the Formation of a Chinese Expatriate Community in Namibia', *The China Quarterly,* No. 199, pp. 707–727.

Douglas, K.M., and Saenz, R. (2007) 'Middleman Minorities', *International Encyclopedia of the Social Sciences,* 2nd edition, pp. 147–148.

Dubinsky, A.J., and Levy, M. (1985) 'Ethics in Retailing: Perceptions of Retail Salespeople', *Journal of the Academy of Marketing Science*, Vol. 13, No. 1, pp. 1–16.

Durham, D., and Klaits, F. (2002) 'Funerals and the Public Space of Sentiment in Botswana', *Journal of Southern African Studies*, Vol. 28, No. 4, pp. 777–795.

Eifert, B., Gelb, A., and Ramachandran, V. (2008) 'The Cost of Doing Business in Africa: Evidence from Enterprise Survey Data', *World Development*, Vol. 36, No. 9, pp. 1531–1546.

Embassy of the People's Republic of China in the Republic of Botswana (2008) 'An Over View of the Relations between China and Botswana', online:
<Http://bw.china-embassy.org/eng/sbgx/t404979.htm>
(1 February 2008).

----------(2009) 'Chinese Envoy Tips Batswana Entrepreneurs', online:
<http://bw.china-embassy.org/eng/sbgx/t537319.htm.>
(16 February 2009).

Fan, Y. (2006) 'Branding the Nation: What is Being Branded?', *Journal of Vacation Marketing*, Vol. 12, No. 1, pp. 5–14.

Ferguson, J. (2015) *Give a Man a Fish: Reflections on the New Politics of Distribution*, Durham: Duke University Press.

Giese, K. (2013) 'Same-Same But Different: Chinese Traders' Perspectives on African Labor', *China Journal*, No. 69, pp. 134–153.

----------(2014) 'Perceptions, Practices and Adaptations: Understanding Chinese–African Interactions in Africa', *Journal of Current Chinese Affairs*, Vol. 43, No. 1, pp. 3–8.

----------(2015) 'Adaptation and Learning among Chinese Actors in Africa', *Journal of Current Chinese Affairs*, Vol. 44, No. 1, pp. 3–8.

Giese, K., and Thiel, A. (2012) 'The Vulnerable Other: Distorted Equity in Chinese–Ghanaian Employment Relations', *Ethnic and Racial*

Studies, Vol. 37, No. 6, pp. 1101–1120.

----------(2014) 'The Psychological Contract in Chinese-African Informal Labor Relations', *The International Journal of Human Resource Management*, Vol. 26, No. 14, pp. 1807–1826.

Hanisch, S. (2013) 'At the Margins of the Economy? Chinese Migrants in Lesotho's Wholesale and Retail Sector', *Africa Spectrum*, Vol. 2013, No. 3, pp. 85–97.

Hardouin, P., and Weichhardt, R. (2006) 'Terrorist Fund Raising through Criminal Activities', *Journal of Money Laundering Control*, Vol. 9, No. 3, pp. 303–308.

Haroz, D. (2011) 'China in Africa: Symbiosis or Exploitation?', *The Fletcher Forum of World Affairs*, Vol. 35, No. 2, pp. 65–88.

Harrison, T.P., Lee, H.L., and Neale, J. J. (2003) *The Practice of Supply Chain Management*. New York: Springer.

Hau, C.S. (2014) *The Chinese Question: Ethnicity, Nation, and Region in and beyond the Philippines*, Kyoto: NUS Press and Kyoto University Press.

Haugen, H.Ø., and Carling, J. (2005) 'On the Edge of the Chinese Diaspora: The Surge of Baihuo Business in an African City', *Ehnic and Racial Studies*, Vol. 28, No. 4, pp. 639–662.

Huang, M., and Ren, P. (2013) 'A Study on the Employment Effect of Chinese Investment in South Africa', Centre for Chinese Studies, Stellenbosch University, *Dicussion Paper*, Vol. 2013, No. 5, pp. 1–40.

Kalusopa, T. (2009) 'Chinese Investments in Botswana', in A.Y.Baah and H.Jauch (ed.), *Chinese Investments in Africa: A Labor Perspective,* pp. 124–157, online: <https://www.fnv.nl/site/over-de-fnv/internationaal/mondiaal-fnv/documenten/english/publications/Chinese_investments_in_Africa_final_report1.pdf#search=%27Chinese+Investments+in+Africa%3A+A+Labor+Perspective%2C%27> (6 May 2016).

Khan, M. G. (2014) 'The Chinese Presence in Burkina Faso: A Sino-African Cooperation from Below', *Journal of Current Chinese Affairs*, Vol. 43, No. 1, pp. 71–101.

Klaits, F. (2010) *Death in a Church of Life: Moral Passion during Botswana's Time of AIDS*, Oakland: University of California Press.

Kuang, E.M. (2008) 'The New Chinese Migration Flows to Africa', *Social Science Information*, No. 47, pp. 643–659.

Lam, K.N. (2015) 'Chinese Adaptations: African Agency, Fragmented Community and Social Capital Creation in Ghana', *Journal of Current Chinese Affairs*, No. 1/2015, pp. 9–41.

Laribee, R. (2008) 'The China Shop Phenomenon: Trade Supply within the Chinese Diaspora in South Africa', *Afrika Spectrum*, No. 43, pp. 353–370.

Lee, C.K. (2009) 'Raw Encounters: Chinese Managers, African Workers and the Politics of Casualization in Africa's Chinese Enclaves, *The China Quarterly*, No 199, pp. 647-666..

----------(2014) *The Spectre of Global China*, New left review. Second series, online:
<http://www.sociology.ucla.edu/sites/default/files/u281/nlr_2014_no._89.pdf#search=%27the+Spectre+of+Global+China%2C%27> (4 March 2015).

Lee, S. (2008) *Influence of Moral View and Other Variables on Purchase Intentions Concerning Counterfeits*, A Dissertation Submitted to the Faculty of the Graduate School of the University of Minnesota.

Lesetedi, G.N., and Moroka, T. (2007) 'Reverse Xenophobia: Immigrants Attitudes toward Citizens in Botswana', A paper presented at the African Migrations Workshop: Understanding Dynamics in the Continent at the Centre for Migration Studies, University of Ghana.

Lewis, C.S. (1952) *Mere Christianity*, SAMIZDAT, online:
<http://www.samizdat.qc.ca/vc/pdfs/MereChristianity_CSL.

pdf> (6 May 2016)

Li, A. (2015) '10 Questions about Migration between China and Africa', *China Policy Institute Blog*, online: <http://blogs.nottingham.ac.uk/chinapolicyinstitute/2015/03/04/10-questions-about-migration-between-china-and-africa/> (4 March 2015).

Li, M. (2005) 'Transformation of Contingency into Meaning: Emergence of a New Qiaoxiang in South China', Presented at the CCTR conference *"People on the Move: The Transnational Flow of Chinese Human Capital"*, 21–22 October 2005 at Hong Kong University of Science and Technology.

Li, T. (2010) 'To Make Live or Let Die? Rural Dispossession and the Protection of Surplus', *Antipode*, Vol. 41, No. 1, pp. 66–93.

Lin, E. (2014) '"Big Fish in a Small Pond": Chinese Migrant Shopkeepers in South Africa', *International Migrantion Reivew*, Vol. 48, No. 1, pp. 181–215.

Lin, N., Cook, K.S., and Burt, R.S. (2001) *Social Capital: Theory and Research,* New Jersey: Transaction Publishers.

Lin, Y.-C.J. (2011) *Fake Stuff: China and the Rise of Counterfeit Goods (Routledge Series for Creative Teaching and Learning in Anthropology)*, New York and London: Routledge.

Liu, Y.-L. (1992) 'The Private Economy and Local Politics in the Rural Industrialization of Wenzhou', *The China Quarterly*, No. 130, pp. 293–316.

Ma Mung, E. (2008) 'The New Chinese Migration Flows to Africa', *Special Issue: Migrants and Clandestinity*, Vol. 47, No. 4, pp. 643–659.

Makgala, C.J. (2013) 'Discourses of Poor Work Ethic in Botswana: A Historical Perspective, 1930–2010', *Journal of Southern African Studies*, Vol. 39, No. 1, pp. 45–57.

Makungu, N.M. (2013) 'Is the Democratic Republic of Congo being

Globalized by China? The Case of Small Commerce at Kinshasa Central Market', *Quarterly Journal of Chinese Studies*, Vol. 2, No. 1, pp. 89–101.

Marr, S.D. (2012) '"If You Are with Ten, Only Two Will Be Batswana": Nation-making and the Public Discourse of Paranoia in Botswana', *Canadian Journal of African Studies*, Vol. 46, No. 1, pp. 65–86.

Mathangwane, J.T. (2015) 'The Francistown Oriental Plaza "White Elephant": A Cultural Conflict or What?', *PULA: Botswana Journal of African Studies,* No. 29, p. 1.

Mathews, G. (2011) *Ghetto at the Center of the World: Chungking Mansions, Hong Kong,* Chicago: University of Chicago Press.

Mathews, G., and Vega, C.A. (2012) 'Introduction: What is Globalization from Below?', in G. Mathews, C.A. Vega, and G.L. Ribeiro (eds.), *Globalization from Below: The World's Other Economy,* pp. 1–16, London and New York: Routledge.

Mathews, G., and Yang, Y. (2012) 'How Africans Pursue Low-End Globalization in Hong Kong and Mainland China', *Journal of Current Chinese Affairs,* Vol. 41, No. 2, pp. 95–120.

Mbendi Information Service (2014) 'Manufacturing in Botswana Overview', online:
<http://www.mbendi.com/indy/mnfc/af/bo/p0005.htm>
(15 September 2015).

McNamee, T. et al. (2012) *Africa in Their Words – A Study of Chinese Traders in South Africa, Lesotho, Botswana, Zambia and Angola,* The Brenthurst Foundation, Brenthurst Discussion Papers: News Release [124294].

Min, P.G. (1990) 'Problems of Korean Immigrant Entrepreneurs', *International Migration Review,* Vol. 24, No. 3, pp. 436–455.

Ministry of Trade and Industry (2011) 'Economic Diversification Drive Medium to Long-Term Strategy 2011–2016', *Ministry of Trade and Industry*, Botswana Government, online: <http://www.mti.gov.bw/webfm_send/231>.

Moahi, K. (2015) 'An Analysis of Botswana–China Relations in the Botswana Print Media', *PULA: Botswana Journal of African Studies*, Vol. 29, No. 1.

Mogae, F. (2009) 'A New Development Partner: New Opportunities', in S.T. Freeman (ed), *China, Africa, and the African Diaspora: Perspectives*, pp. 21–27, Washington, DC: AASBEA Publisher.

Mogalakwe, M. (2015) 'Africa-China Relations in the 21st Century: An Assessment of Chinese Development Assistance to Africa – The Case of Botswana', Paper presented at *Southern Africa Beyond the West: Political, Economic and Cultural Relationships with BRICS Countries and the Global South* JSAS/RoPE/SAIPAR, 7–11 August 2015 in Livingstone, Zambia.

Mogape, S. (2005) *Trade Performance Review 2005: Botswana*, SADC Trade, online: <Trade Performance Review 2005: Botswana > (4 March 2015).

Mogapi, S. (2006) 'Intra-SADC Trade Performance Review 2006: Chapter 1: Botswana', *SADC Trade,* online: <http://www.sadctrade.org/tpr/2006/1/botswana> (4 March 2015).

Mohan, G. (2008) 'Social Relationships of New Chinese Migrants in Africa', *The China Monitor – Emerging Chinese Communities in Africa*, No. 26, pp. 6–8.

Mohan, G., and Kale, D. (2007) 'The Invisible Hand of South-South Globalisation: Chinese Migrants in Africa', *A Report for the Rockefeller Foundation,* The Development Policy and Practice Department, The Open University.

Mohan, G., and Tan-Mullins, M. (2009) 'Chinese Migrants in Africa as New Agents of Development? An Analytical Framework', *European Journal of Development Research*, Vol. 21, No. 4, pp. 588–

605.

Mohan, G., Lampert, B., Tan-Mullins, M., and Chang, D. (2014) *Chinese Migrants and Africa's Development,* London: New Imperialists or Zed Books.

Mwobobia, F.M. (2012) 'Empowering of Small-Micro and Medium Enterprises (SMMEs): A Case of Botswana', *Business and Management Research*, Vol. 1, No. 4, pp. 88–98.

Nayyar, G.M., Breman, J.G., Newton, P.N., and Herrington, J. (2012) 'Poor-quality Antimalarial Drugs in Southeast Asia and Sub-Saharan Africa', *The Lancet Infectious Diseases*, Vol. 12, No. 6, pp. 488–496.

Nyamnjoh, F.B. (2006) *Insiders and Outsiders: Citizenship and Xenophobia in Contemporary Southern Africa*, London and New York: CODESRIA.

----------(2010) *Intimate Strangers*, Bamenda, Cameroon: Langaa Research.

Nyíri, P. (2007) *Chinese in Eastern Europe and Russia: A Middleman Minority in a Transnational Era*, London and New York: Routledge.

----------(2011) 'Chinese Entrepreneurs in Poor Countries: A Transnational "Middleman Minority" and Its Futures', *Inter-Asia Cultural Studies*, Vol. 12, No. 1,pp. 145–153.

Omohundro, J.T. (1981) *Chinese Merchant Families in Iloilo: Commerce and Kin in a Central Philippine City*, Quezon City, Metro Manila, Philippine: Ateneo de Manila University Press.

O'Shaughnessy, J., and O'Shaughnessy, N.J. (2000) 'Treating the Nation as a Brand: Some Neglected Issues', *Journal of Macromarketing*, Vol. 20, No. 1, pp. 56–64.

Park, R.E. (1950) 'The Race Relations Cycle in Hawaii', in E. Hughes (ed.), *Race and Culture,* pp. 189–195, Chicago: University of Chicago Press.

Park, Y.J. (2008) *A Matter of Honour: Being Chinese in South Africa*, Auckland Park, South Africa: Jacana Media (Pty) Ltd.

----------(2009) Chinese Migration in Africa, *SAILA Occasional Paper* No. 24, online: <http://dspace.africaportal.org/jspui/ bitstream/123456789/29711/1/SAIIA%20Occasional%20Pa per%20no%2024.pdf?1.>

----------(2013a) '"Fong Kong" in Southern Africa: Views of China-made Goods & Chinese Migrants', *African Studies Association 56th Annual Meeting,* 21–24 November 2013, Baltimore, Maryland.

----------(2013b) 'The Chinese, the Taiwanese, "Fong Kong" and Labour: Complexities & Ironies of the Garment and Textile Industry in Southern Africa, *African Centre for Migration & Society,*13 August 2013, University of the Witwatersrand.

Park, Y.J., and Chen, A.Y. (2009) 'Recent Chinese Migrants in Small Towns of Post-Apartheid South Africa', *Revue Européenne des Migrations Internationales,* Vol. 25, No. 1, pp. 25–44.

Pratt, M.L. (1992) *Imperial Eyes: Travel Writing and Transculturation,* London and New York: Routledge.

Sautman, B,. and Yan, H. (2009) 'African Perspectives on China-Africa Links', *The China Quarterly,* No. 199, pp. 728–759.

----------(2014) 'Bashing "the Chinese": Contextualizing Zambia's Collum Coal Mine Shooting', *Journal of Contemporary China,* DOI, 10.1080/10670564.2014.898897.

----------(2015) 'Regimes of Truth, Localisation of Chinese Enterprises, and African Agency', *Centre for Chinese Studies,* pp. 60-69, online: <http://www.ccs.org.za/wp-content/uploads/2015/07/CCS_ China_Monitor_FOCAC_July-2015.pdf#page=60>

----------(2016) 'The Discourse of Racialization of Labour and Chinese Enterprises in Africa', *Ethnic and Racial Studies,* Vol. 39, No. 12, pp. 2149–2168.

Sayila, A. (2002) 'Foreigners not Very Welcome', *The Free Library,* online: <http://www.thefreelibrary.com/Foreigners+not+very+

welcome.+(Botswana).-a085881530> (1 May 2002).

Schwab, K. (2010) 'The Global Competitiveness Report 2010-2011', *World Economic Forum,* online: <http://www3.weforum.org/docs/WEF_Global CompetitivenessReport_2010-11.pdf#search=%27% E2%80%98The+Global+Competitiveness+Report+20102011 %E2%80%99%27>

Scott, J.C. (1987) *Weapons of the Weak: Everyday Forms of Peasant Resistance,* New Haven: Yale University Press.

Shinn, D.H. (2008) 'African Migration and the Brain Drain', *Paper Presented at the Institute for African Studies and Slovenia Global Action* 20 June 2008.

Skinner, G.W. (1996) 'Creolized Chinese Societies in Southeast Asia', in A. Reid and K. Alilunas-Rodgers (eds.), *Sojourners and Settlers: History of Southeast Asia and the Chinese,* Honolulu: Universtiy of Hawai'i Press, pp. 51–93.

Smith, D.J. (2007) *A Culture of Corruption: Everyday Deception and Popular Discontent in Nigeria,* Princeton, NJ: Princeton University.

Suryadinata, L. (2007) *Understanding the Ethnic Chinese in Southeast Asia,* Singapore: Institute of Southeast Asian Studies.

Swike, E., Thompson, S., and Vasquez, C. (2008) 'Piracy in China', *Business Horizons,* Vol. 51, pp. 493-500.

Tang, X. (2014) 'The Impact of Asian Investment on Africa's Textile Industries', *Carnegie-Tsinghua Center for Global Policy,* online: <*https://pdfs.semanticscholar.org/76d1/e2a65b797cc56a5b51e169f8 39a8373b8a5b.pdf*>

Tanga, P.T. (2009) 'The Contribution of Chinese Trade and Investment Towards Poverty Alleviation in Africa: Evidence of Divergent Views from Lesotho', *Journal of Social Sciences,* Vol. 19, No. 2, pp. 109–119.

Taylor, C. (1994) 'The Politics of Recognition', in C.T. Gutmann (ed.)

Multiculturalism: Examining the Politics of Recognition, pp. 25–73, New Jersey: Princeton University Press.

Taylor, I. (2006) 'China's Policies towards Botswana, Lesotho, Swaziland and Malawi', in *China and Africa: Engagement and Compromise*, London and New York: Routledge, pp.179–190.

Thrall, L. (2015) *China's Expanding African Relations-Inplication for U.S. National Security*, RAND, online: <http://www.rand.org/content/dam/rand/pubs/research_reports/RR900/RR905/RAND_RR905.pdf>

Thunø, M., and Pieke, F.N. (2005) 'Institutionalizing Recent Rural Emigration from China to Europe: New Transnational Villages in Fujian', *International Migration Review*, Vol. 39, No. 2, pp. 485–514.

Tjon Sie Fat, P.B. (2009) *Chinese New Migrants in Suriname: The Inevitability of Ethnic Performing*, Amsterdam: Amsterdam University Press.

Tomlinson, E.C., Dineen, B.R., and Lewicki, R.J. (2004) 'The Road to Reconciliation: Antecedents of Victim Willingness to Reconcile Following a Broken Promise', *Journal of Management*, Vol. 30, No. 2, pp. 165–187.

Tong, C.K. (2010) *Identity and Ethnic Relations in Southeast Asia: Racializing Chineseness*, Dordrecht and New York: Springer.

Tremann, C. (2013) 'Temporary Chinese Migration to Madagascar: Local Perceptions, Economic Imapcts, and Human Capital Flows', *African Review of Economics and Finance*, Vol. 5, No. 1, pp. 7–16.

Wang, G. (1998) (Ed.) *The Chinese Diaspora: Selected Essays* (Vol. 2), Singapore: Times Academic Press.

----------(2004) 'Chinese Ethnicity in New Southeast Asian Nations', in L. Suryadinata (ed.), *Ethnic Relations and Nation-Building in Southeast Asia: The Case of the Ethnic Chinese*, Singapore Society of Asian Studies, pp. 1–19.

Wang, J., and Stenberg, J. (2014) 'Localizing Chinese Migrants in Africa: A Study of the Chinese in Libya before the Civil War', *China Information*, Vol. 28, No. 1, pp. 69–91.

Wang, Y., and Lemmer, E. (2015) '"It's a Lonely Journey": Experiences of Students Learning Chinese as a Foreign Language at South African Universities' *PULA: Botswana Journal of African Studies*, Vol. 29, No. 1. pp. 76–86

Wertheimer, A., and Norris, J. (2009) 'Safeguarding against Substandard/Counterfeit Drugs: Mitigating a Macroeconomic Pandemic', *Social and Administrative Pharmacy*, No. 5, pp. 4–16.

Wilhelm, J. (2006) 'The Chinese Communities in South Africa'. In S. Buhlungu, J. Daniel, R. Southall and J. Lutchman (eds), *State of the Nation: South Africa, 2005–2006,* pp. 350-368. Cape Town: Human Sciences Research Council.

Xiang, B. (2003) 'Emigration from China: A Sending Country Perspective', *International Migration*, Vol. 41, No. 3, pp. 21–48.

Xiao, A.H. (2015) 'In the Shadow of the States: The Informalities of Chinese Petty Entrepreneurship in Nigeria', *Journal of Current Chinese Affairs*, Vol. 44, No. 1, pp. 75–105.

Yan, H. (2003) 'Neoliberal Governmentaity and Neohumanism: Organizing Suzhi/Value Flow through Labor Recruitment Networks', *Cultural Anthropology*, Vol. 18, No. 4, pp. 493–523.

Yang, L., and Doh, C.N. (2013) 'China and Botswana: Legal and Cultural Differences in Labour Laws', *African East-Asian Affairs,* No. 4, pp. 50-71.

Yao, S. (2002) *Confucian Capitalism: Discourse, Practice and the Myth of Chinese Enterprise*. Oxford: RoutledgeCurzon.

Youngman, F. (2013) 'Strengthening Africa-China Relations: A Perspective from Botswana', Centre for Chinese Studies, Stellenbosch, *Discussion Paper,* pp. 1–19.

Zheng, Q. (2014) 'China and Botswana: 40 Years of Friendship and

Cooperation', *Speech at University of Botswana*, 11 November 2014.

Zhou, M., Shenasi, S., and Xu, T. (2016) 'Chinese Attitudes toward African Migrants in Guangzhou, China', *International Journal of Sociology,* No. 46, pp. 141–161.

Zi, Y. (2014) 'Unravelling the "Fong Kong" Phenomenon in Botswana through Analyzing the Relationships among Mass Media, Governmental Activities and Local Voices', *Psychologia*, No. 57, pp. 259–274.

----------(2015a) 'The "Fong kong" Phenomenon in Botswana: A Perspective on Globalisation from Below', Centre for Chinese Studies, Stellenbosch University, *African Eastern-Asian Affairs*, 2015, No. 1, pp. 6–27.

----------(2015b) 'The Challenges for Chinese Merchants in Botswana: A Middleman Minority Perspective', *Journal of Chinese Overseas*, No. 11, pp. 21–42.

NEWSPAPER ARTICLES

Anonymous. (21 June 2010) 'Fongkongs...' *Mmegionline*, online: <http://www.mmegi.bw/index.php?sid=6&aid=3072&dir=2010/june/friday18>, retrieved 2 January 2012.

Batlotleng, B. (18 July 2013) 'China, Botswana Ties … an Inspiring Dream', *DailyNews*, online: <http://www.dailynews.gov.bw/news-details.php?nid=4178>, retrieved 14 October 2015.

Bule, E. (13 November 2009) 'Shop Assistants in Chinese Stores Maltreated?', *Mmegionline*, online: <http://www.mmegi.bw/index.php?sid=1&aid=46&dir=2009/November/Friday13>, retrieved 2 January 2012.

Botswana Press Agency. (13 July 2014) 'Where There Is a Will ...' *DailyNews*, online: <http://www.dailynews.gov.bw/>, retrieved 18 October 2014.

Chube, L. (13 January 2014) 'Cross Border Business Booms at Kazungula', *DailyNews*, Online: <http://www.dailynews.gov.bw>, retrieved 18 October 18 2014.

Ebrahim, I. (7 August 2015) 'Of Anti-business Rhetoric ….', *Weekendpost*, online: <http://www.weekendpost.co.bw/wp-news-details.php?nid=1458>, retrieved 10 September 2015.

Gabotlale, B. (27 May 2005) 'Botswana Affected by Chinese Imports', *Mmegionline*, online: <https://www.mmegi.bw/2005/May/Friday27/9498841761763.html>, retrieved 10 September 2015.

----------(8 May 8 2006) 'Botswana To Benefit from Chinese Windfall', *Mmegionline*, online: <https://www.mmegi.bw/2006/May/Monday8/274371471408.html>, retrieved 10 September 2015.

Gaotlhobogwe, M. (27 January 2009) 'Government Moves to Ban Chinese Trade in Clothes', *Mmegionline*, online: <http://www.mmegi.bw/index.php?sid=1&aid=2&dir=2009/January/Tuesday27>, retrieved 10 September,2015.

----------(9 April 2009) 'Fake Chinese DVDs, CDs off the Shelves', *Mmegionline*, online: <http://www.mmegi.bw/index.php?sid=1&aid=6&dir=2009/april/thursday9////>, retrieved 10 September 2015.

----------(4 June 2012) 'Underground Chinese Warehouse Raided', *The Monitor*, online: <http://www.mmegi.bw/index.php?sid=1&aid=743&dir=2012/June/Monday4///>, retrieved 10 September 2015.

Keoreng, E. (30 January 2009) 'Chinese Shops a Relief, But They Must Behave', *Mmegionline*, online: <http://www.mmegi.bw/index.php?sid=6&aid=14&dir=2009

/January/Friday30/>, retrieved 10 September 2015.

Liu, H. (6 January 2010) 'Memories and Blessings of China-Botswana Relations', *Mmegionline*, online: <http://www.mmegi.bw/index.php?sid=2&aid=16&dir=2010 /January/Wednesday6>, retrieved 10 September 2015.

Masokola, A. (9 November 2015) 'Botswana Rejected Two Soft Loans from China', *Weekendpost*, online: <http://www.weekendpost.co.bw/wp-news-details.php?nid=1874>, retrieved 7 May 2016.

Mbeki, T. (20 July 2007) Address at the Launch of SABC News International. Johannesburg, South Africa, online: <http://search.yahoo.co.jp/search;_ylt=A2RCxAmhzxRYjUs AzaCJBtF7?p=Address+at+the+launch+of+SABC+News+I nternational&search.x=1&fr=top_ga1_sa&tid=top_ga1_sa&ei =UTF-8&aq=&oq=&afs=>, retrieved 6 May 2016.

Moeng, G. (11 March 2013) 'Govt Urged to "Investigate" Chinese', *Mmegionline*, online: <http://www.mmegi.bw/index.php? sid=1&aid=1709&dir=2013/March/Monday11>, retrieved 5 June 2016.

Mosikare, O. (19 July 2013) 'Sinohydro Relocates from Botswana', *Mmegionline*, online: <http://www.mmegi.bw/index.php? sid=1=6=2009/June/Tuesday23&aid=1498&dir=2013/July/ Friday19>, retrieved 6 May 2016.

Motlogelwa, T. (2 May 2007) 'Chinese Offer to Curb Piracy in Botswana', *Mmegionline*, online: <http://www.mmegi.bw/index.php?sid=1&aid=79&dir=2007 /may/wednesday2>, retrieved 10 September 2015.

Motsamai, M. (1 July 2015) 'Botswana Reduces Retail Licences for Chinese', *DailyNews*, online: <http://www.dailynews.gov.bw/news-etails.php?nid=21146>, retrieved 10 September 2015.

Nadalet, I. (27 July 2012) 'The African Aviation Tribune, *BOTSWANA: Government Fires Chinese Firm Sinohydro over Delays to Gaborone Airport Expansion Project*', online: <http://www.theafricanaviationtribune.com/2012/07/botswana-government-fires-chinese-firm.html>, retrieved 2 May 2016.

News of the Communist Party of China (22 November 2010) 'China, Botswana Sign Cooperation Deals', *News of the Communist Party of China*, online: <http://english.cpc.people.com.cn/66102/7206452.html>, retrieved 10 September 2015.

Piet, B. (16 February 2016) 'Fengyue Glass Project to be Auctioned This Week' *Mmegionline*, online: <http://www.mmegi.bw/index.php?aid=57827&dir=2016/february/16>, retrieved 29 April 2016.

Rasina, R.W. (20 June 2013) 'We Are Not a Chinese Colony ... to Hell with the Chinese', *Echo,* online: <http://www.echoonline.co.bw/index/index.php/columns/item/34-we-are-not-a-chinese-colonyto-hell-with-the-chinese.>, retrieved 10 September 2015.

Seretse, L. (28 March 2014) 'Chinese Want BPC Out of Morupule B', *Mmegionline*, online: <http://www.mmegi.bw/index.php?aid=12693>, retrieved 6 May 2016.

INDEX